With the
3rd Wisconsin
Badgers

Life In Camp,
Or,
Scenes By the Wayside.

A Sketch Of Life As A Soldier,

With Scenes And Adventures In the Valley Of The Shenandoah.

How short is life—'tis but an empty dream,
And we, the creatures of an hour,
Like shadows, flitting oer a stream
Transcient as a Summer flower.

Dark are the shades oer my countrys setting
"Blighted Columbia;" once happy and fair,
While oer sweeps the storm-cloud, darkly, appalling,
And the bold Eagle droops his broad wing in pr...

Frederick City Hospital, Maryland,
October the 14th
1862.
Vol. No. two.

Van R. Willard,
Co. G. 3d W.

With the 3rd Wisconsin Badgers

The Living Experience
of the Civil War
Through the Journals of Van R. Willard

Edited by Steven S. Raab

Foreword by William C. Davis

STACKPOLE
BOOKS

Copyright © 1999 by Steven S. Raab

Published by
STACKPOLE BOOKS
5067 Ritter Road
Mechanicsburg PA 17055
www.stackpolebooks.com

Printed in the United States of America

10 9 8 7 6 5 4 3 2 1

FIRST EDITION

Library of Congress Cataloging-in-Publication Data

Willard, Van R., 1841–1898
    With the 3rd Wiconsin Badgers: the living experience of the Civil War through the journals of Van R. Willard / edited by Steven S. Raab; foreword by William C. Davis. — 1st ed.
        p. cm.
    Includes bibliographical references (p.) and index.
    ISBN: 0-8117-0002-X
    1. Willard, Van R., 1841–1898. 2. United States. Army. Wisconsin Infantry Regiment, 3rd (1861-1865) 3. United States—History—Civil War, 1861-1865 Personal narratives. 4. Wisconsin—History—Civil War, 1861-1865 Personal narratives. 5. United States—History—Civil War, 1861-1865 Regimental histories. 6. Wisconsin—History—Civil War, 1861-1865 Reg imental histories. 7. Soldiers—Wisconsin—Neenah Biography. I. Raab, Steven S., 1949-   . II. Title.   III. Title: With the third Wisconsin Badgers.
E537.5 3rd.W55   1999
973.7'475'092—dc21
[B]

                                                                99-36030
                                                                CIP

This book is dedicated to my wife, Susan, who encouraged my interest and absorption in the Civil War, the greatest of all dramas.

Although we are heirs to the bravery and high example of men on both sides of the conflict, I also want to dedicate this book to the Union soldiers such as Van Willard, without whose sacrifice we would not have our nation as it is today.

CONTENTS

FOREWORD

"When the time has hung heavily upon my hands, and the hours have been long and lonely, I found pleasure in scribbling down my thoughts." That was what Van R. Willard of the 3rd Wisconsin Infantry wrote in introducing his personal narrative of his Civil War experience, written as the war itself was unfolding. Like all Civil War soldiers, he spent weeks in camp for every hour of actual combat, and yet he chose to improve his idle time rather than waste it, and the result is this splendid account of his service.

And what a war he had. There may have been times of tedium, but he saw some of the most active and challenging service of the conflict. The Shenandoah Valley, South Mountain, Antietam, Chancellorsville, Gettysburg, service in Tennessee, the Atlanta campaign, and Kennesaw Mountain—some seventeen battles in all made up Van Willard's combat service, and through them all he recorded his experiences and thoughts, not in a conventional diary, but more as a running narrative.

This is the sort of book that lets us peer into the mind of the Civil War soldier to see how he felt about his cause, slavery, the Union, the nature of soldiering, and so many more of the things that most soldiers never commented on in writing. His battle accounts are good, but his musings on life, the human condition in his era, and the great issues of his time are even more worthwhile. They reveal a thoughtful young man fully aware of the greater issues at stake in the fight for the Union and of the soldier's place in that endeavor.

Entertaining, enlightening, consummately human, Van Willard's war may have had days when time hung heavily on his hands, but no reader will suffer his boredom in reading this narrative.

INTRODUCTION

"We cannot escape history . . . we will be remembered in spite
of ourselves. No personal significance, or insignificance, can
spare one or another of us. The fiery trial through which we
pass will light us down, in honor or dishonor, to the latest
generation."

—Abraham Lincoln

Van Willard's work, in keeping with Lincoln's prediction, has immea-
surably "lighted down" the lives and experiences of those who participated in the fiery trial of the Civil War. It is of compelling importance
as a historical narrative and places the reader in the eye of the Civil War
hurricane. This is a unique work, and Van Willard was an extraordinary
man. Virtually all Civil War narratives that have come down to us were
written years or even decades after the war. Thus they lack immediacy and
are susceptible to the inaccuracies that inevitably result when recalling
events that happened long ago. And so often there were axes to grind.
Most surviving materials written during the war, with just a few famous
exceptions, are in the form of letters and diaries. Although recollections in
letters and diaries are fresh, they are frequently short and have much extra-
neous and family-related material, rather than being in-depth narratives.
Most of the few books actually written during the war are well known,
and their authors were not combatants.

Willard's work, however, is an exception. He was a soldier in a major
combat unit and a sensitive, keen observer. His volumes contain a narrative
of his living experience of the Civil War, completely written during the
war. It is immediate, powerful, well written, and exciting. It should prove
to be an important reference work in years to come for all who want to
know what it was really like to be in the Civil War.

Van Rensselaer Willard was born in Buffalo, New York, on June 8,
1841. When he was four years old, his parents moved to Wisconsin. He
grew up in Neenah, a town on Lake Winnebago just south of Appleton.

On April 15, 1861, three days after the Confederates fired on Fort
Sumter, President Lincoln issued his proclamation asking the states for

75,000 men to suppress the rebellion. The governor of Wisconsin, Alexander W. Randall, received a telegram from the president requesting one regiment of about 780 men as his state's contribution. Responding to the crisis the very next day, Randall issued his own decree inviting Wisconsin's patriotic sons to enlist for service to sustain the U.S. government. This decree was published in the newspapers on April 17.

More than 2,500 Wisconsin men enlisted in response to this call, and the state found itself with an embarrassment of riches. Twelve companies were needed to fill a regiment, and thirty-six full companies actually tendered their services before April 22. One of these, the Neenah Guards, was a local militia unit that had fallen into inactivity. On April 19 it was resurrected in answer to the governor's call, and that night Van R. Willard signed his name as a volunteer, thus beginning his military career. The Guards were ultimately assigned to the 3rd Wisconsin Volunteer Regiment as Company G. Willard was truly one of the "Boys of '61."

Willard served continuously until July 1, 1864, when he was mustered out. His official military records show that he was with his regiment from his muster in until he became sick and was sent to the military hospital at Frederick, Maryland, in October 1861 until February 1862. He became a nurse there after his recovery in December, caring for ill and dying soldiers. Willard then rejoined his unit and served in the Shenandoah Valley campaign. He was wounded in action at Antietam and spent time in the hospital recuperating until returning to the front in early 1863. He was present at Chancellorsville, Gettysburg, and Sherman's Georgia campaign. He was again wounded at Dallas, Georgia, in May 1864, just before returning to civilian life. Willard states that he was involved in seventeen battles.

Willard arrived home in Neenah in July 1864. He was eager to further his education, and he attended and graduated from Bryant & Stratton Commercial College in Milwaukee. In May 1867 he married Cynthia E. Perkins of Cayuga County, New York. They had a son, Lee, born on October 2, 1868, who eventually became a physician. Willard later decided to study law and was admitted to the Wisconsin bar at Green Bay in March 1873.

Van Willard showed the same industry and intelligence in his civilian pursuits that he manifested in his Civil War writings and soon put his skills to work. A new county named after President Licoln was being organized in the middle of Wisconsin, and its seat was the town of Merrill.

Willard moved there in 1874 and took a prominent part in civic affairs in the town and county. His obituary in the *Merrill Advocate* stated that "he was a public spirited man and took a great interest in the advancement of everything that would benefit the community." He was Lincoln County's first recorder of deeds and owned the first land abstract in the county. He practiced law, owned the local newspaper, and speculated in real estate. Willard also was very active in the Grand Army of the Republic (GAR) and must have enjoyed the company of his wartime comrades.

In the fall of 1886, he and his family moved to Chicago, where he engaged in business for six years. They then returned to Merrill, where Willard practiced law until 1897. Apparently as a result of a health problem, he sought a warmer climate and purchased land at Madison Station, Mississippi. He was in the process of having a house built when he died on September 12, 1898, of what his doctor called "cerebral apoplexia," most likely a stroke or cerebral hemorrhage. He was fifty-seven years old. Willard was buried in Mississippi. The newspapers reported that his wife intended to move his body to Wisconsin, but where he rests today is not known. Cynthia Willard died just five years later. Their son, Dr. Lee Willard, was active in the Wisconsin Medical Association. He died childless in 1929, so Van Willard has no living descendents.

>-+-+>-·O-·-<+-+-<

Willard's books reveal him to have been sensitive, intelligent, and thoughtful. Although he was young at the time, he wrote maturely and with humor. His work consists of five separate books, each written at a different time and place during the war, and each with its own distinct personality. They reflect the stages of the war and the moods and experiences of Willard and his compatriots. We can follow his progression from novice to veteran and see how exposure to the experiences and harsh realities of war brought out in him the historian, humanist observer, military scientist, philosopher, poet, theologian, and just plain storyteller.

Book One has an ownership signature and date on the first page of Frederick, Maryland, September 26, 1861. This is most likely when he first bought the book, doubtless intended to replace a diary he lost at Antietam. It covers the period from his enlistment during the first week of the war to February 1862 and reports on his going off to war and life as a soldier.

Book Two has an ownership signature and date on the first page of Frederick City Hospital, Maryland, October 14, 1862. It covers the period from March 1862, when Willard's unit participated in the Shenandoah Valley campaign against Stonewall Jackson, through September of that year, when he fought in the cornfield at Antietam and was wounded. He wrote this book primarily in Frederick in October and early November of 1862, while recovering from his wound. In mid-November he transferred to the Summit House Hospital in Philadelphia, and probably completed it there. The book is fully written in narrative style and has lost all resemblance to a diary. It is exciting, detailed, and has great battle descriptions, and Willard has developed a somewhat humorous tone. In this volume he is very much the historical reporter and no longer displays the melancholy mood of his first book.

Book Three contains a stationer's bookplate indicating that it was obtained from W. F. Murphy & Sons in Philadelphia and was purchased about the third week of November 1862. In the manuscript Willard states that he arrived at the Summit House Hospital in mid-November and remained there until December 29. The entire book was written during this five- or six-week period in 1862, with the exception of the very end portion, which Willard wrote in Washington and Virginia during the week after he left Philadelphia. The book's coverage is limited in time (though not in scope) to the period from his arrival in Philadelphia until he traveled to rejoin his unit in early January 1863. Willard was in the hospital, bored and with a lot of time on his hands—time to reflect on the suffering he saw around him, the country for which the sacrifices were being made, and the nature of God. He disliked what he saw in the military hospital and was unhappy being relegated to the sidelines, far from the scene of action in Virginia. He anxiously followed the news as it arrived from Fredericksburg and went to visit Independence Hall. This volume is full of philosophy, theology, military science, and poetry.

Book Four has an ownership signature and date on the first page of Wartrace, Tennessee, where his company was stationed from November 1863 until early February 1864. The book likely was written in December and January, when most of the regiment was away on leave and the remaining men, including Willard, were given little to do. It covers the period from April through September 1863. This is Willard at his most vivid, and he is a superb narrator. You stand with him at the Chancellor Mansion in Chancellorsville in the midst of the swirl of battle; experience a charge by Stonewall Jackson's corps, complete with Rebel yells; support the cavalry at the key Brandy Station fight; pursue the Confederates into Pennsylvania and try to calm the frightened citizens there; participate in the battle of Gettysburg, including the fight at Culp's Hill and Pickett's Charge; and walk that battlefield in its aftermath. The mood of this volume is determined, patriotic, and intent on winning the war. There is little time for the kind of philosophizing done at the Summit House.

Book Five indicates no date or place of authorship. It is clear from the context, however, that it was written entirely after Willard was discharged on July 1, 1864, and had returned to his beloved Wisconsin. It is also evident that he considered the war's ultimate resolution to be uncertain, so this volume must have been written before the war ended. The period from July to September 1864, when Atlanta fell, was an uncertain one for Union arms, and quite probably the book dates from that time. After Lincoln's reelection in November, the result of the war was a foregone conclusion, and it is unlikely the book postdates that event. Also, Willard began college in September 1864 and would have had less time to devote to writing a book. This volume covers the period from his regiment's trip to fight in the Western theater in late September 1863 to his muster out while campaigning with Sherman in Georgia. It contains some wonderful descriptions of the war against the partisans, Northern soldiers' relationships with Southern civilians, and the early months of the battle for Atlanta, including the fights at Resaca and Dallas. This book is just as interesting as the others, but one can sense that Willard is now writing while out of harm's way.

A NOTE ON THE EDITING

Reading Civil War manuscripts can be a challenge. Grammar and punctuation are often bewilderingly different from today's, spelling is likely to be atrocious, and there are frequent redundancies. Editing such a manuscript therefore requires some fundamental decisions on how to present the material. To leave the text in its original state hinders smooth reading and enjoyment, but to make wholesale changes in the work to modernize it would risk losing the legitimacy and flavor of the manuscript. I have chosen a middle road, striving to maintain the integrity of the manuscript by making as few revisions as possible while still enhancing readability and comprehension.

Willard's spelling and grammar were much better than most writers of his time, but there still were many cases of incorrect spelling and archaic grammatical usages. I have corrected most of the misspellings but have changed the archaic usages only where it seemed necessary for clarity and readability, and have left the rest as originally written. Numerous redundancies have been removed and some material has been reorganized mainly to place related portions together. The original manuscript contains a blizzard of confusing commas and other punctuation, and I have cleaned these up to the best of my ability. Preferring to let Willard speak for himself, I avoided changes to his text otherwise. My purpose in adding material to Willard's narrative has been to place his experiences in context and provide perspective. My intention was not to fashion a comprehensive history of the war or any aspect of it. The portions of this book exclusively in italics and the notes are my work; the balance is Van Willard's.

In 1891 Edwin E. Bryant, a veteran of the 3rd Wisconsin, published his excellent *History of the Third Regiment of Wisconsin Veteran Volunteer Infantry*. I have gathered much valuable information from it and also made use of its muster rolls, statistics, and maps. Any reference in this book to Bryant refers to this fine regimental history.

I would like to thank researchers Sharon Karow and Jeanne Chrudimsky of Wisconsin for developing the details of Van Willard's life after the war.

WILLARD'S INTRODUCTION

The soldier is cut off from society, shut out from the world and all its joys. Often he is living a life of loneliness and should have something with which to occupy his time, his leisure moments, aside from the card games and degrading habits so prevalent. The temptations that surround the soldier's pathway are indeed numerous. They beset him on every side and meet him at every turn, and he must have a true heart and an iron will to resist them.

I have found that writing has not only been a benefit to me but has been a pleasure also. Often when the time has hung heavily upon my hands, and the hours have been long and lonely, I found pleasure in scribbling down my thoughts.

Every soldier, especially the young, should keep a book of this kind. After a little practice, he will find it to be no very difficult task to write several pages. If he keeps a record of events and makes remarks thereon, it will soon become a habit, and he will often find his book to be a friend and companion to him.

So let the thoughts have full play, and chronicle them as they come.

BOOK ONE

A Perfect Madness

Our war drum has sounded,
Our flag is unfurled,
And our vengeance of wrath
On the foe shall be hurled.

Then awaken every brave heart,
Each strong heart and true,
And strike for our country
And the red, white, and blue.

*T*hroughout the momentous year of 1860 the danger to the unity of the nation had been increasing. Southerners were fed up with what they saw as Northern interference, constraints, and hypocritical morality, and they feared being relegated to a powerless minority if the Western territories were not open to slavery but were admitted to the Union as free states. The election of Abraham Lincoln as president on November 8 was to them the final provocation and proved to be the catalyst for bringing the forty-year antagonism between the South and the North over slavery to a head. "Fire-eating" secessionists, men who would split the nation asunder, long on the fringes of Southern society and looked on by many as crackpots, rose meteorically to positions of influence. Their vision of an independent South was taken up by mainstream leaders and made instantly respectable. Some even dreamt of a rich, powerful, expansionist South creating an empire and a new Roman-style "classical age" centered around the Caribbean

From election day in November through the long winter of 1860–61, the South staged an uprising, and the excitement built. Its people were delirious with joy; strangers embraced on the streets. What seem today to be questionable premises and even fantasy appeared then to be imminent, if not already reality. The break promised the South not only political independence but financial freedom, and could be very profitable besides if the South used the occasion to cancel its debts to the North. As William Glaston wrote from Charleston, South Carolina, on November 8, 1860, "One of the most prominent firms in the city talks to me about repudiation of Northern debts as involving little censure in this condition of revolution."[1]

In the North the anxiety and confusion over the deteriorating state of the country and what to do about it developed into panic and desperation, as more and more Southern states seceded and it became evident that there was no clear way to hold the country together. Northerners believed that the South had maintained an unfair stranglehold on the federal government for decades and that they had been constantly called upon to compromise their principles to appease slaveholders. Now it appeared that all their efforts and painful accommodations had been for nothing. Many felt that the Southerners had played them for fools. Worse, cocky U.S. government functionaries from the South sported secession badges and publicly proclaimed loyalty to the South, some swearing to prevent the inauguration of the lawfully elected President Lincoln.

The clamor that something be done grew with every "treasonable" act the North saw taken by a Southern state or politician, and perceived inaction in the face of escalating Southern actions created overwhelming frustration in the North. As the winter turned into spring, Southerners became more confident and bellicose and con-

sidered their independence a fact, while Northerners felt ill used and grew increasingly sullen and enraged. By April 1861 the situation was tense in the extreme, and emotions built to a crescendo. On April 12 a Confederate cannon fired on Fort Sumter. The country was plunged immediately into a hysteria the likes of which we can only imagine today. Swept along in this perfect madness were the citizens of Wisconsin, including those in the town of Neenah. One of them, twenty-year-old Van R. Willard, determined to enlist to save his country. And so his tale begins.

>-+→-·-0-·-‹‹+-‹

The "Neenah Guards" (Co. G) was reorganized on the eve of the 19th of April, 1861, by Captain E. L. Hubbard. The company was one of old standing, but as it was of little use in a time of peace, it had nearly become extinct. On the breakout of the Rebellion, the company was again called together. I enlisted in the company on the night of the 19th. Our enlistment was for three months; but finding that there was no opportunity of getting into the service, we reenlisted for three years.[2]

On the night of the 22nd we began "drill" in Babcock hall. As soon as the weather became suitable, we began drill in the open air on "The Point" on the shore of Lake Winnebago.[3] On the 14th of June we received "marching orders" and went into camp on the night of the 15th. We arrived at Camp Hamilton,[4] Fond du Lac, just at dark. Now began "life in camp." It was Saturday night, and a cold one it was, too. We passed the first night shivering.

Neenah, Wisconsin. June 15/61. Having received orders to march at 10:00 A.M. I arose early in the morning on the 15th and completed the necessary preparations, for leaving home to go into camp at Fond du Lac. It was one of the loveliest of mornings; the sun arose with unusual splendor over the little town where I had lived for years. The village, resting so quietly at the head of the romantic little lake, looked more lovely this sunny morning than it had ever done before. All preparations were soon completed. Bidding the folks "good by," I hurried to the village to join the company.

The streets were thronged with those who had come from their homes in the country and in the village to talk and shake hands, perhaps for the last time, with those who were about to leave home and friends and all the quieter joys of civil life to endure the hardships of the camp and to brave the dangers of the battle field.

As fortune would have it, the cars that were expected to carry us to head quarters did not arrive; hence we were compelled to wait until two o'clock P.M. The company, however, fell into line in front of the Winnebago and marched up to the Point, our old drill ground, where we had labored day after day in learning the rudiments of war. Many of the friends of those who were about to go away came up, and the remainder of the forenoon was passed in wandering through woods or strolling along the shores of the lake.

About noon we all returned to the village and waited with some impatience the arrival of the train that was to convey us to head quarters. As the time of our departure drew near, the throng upon the streets began to thicken, and before the time arrived the streets were crowded with interested spectators. At two o'clock we fell into line in front of the Hotel and started for the depot, towards which the crowd hurried. When we arrived the platform and every available place for a long ways around was thronged.

The train soon arrived and we were ready to go; hands were shaken and the last good by was said, and as the train moved off, friends parted with friends, perhaps never to meet again. Onward we went over the rough road between Neenah and Oshkosh. We arrived at the latter place about 5:00 P.M., where we remained until six, and then resumed our journey towards Fond du Lac, where we arrived about seven o'clock; took supper in the mess house, consisting of bread, applesauce, and coffee.

The boys were in the best of spirits. As night came on, a storm set in; the wind blew, and it was cold and disagreeable. *This* was the introduction to camp life; it was our first experience, and a rather sad affair it proved to be. The walls of our tent were thin, and the wind and the rain came through it, and it was cold and chilly.

There was considerable novelty about it, however. After wandering about the encampment until bed time, we "turned in," arranged our bed, spread down our blankets, and stretched ourselves out for a night's repose. We were weary and soon fell into a sound sleep, from which we were awakened by the loud beating of drums and the stentorian voice of our orderly calling out at the top of his voice, "Turn out to roll call." This to us was rather new, if not comical. We were at a great loss to know why we were called up at such an hour. It was a duty that we had not yet learned, but since then we have learned it to our heart's content.

Well, after "roll call" we returned to our nests. The wind continued to blow, agitating our little canvas house in the most frightful manner. But the night passed away, and the morning dawned, bright and cloudless but cool.

It was the Sabbath, and the sun rose above the "Fountain City" in cloudless splendor. The camp was soon a scene of life and activity; several companies had arrived during the night, and the camp was soon crowded with curious spectators who came in to look with curiosity, and admiration no doubt, at the hundreds who had left home and friends and all the hallowed joys and associations of domestic and civil life. All the forenoon they continued to come: the old, the young, the rich, the poor, and those of every class and clime, until the camp grounds were completely thronged. As the forenoon advanced, the bells of the various churches began to ring out over the city, their musical chimes like the sweet voice of angels inviting those of every class and station, the sin stricken, the unfortunate and heart broken, to leave the busy haunts of men and seek within its hallowed walls those quieter pleasures such as can be found, not amid the scenes of drunkenness and rivalry, but within its peaceful walls. As I thought of the quiet church and the ringing church bell in my own native village, and the pastor to whose voice I had listened so often, I could not but contrast the noisy excitement, the activity and bustle of the camp, with that of the more peaceful and quieter scenes presented within the walls of the little church.

Nearly the whole day passed in the same lively manner. As the afternoon advanced the crowd rather thickened than otherwise. People amused themselves in various ways, roaming about the encampment, conversing with some new made acquaintance, listening to the stirring strains from several bands that were continually playing or gathering in groups to talk over the past and conjecture of the future.

About six o'clock, the companies, as was the custom, "fell in" for supper and were marched off to the mess house. This was an establishment built more for use than beauty, as one might guess at first sight. It was a long building of boards in which long tables were arranged, and seats for the accommodation of the soldiers. Supper being over, we got ready and marched up to church. Thus passed the first Sabbath in camp. Since then I have passed many Sabbaths under many different circumstances. In the army, however, the Sabbath is hardly known, yet within the human heart there is a feeling always dwelling that speaks of Sabbaths that have been passed in other and more peaceful times. Oh yes! The memory of these Sabbaths still will come, though far away amid the bustle of the camp or the hurry of the march.

The companies having now arrived and their positions being assigned them, regulations were made and business began. As then there was work to be done, a system of drills were commenced that left us but little time for ourselves. We were awakened every morning at five o'clock, had breakfast at seven, between breakfast time and six o'clock was spent in drilling. This, however, was soon done away with, and the time for drilling was between eight and half past nine and from eleven till one, again from four till six, after which we had our dress parade. Every thing went on swimmingly in camp. Nothing occurred to mar the pleasant excitement which reigned.

A fight occurring, or some of the boys boldly overstepping the rules of the encampment, afforded topics of amusement and conversation. For instance, on the night of the 22nd some boys who were out after roll call in the evening, and being a little in liquor, thought that it would be fine to amuse themselves by running the guard. They attempted to do so, but the watchful sentinel detected them in the act. They then attempted to drive him away with clubs; the fellow was not to be easily frightened but stood his ground with firmness. In the fray one of the intruders received a bayonet thrust in the side and another had his hand severely cut. The guard lost his gun, but the intruders were finally taken and put in the guard house. Some of the men (though allowed every privilege that could be expected under the circumstances) were continually breaking the rules of the camp by going out without permission. The unrestrained life which they had been accustomed to, their wild and reckless habits, would not allow them to be confined within the narrow limits of the camp, thus furnishing the guard house with inmates continually.

The "Guard House" is one of necessaries of camp life, and I don't know as I shall have a better time to explain the term than now. The term "guard house" implies several tents standing by themselves, erected for the purpose of containing those who have been arrested and condemned as prisoners. The treatment of those who have been so unfortunate as to be confined therein depends upon the nature and magnitude of the offense committed and the manner in which they conduct themselves while there. For common offenses they are simply confined within the limits allowed them by the guards, who are placed within a short distance from the guard tents. If the offense is great or the conduct bad, they are "bucked." This is performed in the following manner. The victim is held firmly while his hands are tied and slipped down over his knees, and a stick thrust through over his arms and under his knees. They are sometimes gagged by putting a bayonet into their mouths and tying it. In addition to this, a block of wood is lashed to the back. This is a painful operation, one that I do not wish to experience. There were other modes of punishment, however, such as loading the prisoner down with chains and handcuffs.

Our camp at Fond du Lac was a pleasant one, yet the life of idleness and inactivity which we were obliged to lead was not agreeable to us—at least to me. There was too much sameness, too much monotony. Days and weeks came and went but brought with them no change.

But by and by the orders came that we had waited for so long and somewhat impatiently. We were to march without delay to join General [Robert] Patterson's (then in command) division on the banks of the Potomac.

The orders came on July 5, and now the men would go to the front and get a chance to see what soldiering was all about. The next week the camp was a beehive of activity, with everyone preparing to pull up stakes. For many Civil War soldiers, the train ride to the seat of battle was their first trip away from their native state. Willard paints a particularly vivid picture of what it felt like to leave home for the first time.

On July the 12th we began our journey for the *South*. The day was one of nature's loveliest. The sun rose that morning in cloudless splendor, the sky was clear, and indeed, all nature seemed to smile upon us who were leaving to endure the hardships and trials of the camp and to brave if need be the dangers of the battle field.

Nearly the whole day was spent in preparations for our departure. At five o'clock the regiment was formed into line with knapsacks packed and slung upon our backs like regular "troopers." Though we were still unarmed, we felt like real soldiers. Soon the march to the depot was begun, and every heart beat high, filled with strange emotions. We were about to leave our own dear homes and friends, our loved ones, our firesides, and all the happy scenes and associations that have been so dear to us in former days. All these now we were about to bid adieu—perhaps forever!

Yet our hearts were light and we could bid adieu to all of these with cheerful hearts, for we knew we were engaged in a just and noble cause. We marched to the depot amid the cheers of a dense crowd who thronged the walks on either side. On account of some delay the train on which we were to take our departure from the "Fountain City" did not arrive until nearly seven o'clock.

We stepped aboard the train and were soon being borne away—"southward bound!" As the long train of twenty-seven cars moved away, bearing within the pride of the "Badger State," we were greeted with such a round of cheers as drowned out the roar of the heavy train as it rattled on over the iron rail. On we sped, soon leaving the beautiful city of Fond du Lac behind us, and as the train swept around a curve in the road, we could see from the car window the city far in the distance, with its towering spires glittering with the tints of the setting sun. Long and sadly we looked upon the lovely city where we had passed so many hours, some lonely and some cheerful, as it faded away, fast becoming lost to our view.

It was a lovely evening, clear, serene, and beautiful. The sun had nearly set, going down in the west like a great red ball of fire, shedding its golden light over the scene, transforming every thing into gold. I could not but be sad as I looked from the car window upon the scene and thought perhaps that this would be the last golden sunset that I should look upon in my own dear Wisconsin. But the sun went down, darkness came gently on and hid behind its nightly veil the last glimpse of the groves and hills of the Badger State. Sadly I turned away, and as I closed the window, I could not but shed a tear as I bade adieu (perhaps forever) to my native state and all the loved and loving ones contained therein.

Darkness soon hid from view every object by the wayside. Silence reigned through the car, and everyone seemed wrapped in the mantle of his own musings. We were leaving our own dear homes and their endearments; we had quitted the cheerful firesides with all their pleasures and quiet joys. We were on our way to a hostile country; we were about to plunge into the midst of dangers, perhaps to become early victims to the grim *malice* of war. But the silence was soon broken, and the car, which was so short a time before wrapped in silence and gloom, was now the scene of mirth. As for me, I felt no desire to join them. I knew that their laughs were feigned and felt that their mirth was but a mockery.

The moon was shining brightly, and stars were twinkling way up in the dark blue sky above. I left the car, for the air was close and warm within, and went out upon the platform. The evening was indeed a lovely one, warm, calm, and moonlit. For a long time I stood upon the platform musing of the past and present and dreaming of the future. Deep emotions were swelling within me as the car rushed madly along its iron pathway.

The past appeared all checkered over with good and ill, with joys and pleasures, filling my heart with a thousand varied emotions. My heart was filled with sadness at the thought of leaving home and those I loved so well. The happy scenes of other times and the dear associations of the past were very vivid in my memory—the home of my childhood and its surroundings, the silvery lake and the deep, tangled wildwood, the friends of my youth and the associates of my schoolboy days. The present was rich with stirring events. The tocsin of war had been sounded, and the booming of cannon was heard in our own land, and thousands were leaving their homes and happy firesides. Not to sail for a distant shore—not to resist a foreign invader—but to stay the fearful tide of Rebellion that threatened our fair land with desolation and ruin. The future lay before me, vague and uncertain. Dark, heavy clouds hung around it. Yet far in the dim distance one bright star arose, and hope smilingly whispered of a happy termination which would bring once more peace and joy to our stricken land.

But why dwell on the thoughts of that time, as I stood there alone on that lovely evening? The air was growing chilly, and I was glad to return to the crowded car. The mirth had subsided, and all was still. Many, as the evening advanced, sank to slumber as quietly as if at home. Soon the car was wrapped in unbroken silence. But I could not sleep, for my mind was too busy with thoughts.

Long before sunrise the next morning we were astir again, and the car resounded with the hum of many voices. Songs were heard, and all seemed as happy as if on their way to a wedding scene. Just after daylight we arrived in the great city of the West—Chicago. We saw but very few people as we passed through the city. They were all asleep. The Badgers came on them unawares and caught them napping. A few, however, made their appearance as we passed through the principal street, bearing the unmistakable appearance of having been roused from their slumbers at an unusual hour. We remained at the depot for a short time, where we tried our best to obtain some thing in the way of eatables to satisfy the cravings of our outraged stomachs, for we had had nothing to eat for a long time and were as hungry as Badgers ever were. But there was nothing but whiskey or lager to be had. The "Suckers"[5] seemed to care but little for our hunger, though they were *very* anxious to become acquainted with our specie. We did not make a very long stay in this inhospitable city and were glad to get aboard the cars again. We could not but think of the instructions that Christ gave to His Apostles, and we shook the dust from our feet "as a testimony against them."

About seven o'clock we were again on the road for "Dixie." The day was a lovely one; the sky was clear and cloudless, the sun shone warm and brightly, and all nature wore her most becoming look. Onward we sped, passing through a country at times smiling in all the loveliness of broad prairies, shady groves, and fields of ripening grain. All along the line, wherever we made a pause (with but one exception), the people came out in crowds to welcome us. At almost every station refreshments were passed through the cars by the citizens, and at several places public receptions were given us.

On the 17th of July, 1861, we arrived at Hagerstown, Maryland. The country around about wore a strange, wild appearance. It was with a feeling somewhat peculiar that I stepped from the platform and stood for the first time upon the soil of a—"*Slave State!*" The country around had, to me, an appearance of desolation. Just down below us lay the city of Hagerstown, looking more like a ruined city of ancient times than one of the present day. Hagerstown contains about eight thousand inhabitants and is built on rather low ground. It wears an appearance of old age. The buildings are time worn, the moss has grown upon the walls, and they look as though they were about to fall to ruins. After resting for a short time, we fell into line and marched through the city.

We camped for the night just outside of the city in an open field. We remained at Hagerstown until the 23rd, when we (having received our arms[6]), took up our line of march for Harpers Ferry. The morning was warm and bright, and the sun was shining in all its summer splendor. Although our knapsacks were heavy, our hearts were light and happy, and we trudged on with a light step and a merry heart.

The road to Harpers Ferry was a rough one, leading up over high bluffs, down deep ravines, and along dusty plains. We halted at noon beneath the shade of a ledge of overhanging rocks and partook of a dinner consisting of hard bread, cold meat, and a cup of water. About two o'clock we again began our toilsome march. We halted at evening and pitched our tents in an open field on the side of a little hill. The night was warm and moonlit without (to us) the slightest indication of a storm; therefore we neglected to put our tent up as it should have been or to dig a trench around it as is the custom. We had not learned the changeful nature of Maryland climate and had yet to learn that there was no dependence to be put on sunny skies or cloudless evenings, for the smiling sky of the morning is often superseded by clouds and storms at night. We paid dearly for our neglect.

Things went swimmingly until about three in the morning, when I was awakened from a sound slumber by a sensation such as one might be supposed to feel if suddenly being lain in a tub of cold water. In fact, it was raining at a furious rate, and the water was pouring into our tent in a manner truly shocking. Everything was afloat, the water standing at least four inches deep in our tent, which, by the way, stood in a little hollow on the hill side. What was to be done? What could be done but to lie down and take it with the best possible grace. The morning found us wet and cold as Badgers ever were. But it cleared off in the morning and proved to be a pleasant day.

About 9:00 A.M. we began again our march. At three o'clock in the afternoon, after descending a long, steep hill, we found ourselves for the first time on the banks of the grand old Potomac. We turned up the river, passing through the little villages of Lenoxville and Weaverton. These are two little villages looking so old and time worn that one can hardly calculate their age. Passing on up the river for a few miles, we arrived, almost before we were aware of it, in the wonderful little town of Sandy Hook, near Harpers Ferry. This little prodigy of a town consists of a few dilapidated structures looking so ancient that one might imagine that they were built previous to the Flood.

Just above Sandy Hook is Harpers Ferry. It is located on a point of land lying between the Potomac and the Shenandoah, just where they mingle their waters together. It lies in a little nook in the mountains, which rise around it in all the grandeur of their rugged beauty. Just behind it is Jefferson's Rock, where it is said the immortal Jefferson made his first speech.

I had but little time to make observations, as we did not pause for a moment but pushed on up the hill. The road wound among the rocks and crags for about half a mile. On arriving at the top we found ourselves at the head of what is called Pleasant Valley. There we halted and made our camp. It was indeed a "pleasant valley," lying so quietly among the mountains along the banks of the Potomac. It is nearly surrounded by mountains. We pitched our tents almost under the shadow of the Heights of Maryland.[7]

We remained at Pleasant Valley for four weeks, during which we were called to arms several times, the alarm always proving a false one. We had quite a number of surprises, but always without the party. Being on guard down on the river opposite Harpers Ferry, and having nothing to do at that time, Corporal Dodge[8] and myself took occasion to climb up the steep, rugged side of the heights opposite the Ferry. Way up several hundred feet, at the top of the bluff, is a huge rock which seems about to fall to the ground, so much does it project beyond the side of the cliff. To gain the top of that rock was our intention. We began the ascent, which, for a time, was not very difficult, but on reaching a little shelf on the side of the cliff, we found ourselves in the shade of huge rocks which seemed about to tumble down upon our heads. The ascent now became very difficult, and we were obliged to take off our shoes before we could go farther. But we were bound to go up, and so we climbed on from rock to rock until we stood directly under the huge rock which crowned the summit of the cliff. To go farther seemed to be impossible, but on looking more closely, we discovered a crack in the rock. After climbing up forty or fifty feet we got into the crack, which proved to be a narrow channel worn by the water rushing down the side of the mountain. We followed this channel up to the top of the rock. We found ourselves, as it seemed, standing almost directly over the river, which was in reality several hundred yards from its base.

We had a view which was indeed a sublime one. To the north and west lay the valley of the Potomac, through which ran the grand old river, sparkling in the sun light like a belt of diamonds. To the south west lay the valley of the Shenandoah, watered by a river of the same name. To the south loomed up the dark blue heights of Bolivar and Loudens, beneath the shadows of which lay the little but ruined town of Harpers Ferry.

Here then was the scene of the "John Brown drama." I could almost imagine that the spirit of the old Hero and Martyr was hovering around these heights or resting on the doomed town like a blight. Harpers Ferry consists of old, ruined structures lying in the shadow of the mountains. Along the river bank stretches a long line of half burnt buildings which mark the spot where stood the armory and arsenal. But we had little time to remain on the cliff, for a storm arose in the north west which came rolling up the valley with fearful rapidity, and we were compelled to hasten down the mountain side.

After we had been at Pleasant Valley about four weeks, we received orders to march to Edward's Ferry. The Rebels, it was supposed, were about to attempt to cross, but when we arrived there, all was quiet. We left the Potomac and marched back into the country and camped on the banks of the lovely little Monocacy near Buckeys Town. Here we remained for a short time, when we again received marching orders to go to Camp Crane near Darnstown. Nothing of importance occurred while there. We again received marching orders. This march brought us to the city of Frederick.[9] Here I have been ever since.

Frederick City is a very pretty place, located in the midst of the beautiful valley of Frederick. It contains about ten thousand inhabitants and is a thriving little city. On the 30th of September we were detailed to guard the bridges at Frederick Junction, about three miles from the city.

The above is but an imperfect outline sketch which I have given of our wanderings and doings from the time we left Fond du Lac up to the first of October.

Names of places which we passed through on our way from Wisconsin to Maryland. We left Fond du Lac on the 12th of July about six o'clock P.M. after day light, changed cars, and pushed on into Indiana. Passed through the following towns: White Rose, White Pigeon. Towns in Michigan, Coldwater, Jonesville, Perrysville, Hillsdale, Hudson, Adrian, Palmyra. In Ohio, arrived at Toledo 6:30 P.M. Elmore, Fremont, Cleveland 2:00 A.M., Painesville, Ashtabula, Grant Station. Pennsylvania, Sun Station, Erie, Arrow Creek. New York, Dunkirk, Troy, Painted Post, Buffalo, Lancaster, Attica, Corning, Elmira. Took breakfast there. Pennsylvania, Williamsport, Watsontown, Harrisburg. Arrived in Hagerstown, Maryland.

Frederick City, Camp Banks, September 30. Morning fair and warm, contrasting most agreeably with the cold, wet, and gloomy mornings that had dawned on us for the last few days. The sun, rising slowly above the Southern city of Frederick, shed a flood of golden light upon the encampment, warming it into life and activity.

It was truly refreshing after a sleepless night, on account of the cold (the night having been very cold and chilly), to "turn out" and sun oneself. Oh! Sunshine, what a blessing to the children of the cold earth. Were it not for thee, cold indeed and cheerless would be this world of ours, and dark and night would reign supreme and unbroken. Sunshine! It comes to the cold earth with its cheering rays of golden light like hope to the crushed and broken heart.

Having received orders to be in readiness to march this morning, we soon had our effects safely stowed away in our knapsacks and our tent ready to be taken down. At eight o'clock our tents were struck, and we fell into line in company, along with Co. B and K, who had been detailed with us to act as pickets to guard the rail road and bridges at Frederick Junction, about three miles from Frederick City.

We came to take the place of a detachment of the Massachusetts 13th, who, on our arrival, got aboard the cars for Harpers Ferry. Our camp is finely located, lying upon the green hillside sloping down to the south, terminating in the green and pebbled banks of the sparkling Monocacy. This is a stream of great beauty winding about among the mountains through the green glades and meadows, now resting quietly beneath the shade of some overhanging rock, now dancing among the trees or flashing like a band of silver as it sped onward through the open country.

The day since our arrival has been passed in pitching tents and fixing up our quarters as best we could under the circumstances. The day, as the morning augured, has been one of the pleasantest that we have had for a long time, warm and balmy, reminding one of the days of an "Indian Summer" in our own fair Wisconsin. At sunset we had dress parade, Captain Scott[10] acting in the capacity of colonel. It was rather a small affair, there being only three companies present.

Frederick Junction, October 1st. Morning very fair but cool. A heavy fog hung over the country, wrapping the hills and forests in its folds, hovering over the river like a thousand white winged fairies. As the sun arose the mist disappeared, revealing a sky clear and cloudless. Notwithstanding the cold and chilly night by which it was preceded, the day has proved to be one of warmth and beauty. Such days are common after the burning of the summer has passed; there follows these bright, golden days of sunshine. But the nights are very cold, much colder than they are in Wisconsin. Heavy dews are also a characteristic of this country; they fall so heavily as to resemble a small shower of rain.

This renders it very unpleasant for those who are on guard. Their blankets and clothing become very damp, and the nights being cold and the ground damp, one soon gets cold and chilly. Those on guard often have no other bed than the ground and are sheltered only by a single blanket and the blue sky. This on a warm summer night is not so disagreeable. It is to me something of a pleasure to lie and look way up into the deep sky, bespangled all over with myriads of bright, glittering stars. But at this season of the year, one can find little to interest him in either sky or stars under such circumstances. It is truly outrageous that men, many of them in indifferent health, should be compelled to endure such hardships and expose their health with such impunity.

For two weeks while at Camp Banks, no shelter whatever was afforded the guards, not even a tent. One could not but look with pity upon the poor fellows as (when relieved) they wrapped their blankets about them and lay down upon the damp, cold ground to try and snatch a few moments' slumber, even while shivering with the cold. But the soldier is not his own master; he has no choice of his own, he is dictated to by his superiors, he has no alternative but to obey. He must console himself by remembering that he is doing his duty, and *perhaps a little more*, that he is serving his country, and that such are the vicissitudes of war.

We received our overcoats today, which are gray and very good articles; our blankets have also arrived. We shall sleep warmer in the future, I hope. I was out on a pass today and bathed in the Monocacy.

The monotony of the camp was broken today by an occurrence the likes of which are not infrequent. A fellow with a temper not the mildest and a disposition something like that of a mule refused to do duty, and not having been excused from so doing, he was given his choice: to do his duty like a man or to go to the guard house like a felon. He refused to do either, remarking that there were not men enough to take him there, i.e., to the guard house. Corporal Dodge was ordered to take him prisoner. He requested him to go with him to the guard house in a kind and gentle manner, but the fellow made some insolent reply, refusing to go. The corporal then called upon one Prouty[11] and myself to assist him, which we did. The victim made all the resistance and noise in his power, which created quite an excitement. He was soon overcome, however, and taken to the guard house, where he was bucked and tied to a piece of machinery, where he was to left to sweat for his insubordination.

Frederick Junction, October 2nd. Morning fine and cool as usual. I arose this morning more tired than refreshed after my night's rest—or rather unrest. In fact, I am quite unwell today and indeed have been so for some time past. The health of the regiment in general is very bad. The diarrhea is almost universal, and many are troubled with bilious complaints, while all are suffering with a cold.

It is reported that heavy cannonading was heard by those at [Maj. Gen. Nathaniel] Banks's head quarters in the direction of Chain Bridge. It is said that there is much excitement in Washington. Troops are gathering in great numbers along the banks of the Potomac. A forward movement is soon expected.

Frederick Junction, October 3rd. Things have progressed in camp today about as usual. The same routine of duties occurs as regularly as the sun rises. The day has been warm and sunny, but I have been too much unwell to enjoy it. What a disagreeable thing is disease. It destroys all the beauties of nature and casts a shadow upon her fairest features. The sun may shine as brightly and the sky look as blue and fair; the birds may sing as sweetly and the brooklets murmur as softly. Ay, nature may be in her loveliest mood, yet if disease is in the system, if the fever is burning in the veins and throbbing in the head, under such circumstances all this will fail to be of interest. I am supernumerary of the guard today. G. W. Dodge is acting as sergeant.

Frederick Junction, October 4th. I slept soundly last night and arose much refreshed this morning but still feel weak. I sent home eleven dollars by express. The day has been one of the warmest and fairest that has smiled upon us for a long time. Nothing has occurred in camp today worthy of notice, except a fight which took place between two of the men in Co. B. Such instances, however, are very rare. There was a time when such events were very common. It was no strange sight to see fighting in any of the companies, especially in Co. G. But since the men have been together so long, they have learned to look upon one another almost as brothers. The afternoon passed without the usual drill, and dress parade was also omitted.

Frederick Junction, October 5th. The sun presented a very fine appearance this morning as it rose slowly above the little wood covered hill just east of our encampment. There are a pair of these little hills that nearly join. Every morning a heavy gray mist hangs in between these hills as though a dozen truant clouds had stolen away from up above and hidden away down among the hills. But the sun, when he wakens up in the morning and discovers these little runaways, just darts a few of his brightest rays down among them, which causes this mist to disappear in no time. About noon orders came to strike tents in order to let the ground dry. The afternoon was cloudy with prospects of rain.

Sunday, October the 6th/61. Today has been the Sabbath, and a beautiful one has it been. It has dawned upon us as brightly as though a dark war cloud was not hanging above us like a pall. Yes, the blessed Sabbath comes to give rest and quiet, for even here in the army that day is observed and is, as in civil life, set apart for rest. Last night a little fight took place in our street between one Robbins and Mr. R. Longstaff.[12] It was not a serious encounter, however, and resulted in nothing. The loss of a little blood, and more breath, were the greatest damages. I am on guard today, evening cloudy with prospects of rain.

Monday, Frederick Junction, October 7th. Morning cloudy with a little rain, but towards noon the clouds cleared away, and for a time the sun shone as brightly as ever. But this was only for a short time, for about the middle of the afternoon, dark clouds overcast the sky, the red lightning was seen to dart from cloud to cloud in the most vivid manner, and heavy, rolling thunder was heard in the distance, threatening a storm the like of which we had not yet experienced. As fortune would have it, the heaviest part of the storm passed around to the west. But we were not so fortunate as to escape this easily, for just after dress parade, dark, heavy clouds came rolling up over the hills, laden with wind and rain. Soon it came, the storm bursting upon our little encampment in the most fearful manner. The wind blew and the rain fell in torrents. With the darkness, the storm increased in force and violence; and in fact, so violent had been the storm that the encampment in places was flooded with water. Many of the tents, through the negligence of their inmates, had not been prepared for such a storm, and the wind blew the rain through their canvas walls almost unresistingly. At roll call we all turned out in the rain to answer to our names, as is the custom, let the weather be what it may. During the night one of the wigwams blew down, leaving the unfortunate inmates in a plight not the most desirable. Our wigwam remained all right, however, and the morning found us dry and comfortable.

I came off guard at 11:00 A.M. Heard cannonading about noon in the direction of the Potomac. A little engagement has doubtless taken place. Had much rather participated in it than to have been here doing nothing.

I find myself very much unwell and have no appetite.

Willard became seriously ill and was taken to a large hospital in Frederick. There he found himself in the midst of a mass of suffering humanity and was profoundly moved by what he saw. Sickness was rampant in Civil War camps, and about twice as many men died of illness as were killed in action. This occurred for three reasons. First was the lack of immunity. Most of the new recruits were country boys who had not been exposed to many common diseases, such as measles, and so had not built up antibodies to make them immune or resistant. This meant that they were ill equipped not only to fight off the sickness but also to mitigate its severity. Second was an almost total lack of sanitation. Untold thousands died of typhoid and dysentery from drinking polluted water, which often contained sewage, and the filthy conditions made a perfect breeding ground for bacteria. Third was the primitive state of medical knowledge. Doctors were ignorant of the nature and cause of infection and disease, making effective treatment virtually impossible. A doctor who did no harm was the best that could frequently be hoped for by the patient. Louis Pasteur's paper showing that germs cause disease was not issued until the very end of the war—and not accepted by the medical profession until later still—and Joseph Lister's description of how antiseptic conditions could prevent infection, and thus save many of the wounded, was still years away.

Within a few decades after Appomattox, it was generally recognized that many Civil War soldiers had died unnecessarily from conditions already seen as primitive. Gen. O. O. Howard wrote between 1890 and 1900 of the Civil War that "the loss of life on our part which follows any successful strife is appalling, mostly due to the want of the knowledge of hygiene and of self-care in the field and in camps."[13]

Willard eventually recovered, but instead of returning to his regiment, he was unable to walk away from those so desperately in need and chose to remain at the hospital as a nurse. His military records show that he was officially detailed to this duty.

Frederick City, November 11. Since the 7th of last month I have had a very severe time. Was very sick on the morning of the 8th. A burning fever set in, and I was very much indisposed indeed. On the 10th I was removed to the hospital in Frederick City. This building in which the sick are placed is the old barracks built in the days of George III which had been fitted up for a hospital, as there were a great many sick in our regiment. It is a large, stone structure just north of the city and consists of two long buildings separated only by a small wooden structure, the use of which I cannot tell. These buildings together are at least 225 feet in length by 40 in width and are two story and a half high. The building on the west has a wing half as large as the main building. It is inclosed by long rows of stalls for the use of the cavalry, except on the west side, which is inclosed by a high board fence. This side of the inclosure borders on Market Street, the main thoroughfare of the city. This inclosure around the old barracks contains about fifteen acres of the prettiest grounds to be found anywhere.

In this building are the sick and the wounded ones of our regiment. Here have I been housed ever since the 10th of last month. For two weeks the fever, with its horrible delirium, burned in every vein and throbbed in the head as though it would consume my very life. But it is now passed and I am recovering very fast. While I have been here, five have died with the fever[14] and five others were buried who were killed in the engagement near Harpers Ferry.[15] Our troops, however, were victorious. Things in the hospital are progressing finely, the sick as a general thing are recovering.

Frederick City, November 12th. The morning was fine and the weather promising. Was down in the city in the forenoon, also in the afternoon, had my miniature taken. Called, with my friend the fife major Rodgers,[16] on Mrs. Suman and had a very agreeable time; was strongly urged to come again.

The day, as it began, ended in beauty. The evening was clear and serene, the sun setting in cloudless splendor shed a flood of golden light over the lovely valley, lighting up the dark blue hills in the distance, resting upon their tops like a crown of gold; resting there for a moment, then fading gently away into the gloom of twilight.

Frederick City, November 13th/61. Morning fair and pleasant as usual, my health still recovering. An accident occurred here today of the most shocking kind. One of the Maryland Cavalry was accidentally shot by one of his comrades. The ball entered the side of his head near the temple and came out at the top. He only survived a short time. He was a lieutenant and was well thought of by the regiment. It was a painful casualty and seemed to fill the hearts of the soldiery with sorrow. A gloom spread throughout the whole encampment. The Maryland boys are a happy, musical set of fellows as I ever saw, but now their mirth was turned to sadness and their music was hushed in silence. He was a native of Maryland and lives about five miles from the city. He will be taken home tomorrow.

Frederick City, November 14th/61. The unfortunate man who was shot yesterday was taken home today, accompanied by the Maryland Cavalry. The day, which had been so warm and bright, ended in clouds and rain. One of our men is supposed to be dying by inward bleeding.

Frederick City, November 15th/61. The rain, which began last evening, continued all night. The morning came cold, wet, and dismal, affording a strong contrast to the bright, sunny days that have preceded it. Thus are the changes in human life; now bright and sunny, now dark and cheerless. Hope for a time lights up the human heart, then dies away like the evening twilight into the gloom of night. Yes, hopes wither and die and we are left to misery and despair. The man (Austen[17]) who was thought to be dying last evening is dead. He died about eight o'clock.

He is to be buried today at three o'clock. His death was very much unexpected; he was well and healthy only a few days since. He was one of the best of nurses. Another of our men is very sick; there is not much hope of his recovery. He is very young. It seems hard, very hard that he should die.

Afternoon. The funeral of Mr. Austen took place this afternoon. He was buried by the Maryland Home Guards. The weather continues disagreeable, raining continually, with a little snow. But there are signs of a fair day tomorrow. Things are prospering as usual.

Frederick, Sunday morning, November 24th. An interval of several days necessarily occurs since the date of my last notes. This indeed is the result of a visit with a family in the country, where I and one Rodgers, the fife major, have been spending several days. And a most pleasant and agreeable time we have had of it. Never were there kinder or warmer hearted people than the Bengle family. Their residence is about four miles from the city. They have a fine, large farm and every thing that a farmer can wish. We remained with the family from the 16th to the 23rd. While there, we amused ourselves in various ways, hunting, rambling through the groves, and clamoring over the hills among the rocks and crags. We returned to the hospital Saturday the 23rd. Today is dark, cold, and stormy. The wind blowing from the west bears with it snow and rain. One of our men has died during our stay in the country.[18]

Frederick City, November 25th/61. Morning cold and cloudy. Had quite a snowstorm last night. The ground this morning was covered with snow, reminding one of his Northern home, where the snows fall heavy and deep and the winter is severe and cold. The leafless trees, the cold, bleak sky, the ground covered with snow reminds one that winter is near. Soon the bright, beautiful days will be gone and the winter with its chilling breath will be upon us. But—

> Welcome Spring with its balmy breath
> And the Summer with its golden bloom,
> Welcome Autumn with its golden fruit
> And Winter with its storms and gloom.

Was down in the city this afternoon; got lost and had to enquire my way out. The evening was quite pleasant.

Frederick City, November 26th/61. Morning warm and pleasant. The sun shines clear and bright, affording a fine contrast to the cold, bleak day of yesterday. Thus, the changes come, the warm and bright, the cold and gloomy, sadness and sorrow, joy and gladness. Since last evening two more of our men have passed from life unto death—from this world into that of another, which I trust is brighter and fairer.[19]

Frederick City, November 27th/61. Morning cold and cloudy, with every indication of a storm. It began to rain and snow about ten o'clock. The funeral ceremonies of those who died yesterday took place today. A portion of the Home Brigade[20] were present. They, in the absence of our regiment, have performed the ceremonies of burial over those who have died here in the hospital. Notwithstanding the inclemency of the weather, many of those who had been sick turned out, forming quite a respectable appearance. Quietly we laid them down and discharged our "farewell shot" over their graves, and left them to sleep on in peace. Another of our men is supposed to be dying.

The storm continues, and in fact, it is a cold, gloomy day. Thus it is, sunshine and shade, fair weather and foul!

Frederick City, November 28th. Morning very cold; no sunshine, all clouds and storms. Such weather is very disagreeable, it is so change-able. One day it will be warm, and the sun shines in golden beauty; the next, cold, dark, and stormy.

Never was there a country with lovelier scenery, hills, and valleys; no country with brighter summers or lovelier falls. I am no longer on the sick list, but am acting as *nurse*.

Frederick City, November 30th. The day has been very fine. Once more the sun has made its appearance and has smiled down upon us so benignly as to make us forget that he had been playing truant for the last three or four days. Yes, old Sol looks so bright and smiling that we cannot help but forget his past inconstancy. Nothing of importance has occurred today. (I have forgotten to mention the death of another of our men; he died Thursday evening, the 28th. He was buried today.)[21]

Frederick City, December 2nd. Weather agreeable. Went down to the city with one Braynard[22] who, by the way, got somewhat intoxicated, the result of which was I had a crazy man to deal with. Our regiment is reported to be on the way to this place.

Frederick, December 9th. Since the 3rd I have been very busy, having had a large number of new patients to care for. A number have been added to the sick list from the several regiments of General Banks's division. Dr. Stone is in charge of the sick in the hospital. The weather has been very fine indeed. Our regiment has returned to the city again; they came here on Thursday last. The ward master just came in to get assistance to "lay out" a young man (a Pennsylvania soldier) who has just expired. Deaths are quite frequent here. Some die after a long and painful sickness, others drop away hardly without a moment's warning.

December 12th, 1861. The weather still continues remarkably fair. There have been no storms to speak of for a long time—all has been sunshine, warmth, and beauty. The hospital has been enlarged. It is now a brigade hospital. The men of the Wisconsin 3rd who are in the hospital are all getting along finely. There is, however, much mortality among those of other regiments; deaths are not infrequent. The Wisconsin 3rd is now encamped just on the outskirts of the city. Colonel Ruger has been appointed provost marshal, and our regiment is acting provost guard of the city.

Frederick, December 19th/61. The weather has been very fine since the date of my last entry; there have been no storms or cold weather. Our regiment is still encamped near the city. They are to go into winter quarters here. Barracks are being built for them to winter in. The hospital has been changed from a brigade to a division hospital. There have been no deaths since the 13th. At that time three men died; one was Wisconsin 3rd,[23] one Pennsylvania 29th, and one New York 9th. There was also a teamster who died at the same time. All four of them were buried side by side in the city cemetery.

There are now twenty of our men (the Wisconsin 3rd) buried here side by side.[24] Oh! How sad, how *very* sad that they should be thus called away from their homes and firesides to die almost alone, far from home and friends, with no loved one near to soothe them in their hours of sickness and pain, with no friendly hand to clasp their own when the dark hour approaches, when life is swallowed up in death and they pass from time to eternity. Oh! It is hard to die anywhere or under any circumstances, but to die here in such a place, among strangers, almost alone! Yet such are the vicissitudes connected with the soldier's life. 'Tis not that death is terrible or that the grave is dark and lonely. No, 'tis not this. For beyond the grave there is a world more fair than this, a land where all is sunshine, a land where death can never come, where hopes are not crushed and blighted and hearts do not wither and die! Yes—

'Tis sweet to think there is
A better land than this,
Where pain and sorrow cannot come
To taint unmingled bliss.

December 21st/61. Weather fair as usual. Many improvements are being made here at the hospital. One of the Wisconsin 3rd[25] died this morning and was buried this evening. I could not but shed a tear of sadness as I thought of his family and the stricken ones at home. Ah, how sad they will be, and how lonely! The wife—the partner of his bosom, and little ones—the offsprings of their love. Ah! Will not they be stricken with sorrow?

Names of those in my ward, December 21st, 1861

William Hoppel	Pennsylvania 29th
Thomas Moore	Pennsylvania 30th
A. Bullock	Michigan Cavalry
Simon Marvin	Wisconsin 3rd
[Abner] Gould	Wisconsin 3rd
Marshal Hane	
William Conley	Wisconsin 3rd
Orlando Rodgers	Wisconsin 3rd
F. C. Foltz	Wisconsin 3rd
Godfry Becker	Indiana 27th
John Donnelly	Maryland 1st
Godfrey Baker	[died January 1st, 1862]

December 22nd/61, Sunday afternoon. Today has been cold and windy. The sun shines dimly through the leaden sky, and dark, heavy clouds hang upon the horizon's hem, giving strong indications of a storm. Today is the Sabbath, but were it not for the chiming of the church bells, it would be hardly known, for we are very busy here today, as there is to be an inspection of the hospital generally.

Evening—inspection has taken place, and "well done" has been said of us. Thanks to you, kind Doctor, certainly I have labored hard enough to win some praise.

Monday morning, 23rd. Weather cold and stormy. The storm began just after dark and continued during the night, and it has stormed all day. Last night was a wild one, indeed. It was intensely dark, the wind blew fiercely, dashing the sleet against the wooden panes and whistling around these old barrack buildings like the wail of a thousand fiends.

Today was the execution day of John Lanagin, the murderer of Major Lewis[26] of the 46th Pennsylvania Regiment. He was hung today about two miles from the city. I was present at the execution, and never did I witness a more revolting spectacle. A man hanging by the neck, being murdered by authority! He was young and possessed intellectual appearance but was addicted to the use of strong liquor. This is the cause of all!

Christmas Eve, Frederick, December 24th. The weather today has been cold, but the sky has been clear. The storm of yesterday terminated in a gentle fall of snow. Yesterday was indeed a wild and stormy day. The wind blowing from the west drove the sleet with terrific velocity. Yesterday was the execution day of John Lanagin. It was a sad affair to see him hung—he was so young, so interesting in appearance. There was not a soldier's heart that did not throb with emotions of sympathy. As the carriage in which he was approached the place of execution accompanied by the Wisconsin 3rd, the band played a solemn death march and the long line marched slowly on, forming a hollow square around the scaffold. The prisoner viewed the preparations for his death calmly and without a shudder. He was very cool and self possessed and walked up the scaffold with a firm tread, and looked calmly around the long lines of soldiers below. He was very pale but bore his fate without a murmur. When upon the scaffold, he was asked if he was ready. He said that he was, that he was ready and willing to die, and that he had nothing to say only (said he) tell the soldiers to shun the use of intoxicating liquor. All then descended from the scaffold and he was kept standing alone. The trap was sprung—he fell, his neck was broken, and after a few slight struggles he was dead. He died a victim of intemperance.

Christmas, December 25th/61. 'Tis Christmas day, but to me it has not been a merry one. All day have I been in my ward room with the sick. One year ago today I was at home with my friends, enjoying the blessings of civil life. But what a change! Today I find myself a thousand miles from home, an attendant in a hospital, my home the sick room, my companions the sick, the dying, and the dead! Yet I am happy, for I am in the discharge of a high and noble duty. To take care of the sick and afflicted is now my duty, and it gives me pleasure to care for them and provide for their wants. Two more poor soldiers have died today. They have been sick for a long time, wasting away slowly by disease. But now they have gone, dying together, sinking hand in hand in death!

Frederick, December 26th/61. Another has gone to that better land beyond the grave. He died this morning at five o'clock. Calmly and gently he died, and we folded his white hands over his breast. Poor fellow! He has suffered long but is now at rest. Sleep on, poor soldier, though far from home and among strangers; yet often will the stranger come and shed a tear over thy grave. Yes,

> Soldier rest, thy war's o'er
> Sleep the sleep that knows no waking,
> Dream of battle fields no more
> Days of danger, nights of waking.

December 28th. Today has been very busy to me, as it has been the general cleaning up day. Tomorrow we are to have an inspection of the hospital. Another poor soldier died today, and there are still others who are not expected to live.

Frederick, December 30/61. Sunday evening. Today has been warm, bright, and lovely. It has seemed more like a summer's morning than a day at this time of the year. Today has been the Sabbath, and bright and beautiful it has been, the sky clear and cloudless, the sunshine golden, in fact, all nature seemed to be wearing its loveliest garb. The rich but solemn music of the church bells has been ringing out over the city, reminding me of the little church way down in Wisconsin where I have passed many pleasant hours in the quiet enjoyment of Christian society. Was over to the barracks yesterday. Another man died yesterday and is to be buried today.

Frederick, December 31st. Today is the last of the old year, quietly and calmly 'tis passing away. It's a lovely evening, the sky is clear and cloudless, the sun is sinking in the crimson west, lighting up the dark blue hills and shedding a flood of golden luster over the quiet valley. Yes, the gray old year is dying, passing away, to give place to the new one. Fare thee well! Thou hast brought us many changes, some for good and some for ill; thou hast seen us joyous and happy, and thou hast seen us when sorrows cast their shadows darkly about the heart. Yes, many are the changes that have occurred since thy birth. Friends have met—have loved—have parted, never to meet again. Death has taken away the fair and beautiful. War has lain its desolating hand upon our land, and its clouds darken our fair skies.

January 1st, 1862. Today is the first of the new year. Welcome to the bright, young, and lovely "New Year," may thy short reign bring with it peace, prosperity, and plenty. May the dark clouds that have gathered about us pass away, may the sunshine of peace and prosperity illuminate our darkened land. This New Year's Day has indeed been a lovely one; it has been more like the first day of summer than like that of winter. There is no snow or frost, the sun shines brightly and the sky is clear and cloudless.

Another soldier died last night. He died with the old year. Another has died today, he died in my ward. He was young, a mere youth, just beginning life. All night I watched by his bedside, and today I was with him till he expired. This afternoon I was down in the city and had a New Year's dinner at Mrs. Suman's.

January 4th, 1862. The weather has been remarkably fair up to yesterday afternoon. It began to cloud up about three o'clock, giving strong indications of a storm. And it came. It began to snow about eight o'clock, but it was not of long duration. This morning the ground, which yesterday was so brown and bare, was wrapped in a pure white mantle of snow. I could not but pity the poor sentinels as I saw them this morning, pacing slowly up and down along their beats. It began to storm again this morning, and the wind blowing sharply from the west drove the snow fiercely against the face of the guard as he walked slowly up and down, apparently regardless of the storm raging about him. He was doubtless in thoughts of other and better times. Since my last date, two more have gone, it's hoped to the better land. One died on the 2nd, the other this morning. So they go, one after another, into eternity.

Unlike today, in the nineteenth century, people were accustomed to seeing death and living with its presence around them. With medical science unable to diagnose or treat most diseases, no vaccines for prevention, or drugs to kill infection, death could come very suddenly from the most minor of incidents. Typically, a person died at home rather than in a hospital and was made ready for burial and buried by his family and friends rather than by a funeral home. Yet neither Willard nor his comrades were prepared for death on this scale—unrelenting day after day, taking the young in large numbers, far from home and unattended by loved ones. For many of Lewis Hoag's comrades, his death was the first they had experienced in the war.

Frederick City, January 12th/62. Since my last date, another week has come and gone, bringing with it varied changes for good and ill. During the past week death has visited us but twice. One from the Indiana 27th and one from the Wisconsin 3rd have been taken from our midst and have been borne by the "grim ferryman" across death's dark and turbid waters. The first died January the 2nd, the latter January 11th. Though both died in the beginning of the year, yet the manner of their death was very much different. One, the first, died of a long and lingering disease, the other instantly. The first lingered for weeks and days between life and death, wasting away slowly day by day, till at last death came and broke the last bond that bound him to life. Poor Bias! He suffered much, wasting slowly but surely away, racked with pains. His reason died long before the vital spark had left his body, and he lay for a long time madly raving with the horrid delirium of death. But at last he died, and his weary spirit went home to that better land where mortals do not die and where all is bright and fair.

Lewis Hoag of the Wisconsin 3rd was accidentally shot by one of his comrades on the evening of the 11th and expired instantly, hardly without struggle or a groan. The shot entered his left side, passing upward through the heart, out at the shoulder. He was on guard, as also was the one who shot him. They were thoughtlessly amusing themselves, practicing the bayonet exercise. While thus engaged, poor Hoag was shot. The accident occurred early in the evening, and he was immediately brought to the hospital. We took him to the dead room. He was not yet cold, but death had glazed his eye and sprinkled the death dew over his high, white brow. Gently and mournfully we laid him out and dressed him in the snowy habiliments of the grave. One after another of his friends came forward, pushing their way through the crowd. They gazed eagerly down into his pale, ghastly features and gathered around him silently and sadly. The dead room was lighted only by a single lantern, which I held in my hand as I stood at the table by the corpse. The little room was quickly filled by his friends and comrades, who pressed forward, anxious to look upon their dead comrade, for he was one that they all loved. It was indeed a sad sight to see him lying there wrapped in death's chilly embrace—so young—so fair, a sight that brought tears to every eye. It was hard, *very* hard that one so young should come to this untimely end—that one like him should be thus stricken down in the vigor of youth, in the budding of manhood, without a moment's warning, to be hurried into eternity unprepared!

Yet it matters but little how we die, as death must be the common lot of all. Death will come in some form sooner or later, and perhaps it is a mercy to die thus, rather than to linger along, wasting away slowly by disease. Yet it is hard to die with no opportunity of sending a single word or token to the loved ones at home.

They were both young men, just in the vigor of manhood. Poor Hoag! He was an only son, his parents were old and poor, and Lewis was their darling—their pet—the light and joy of their old age. But he is gone and they are left alone. How sad to be thus bereft in old age. How lonely must appear their little cottage in the West, robbed of its brightest light, its only joy! Oh, how many homes are thus made lonely, how many hearthstones are thus robbed of their brightest charms?

The weather during the last week has been somewhat changeable, yet as a general thing it has been very pleasant. Monday we had a little dash of snow. On Thursday the 9th, I visited the barrack and had a good time chatting with some of my old companions. The boys are getting along nicely and appear to enjoy themselves in the best possible manner. Their quarters are very comfortable and are fitted up with taste, and look as though they might possibly pass as an apology for a home.

Willard had been at the Frederick hospital for some three months and seen hundreds of men suffer and scores die of disease and accident. He had nursed them patiently, sat by their bedsides, and felt the pain of their families. This had been the extent of the war to him, and he was filled with empathy for the suffering and consumed with the feeling of looming tragedy. Willard was a thoughtful man, and he began to philosophize on the meaning of life and death.

Frederick, January 19th, 1862. Another week has passed away, and another Sabbath has dawned in beauty upon this dark and stormy world. Thus, week after week and month after month glides by, hurrying us on into eternity. Each week brings with it good and ill and witnesses the budding of new hopes, some to be fulfilled, others to be crushed and blighted.

This, at best, is a world of changes, from sunshine to shade, from darkness to light, and it is well; for who would wish to live a life without change, a dull monotony. Were it always day—a cloudless sunshine, were there no night—no darkness or storms, were there no sorrows—no pains, all joys and sunshine, life would be but one changeless round of pleasures that would soon become insipid, and we would never know how to appre-

ciate them. The sorrows of life only fit us for the full enjoyment of its pleasures; the darkness of night teaches us how much to prize the sunshine.
The storms of winter only make the loveliness of summer more lovely.

This, it is true, is a world of sadness and sorrow; disappointments surround us on every hand, they spring up to meet us. Often, very [often],
our fondest hopes are blighted and the fairest prospects are darkened, misery stares at us at every corner, and the world seems like a wilderness, a
desert, with but few bright spots to cheer us. Yet after all, there is much of
happiness mingled with the sorrows, and the sorrows and trials are given
us only to teach us the true value of the real pleasures of life.

During the week just ended, another soldier has completed his existence in this life and has, like his predecessors, begun a new one in that
bright land across the dark valley of death. His name was Smith. Brought
into my ward—George Sipple, 46th Pennsylvania, came in January
6th/62, Henry Little of the New Jersey 19th on the 18th. He is sick with
the typhoid fever. Henry Burlingham brought into my ward January
21st.

The weather during the week past has been cloudy and rainy nearly all
the time. There has not been one clear, pleasant day during the whole
week, yet flashes of golden sunshine would gleam through the broken
clouds like hopes dimly lighting up the dark chambers of the heart. Things
have progressed here at the hospital about as usual. There have been but
few deaths lately. Have been down in the city several times. It has been
very lonely here the past week. It is a very lonely place to be continually
among the dead and dying.

In war, suffering and death come in such large numbers that it is often hard to
take in the meaning of each individual tragedy. A thousand people killed is an
impersonal statistic, but to observe firsthand the agony of one makes it very real
indeed. Now occurred an event that clearly had this kind of personal impact on
Willard—the death of a young man he had attended with love.

Frederick City, February 1st. The first of the winter months has
passed and another has begun. Thus month after month rolls away, each in
turn bears us nearer to the borders of this life and closer to the dark valley
across which lies that beautiful land where months are never numbered and
where death comes not, and where pain and sickness are never known.

During the week just ended today, only one more of those sick at the
hospital has died. His name was Levi Close.[27] I had often visited him

during his long illness and found him to be a young man of no ordinary quality. His broad, high forehead and expressive eyes—so large, so blue—gave evidence of an intelligence of no common character, while the beauty of his language and the goodness of his heart betrayed a Christian spirit that was truly lovely to witness. It was known that he was dying all the afternoon of Saturday last. He failed very fast, and early in the evening he gave unmistakable evidence of his approaching dissolution. He sent for me to come and see him. I went up into his room. The ward mistress was by his bedside. I went up to him and took his thin, cold hand in mine. "I am glad to see you," said he, for "I wish to say good by to you before I go." "Are you afraid to die, Levi?" said I, putting my hand up on his white forehead and bending close down to him, for he could only talk in a whisper. "Oh! No, Willard. I do not fear to die, for then I shall be at rest. I have been sick a long, long time and I am anxious to go to that better land where there is no pain or sickness, where I hope to meet you all." He was very low and weak, and [it] seemed to hurt him to talk. He closed his eyes and lay for a long time as if resting in a quiet slumber. The room was perfectly still, dimly lighted by a single candle which I held in my hand. It was a wild, dark night without, and the storm was loud and high. The wind whistled around the rough corners of the old barrack buildings, wailing and hammering through the cracks and crevices.

Poor Close was dying! His two brothers[28] were kneeling by the side of his low cot, weeping as though their hearts would break. We thought he would not speak again, but he opened his eyes once more, and turning to his brothers and taking a hand of each in his, said, "Do not weep for me, and when you go home you must tell Mother not to feel bad. Tell Sister good by for me, and kiss the baby for me, too." Then, shaking hands with us all, bade us good by, closed his eyes, and died, hardly without a struggle. We dressed him in his uniform, and he was carried to the dead room, where so many had lain before him. His was the death of a Christian. He died with bright hopes of the future. The grave had no terror for him, though it was deep and dark and clouds dark and appalling hung over the lonely valley of death. Yet through the darkness gleamed the lights of the great city which lies just beyond the dark valley.

This marked the end of Willard's stint as a nurse, and he returned to active duty. His regiment had spent the winter in camp and had yet to fight a major battle, so he likely had seen more death and sorrow than any other man in his unit up till that time.

The weather during the week past has been one of clouds and storms, yet it has not been very cold. Have been down in the city several times. I returned to my company Wednesday last. I found the boys all well and hearty, and apparently enjoying camp life very much.

I have visited the hospital several times since I came away, having taken a deep interest in the welfare of many of the sick in the hospital. There is one especially, his name is Peterson.[29] He has been sick for a long, long time and has wasted away to a mere skeleton. He is the most emaciated human being that I ever saw. It was thought that he could not live. The ward mistress (Miss Fitzroy) came to me one day with the request that I should go and take care of him for a little while. I consented and went to his room. I found him in a most horrid condition. He was entirely helpless and had not been washed for several days. This was a difficult task, and a very disagreeable one, but I went to work with a cheerful heart and soon had him washed, and clean clothes on him and his bed. He had been given up by all, but he soon began to recover. I devoted my whole time to him and watched by his bedside night and day. When I left the hospital he had recovered so far as to be able to eat and talk, and there were hopes of his recovery. He still continues to improve.

I have said that when I returned to my company, I found my old friends and comrades all in good health and spirits. There are two exceptions which I forgot to mention. I found James Scott in the regimental hospital very sick. George Howk, too, was on the sick list, being troubled with fits. I watched with him nearly all day. One Rance Clark started for home on the evening of the 29th, having been discharged on account of ill health. Was down in the city with Lieutenant Giddings[30] and Corporal Dodge. Giddings was the officer of the guard, Co. G was on picket, and we visited them at their several posts.

Camp Ruger, Frederick, February 9th. Today is the Sabbath, and the ringing of the church bells tell of another week that has passed—gone into eternity. Thus they go, week after week, month after month, year after year. Men, too, sicken and pass away, growing old like the year. The day is beautiful and warm, the sky is clear, and the sun shines in all the beauty of golden splendor. Oh sun! How welcome are thy rays after so long a time of clouds and storm. All nature rejoices in thy light. The little valley seems to smile in thy golden beams, and the snow crested mountains look up and thank thee for thy warmth.

I was over to the city burying ground a few days ago and could not but feel sad as I looked over the many graves of those who are sleeping there. Twenty-one of our regiment have been buried here in Frederick. Poor Folts[31] first led the way across the valley of death. Others sickened and died, following one another over the dark waters. Oh! How hard to die thus—almost alone—so far from home and friends and those we love. But death will come, and it matters but little when or where we die. Death at best is but a change, and a change from a land of darkness and sorrow to one of joy and gladness.

The weather during the past week has been, as a general thing, very disagreeable. Sunday the 2nd was a bright, beautiful day, and there was a good chance of having some fine weather, but we were doomed to be disappointed, for before the day was done, the whole aspect of nature was changed. Dark, heavy clouds came rolling up from the west, the air grew colder, the whole sky became overcast, and there was every prospect of a storm. And it came. It began to snow during the night, and in the morning the ground was covered. The storm continued during the whole day and part of the night. It was a real old northwester, such as we often have up in the North. The wind blew furiously, bearing with it a storm of snow that was truly *Northern* in its proclivities.

I was on guard that day, and a rough old time we had of it. This was the first time that I stood guard since I was on guard October the 7th at the Junction. Things have changed very much since then. The lovely little valley has been robbed of its carpet of green, the trees had been shorn of their summer garments, the mountain side was covered with snow, and the flowers had withered by the wayside. The autumn had indeed been a lovely one, but its days of golden beauty had been passed (or at least many of them) by me in sickness and pain. But health had returned again, and on this cold, bleak wintry day, I again found myself performing the act of the soldier.

The storm continued all day, and the night was cold and dark. But the long hours wore away, and the morning came at last. The weather continued stormy during nearly the remainder of the week. There has hardly been an hour of sunshine. Several have died at the hospital whose names I do not know.

Life in camp is a school in which to study human nature. Here are congregated those of all classes and ages. The old and young, the high, the low, the moral, and the degraded. Here one may observe the working of every passion. It is sad—*very* sad to observe how far the rude and demoralizing influences predominate. Drinking, profanity, card playing, and intemperance are almost universal. Yet we have some innocent amusements. Often the whole company join in a dance and seem to enjoy themselves in right good earnest. We have a great deal to do, yet we find some time for amusement.

The company was on provost guard Wednesday the 5th. The object of this was to guard the prisoners confined in the provost guard house. There are 154 prisoners confined there. The principal crimes are those of drunkenness, disorderly conduct, running the guard, etc. There are some, however, who are confined here for desertion. Poor Lanagin was confined there for a long time previous to his execution.

While there, I took occasion to go with Corporal Dodge to the different rooms to see the prisoners. It was a sight of no uncommon interest. Within those dark, dreary rooms were many who had left home respectable and moral, but who had fallen victims to the many degrading vices that continually beset the soldier's pathway.

There were those of almost every clime, class, and age. The gray-haired old man and the youth of tender years, the red-eyed inebriate and dark-browed, scowling villain, side by side with the pale-browed youth of intellect and genius. There were those of every character and disposition—the meek and resigned, the turbulent and boisterous. There were those who laughed at their chains, and there were others who sat down in silent and sullen despair.

There is one who would attract special notice. He is a mere youth with fair skin, a high brow, and a countenance of intellect and beauty. His eyes are large and dark, and his hair hangs in masses of heavy, dark curls about a brow of snowy whiteness. He was arrested for having "run the guard" and has been confined in the dreary place for a long time. He was court-martialed a few days since and sentenced to six days of solitary confinement, to be fed on bread and water, and six dollars taken from his pay. Why such a sentence should be passed on him is more than I can account for. Others of the same company (Co. G of the Wisconsin 3rd) have done things much worse and have escaped punishment. He has unfortunately, by his bold, outspoken way, won the dislike of Capt. E. L. Hubbard[32] of Co. G., and it is a well known fact that the captain is often actuated by a base, low desire for revenge and resorts to the most contemptible methods of spiting someone. Hence he snapped at this as a favorable opportunity of exercising his petty malice. One would think that one in so high a position as he would have something better to think of. Noble captain!

On the evening of the 7th, I attended a party in the country at Fair View Farm. The party went on nicely and I enjoyed myself in the best possible manner. Fair View is the place where I and the fife major Rodgers passed a week so pleasantly last fall. I shall never forget the kindness which they have shown to me. When I was sick they often visited me, and when I was able to ride they came and took me in their carriage to their own home.

The young people of Maryland are not slow in the art of enjoying themselves. The girls seem to think that the soldiers are all right, and of course, the soldiers *know* that the *ladies* are. We remained at Fair View till 11:00 A.M. of the next day, when they brought us back to the city.

The people of Maryland are much more illiterate than those of the North. Their privileges for schooling are very limited. It is not infrequent that I have found young men and women that could neither read nor write. They lack the enterprise of the North. There seems to be a feeling of quiet pervading society which the trumpet of war, sounded so near their own borders, or the tramp of armies, can hardly awaken.

Names of those of our regiment who have died while here in Frederick City.

Foltz	Sept. 18th, 1861	Co. B
Mosier	" "	Co. C
H. Raymond	" "	Co. C
D. Rennels	" "	Co. A
J. Mason	" "	Co. D
S. Williams	" "	Co. D
Buckington	died of the fever	Co. J
Gaston	" "	Co. E
Pierce	" "	Co. H
C. Austin	bled to death	Co. C
Thompson	died of the fever	Co. H
Remele	" "	Co. K
Yarger	" "	Co. K
Northrup	" "	Co. F
I. Narracong		Co. G

Bemis		Co. B
L. Hoag	shot Jan. 11th	Co. I
L. Close	died of the fever Jan. 26th	Co. D

Two are buried in the Catholic burying ground. One died at Baltimore, two at Georgetown, making twenty-two in all.

When in military hospitals with time on his hands, and facing pain, suffering, and death all around him, Willard found in poetry a great refuge. He wrote numerous poems in Frederick, and preceded them with short essays on poetry and his impulse to compose it. A number of the poems that Willard wrote during the war are placed within the body of this book. Many others appear in the appendix.

What a lovely thing is poetry. How expressive! How simple yet how sublime when one feels like going away alone to ponder—to muse of the past, the present, and to dream of the future. When we are happy and light hearted, the poet's muses have the power to please. The true poet weaves his fantasies into a thousand beautiful forms and fantastic imageries. He dreams of joys, of hopes, of gladness. Then he is happy, and the world wears a bright and golden gleam, and the sun light of joy falls about him and illumines his pathway. He sings, and the notes of his songs come abroad in deep and cheerful melody.

When we feel sadness and sorrow, and all the world appears cold and lonely and the heart is sad and weary; at such a time, what is there more soothing than the poet's musings? The poet identifies himself with someone whose hopes he imagines have been blighted, the stricken one of his imagination. His heart grows sad, and he warbles forth his songs, as though he himself had been the victim of some dreadful disappointment. Thus he identifies himself with those of every kind. . . .

It is well that we know not what is in store for us in the future. The veil which hangs before us and futurity was indeed wove by the hand of mercy. . . .

This life, like the poet's dream, is made up of joys and sorrows. The sunshine of gladness and the gloom of despair greet us upon every hand. Today we smile and our hearts are light and happy. Tomorrow we weep with sorrow and our hearts are filled with sadness. Today the sun shines upon us and our pathway is illuminated with its golden luster. Tomorrow the sky is overcast with clouds of gloom. Yet, when taken rightly, we find that even our misfortunes result in good. Yes, life is very fair indeed.

> The poet may sing of the sorrow of life
> And pour forth a dolorous tale,
> He may sing of its sorrows, disappointments, and strife
> And sadly his lot may bewail.
>
> What though he murmurs in joyless despair
> Singing and sighing so sad,
> The world still around us is brilliant and fair
> If we keep our heart right, we'll always be glad.
>
> What though the storm clouds about us should lower
> What though the bright sky with clouds be o'ercast
> What though the tempest around us should roar
> All will be bright—will be sunshine at last.
>
> Then why should we murmur, in grief bending low?
> Why should our hearts be joyless and sad?
> Why should the teardrops so readily flow?
> *If we keep our hearts right, we'll always be glad.*

I have now completed this little volume, in which I have recorded some of the most interesting events which have occurred since I left the little quiet village of Neenah. I am sorry that I could not have given a more interesting account of the Wisconsin 3rd and hope that in my next (if I should write another book, though), I can give an account of some more stirring and interesting events.

To Those at Home

> This book I send to thee
> This simple record of the past,
> This little book so dear to me
> When sadness o'er my heart was cast.

To my faithful friend farewell
Thou no more will with me roam,
Go and of my wanderings tell
To those dear loved ones at home.

BOOK TWO

Life in Camp
or
Scenes by the Wayside
A Sketch of Life as Soldier

With Scenes and Adventures in the Valley of the Shenandoah

How short is life—'tis but an empty dream,
And we, the creatures of an hour
Like shadows flitting o'er a stream
Transient as a summer flower.

Dark are the shades o'er my country now falling,
Blighted Columbia, once happy and fair
While on sweeps the storm cloud, darkly appalling
And the bold Eagle droops his broad wings in despair.

*T*oday we expect to go into the hospital, have whatever is wrong taken care of, and emerge healthier than when we went in. During the war in Vietnam, soldiers who survived long enough to make it to the hospital usually pulled through. In the past, however, this was not the case. Hospitals were seen as dangerous places, as indeed they were. Military hospitals were no exception. When American soldier Paul Lee took sick while defending Long Island in 1776, he fearfully wrote home on August 5, "I heard we are to go to the Grand Hospital all that are sick, and it is the very worst place in the world for we are shure of dieing if we go there."[1]

Willard was wounded at the battle of Antietam on September 17, 1862, and sent to recover in the hospital. He was miserable and found that he had a lot of time on his hands, which he used to write this volume.

>–<>–O–<>–<

Frederick City Hospital, Maryland, October the 14th, 1862. Inasmuch as I am one of those most pitiable of unfortunate creatures, a wounded soldier, and an inmate of that most horrible of all *horrible* places—a military hospital—and as old Father Time, like a wounded serpent, drags his slow length along at a pace almost intolerable, hanging on my hands most heavily; and having nothing to do, and being tired of idleness, I have concluded as a last resort to write a sketch, or at least the penumbra of a sketch or history of the marches and events connected with the regiment of which I am a member, from the time we left this city on the 25th of February last, up to the present time, October the 14th.

The 3rd Wisconsin Regiment was among the first to take the field during the dark days of the Rebellion, when Sumter fell and the old flag was trampled beneath the feet of traitors. The storm which had been so long gathering in the South broke at last upon the walls of Sumter. Long and fearful was the struggle, but in vain. Hundreds of iron monsters belched their deadly missiles amongst the gallant defenders, and a perfect shower of shot and shell fell upon the doomed fortress. Fort Sumter fell, but hardly had the echoes of the fearful strife died away out upon the waters of the deep, ere thousands of strong brave men were hurrying onward to the scene of strife and to the defense of the capital. Not long after the fall of Sumter, the battle of Bull Run was fought and lost by us; the Union seemed on the very brink of ruin.

It was during these hours of darkness that the regiment, having been organized and disciplined, left the camp of instruction and marched to the scene of conflict and danger. After spending the summer and autumn doing picket duty along the banks of the Potomac, we were finally put on duty in this city as Provost Guard, where we went into winter quarters. The long winter months passed slowly but pleasantly away, until at last we grew impatient and longed for more active service. We longed for the novelty and the more exciting scenes connected with life as a soldier in camp and field.

By and by the long wished for time had arrived, and we prepared to bid adieu to the fair city of Frederick and the old barracks where we had passed so many pleasant days, but were glad to exchange the warm comfortable rooms of the old barrack for the tent and the open field.

In the Union army most of the regiments were provided to the U.S. service by the individual states. Early in the war they were constituted by combining companies that had been raised in towns or localities. Thus Van Willard's Neenah Guards, all from his hometown area, was merged into the 3rd Wisconsin Regiment as Company G. Although the number of men enrolled in a regiment should theoretically have been about a thousand (the original strength of the 3rd Wisconsin was 979), in practice it was often half that. Moreover, since not all of a regiment's men were actually available for service, its effective strength was lower still. For example, Thomas Ruger led 340 men into the cornfield at Antietam. A number of regiments were organized into a brigade—ideally four, but because so many regiments were understrength, five or more was not uncommon—and three or four brigades formed a division. There were two to four divisions in a corps, which was the largest unit in the chain of organization. Corps commanders such as John Reynolds and Winfield Scott Hancock answered directly to the general in overall command of the army, such as George McClellan or U. S. Grant.

The 3rd Wisconsin was initially assigned to the 3rd Brigade, 1st Division of Banks's corps. The brigade was under the command of Gen. Charles Hamilton until March 13, 1862, and then placed under the command of Gen. George H. Gordon. During this time the regiment was led by Colonel Ruger, whose leadership so recommended itself to his superiors that he was promoted to brigadier general and assigned to replace Gordon as brigade commander after the battle of Antietam.

The regiment left Frederick by train on February 25, 1862, destined for Harpers Ferry. There they crossed the Potomac for the first time to launch the Valley campaign, which dawned so promising to the Union but ended in catastrophe. It also made the name Stonewall Jackson a household word in both the North and the South. The crossing was a moment of high excitement for the men. Halted at the river, they first watched the engineers build a pontoon bridge and drilled on how to get across it. Then came the long-awaited advance into enemy country.

It was a lovely morning, that on which we bade adieu to the goodly city of Frederick and marched, or rather took the cars, for Harpers Ferry. The night before, however, had been a wild and stormy one indeed. A rude old northwester had been piping up most lustily, howling around the barracks, rattling the loose panes in the windows most merrily and insinuating its breath through every crevice, as though wishing to pinch our ears and sting our noses for the last time, and at least to pay us a parting visit.

But the morning at least was lovely, fair enough to make up for the bleakness of the night. Hardly had the first gleam of morning appeared above the hills in the east before the men were up, and every preparation was completed for our journey. Guns were put in conditions, knapsacks were packed, and haversacks filled. The men were in the best of spirits, for the dull monotony was now to be broken and a life of activity and adventure was now before us, and we were impatient to be off.

Just at sunrise the drum beat, and we were formed in line and were soon moving down toward the cars. The sun rose bright and warm above the blue hills in the distance, and the sky was serene and clear and the air cool and bracing. All that gave token of the last night's storm was the pure white sheet of snow that lay like a spotless shroud wrapping the cold form of earth, and the broken fragments of white clouds that were scattered over the broad expanse of the great blue field of ether above, wandering here and there like "stray lambs."

While passing through the city to the depot, though early in the morning, crowds of citizens came out to bid us good by, for the regiment stood high in the estimation of the people. On board the cars, we were soon on our way towards Harpers Ferry. It was not without a feeling of sadness that we looked (as we thought) for the last time upon the goodly city, watching it as it faded from sight, until even the glittering spires were lost to view.

Our ride was a pleasant one, and though quite unwell myself, I could not but enjoy it. The men were in high spirits and the cars echoed with their songs and laughter. The country through which we passed exhibited all the beauties of art and nature combined, the well cultivated fields and palatial mansions, the tidy farm houses, having all the beauties of taste and refinement.

On our way to the Ferry, we passed what is known as Point of Rocks. This is a place of some interest, as it is not only a very wild and romantic place but is noted as being the scene of more than one sharp skirmish between the then Colonel Gerry and the Rebels under Ashby and the since-noted "Old Stonewall Jackson." The place is indeed one of the most picturesque that I ever saw. It is about ten miles below Harpers Ferry, where the Potomac seems almost walled in by huge, gray, rocky bluffs that loom up on its banks like grim sentries standing along its broken shores. In the centre of the river there is a small island. One house stands upon it but has nearly gone to ruin. On both sides of the river the bluffs are very steep, rising to a perpendicular height of two or three hundred feet. On the Maryland side the rocks project out over the road fifty or sixty feet. There are several old dilapidated buildings, and upon the whole it is, I think, one of the loneliest of places.

The river is at this point very rapid and goes dashing down over the rocks like a cataract. It is narrow, as its channel is only a deep cut through the mountains to let the old Potomac roll onward to the sea. I had but little time to admire the grand, wild beauty of the place, as the cars moved on up the river towards the Ferry, where we arrived about noon.

Harpers Ferry and vicinity. After a slow but pleasant ride of about three hours, we arrived at the much noted place Harpers Ferry. We were camped at this place for a month the fall previous, and as I have already written of this place in a book which I have sent home, I will only glance at some of the most prominent features.

Harpers Ferry is a place of some interest from the fact that it was here that that strange, eccentric yet brave old fellow, John Brown, made his celebrated raid upon the "sacred soil" of the Old Dominion, and

> With his twenty men so true,
> Frightened old Virginia
> Till she trembled through and through.

In addition to this, there is the wild, grandly sublime beauty of the place and its surrounding scenery. It is situated on a point of land just where the lovely, sparkling Shenandoah mingles its waters with those of the grand old Potomac. Then there are the lofty peaks and craggy bluffs that sentinel the shores, casting their shadows far out upon the stream. Maryland Heights on the north and the lofty old Loudon on the south and Bolivar on the west make a wall which nearly surrounds the doomed little village with a circle of rocks.

The town itself presents a picture of rare beauty. Not the beauty, however, of splendid mansions, of shining domes or glittering spires, but the solemn, sad beauty of a ruined city, for such is the condition of this doomed town. The town is an old one, the buildings are overgrown with moss and look as though they were just ready to tumble down. War has done fearful work here. The long mass of charred and blackened ruins is all that marks the spot whereon stood the armory and arsenal of the U.S. The shattered and blackened piers are all that remain of the splendid bridge across the Potomac. But since we were there in the fall of '61, other changes have occurred, for seven of the best buildings in the village have been burned. During the last spring, prior to the advance of the grand army, a young man by the name of Rower was shot by order of Captain Bailey or Balier while crossing the river with a flag of truce. Rower was a native of Maryland and a resident of this city (Frederick) and was in the employment of Colonel Gerry. The colonel was indignant and shelled the town, completely demolishing seven buildings and doing no little damage to several others.

We arrived at Sandy Hook opposite the Ferry on the afternoon of the 25th and camped for the night on our old camping ground at the head of Pleasant Valley. Meanwhile, the pontoon bridge arrived and by noon the day following had been stretched across the river, and by night, nearly the entire corps, under command of General Banks, had crossed, much to the surprise of the inhabitants and consternation of the Rebel pickets at Bolivar. The construction of a bridge in less than ten hours across such a stream as the Potomac, swollen as it was by the heavy rains of the season into a rushing, foaming torrent, was an event which they had not dreamed of.

Willard's mind was alive with curiosity, and he yearned for thrilling experiences. Not willing to pass by interesting sites, he requested and received permission to leave the ranks, find a vantage point, and observe the Union army making this historic crossing. This would not be the last time that Willard went out of his way to watch events unfold around him, even at the risk of exposing himself to danger.

Being quite unwell, and wishing to have a good look at the ruins, I obtained permission to go over in advance of the regiment, which was the first to cross. Though hardly able to walk, yet stimulated by a desire to *see* and explore the ruins, I rambled about among them and visited the old engine-house, the place where Brown and his followers sought refuge and where he maintained his ground for nearly two days, when he at last surrendered. This building is standing yet, though the storms of war have swept around it for nearly two years and all about it is one mass of ruins. Yet there it stands, as if in memory of the brave old fellow who once converted it into a fortress.

About 3:00 P.M. the troops began to cross, and a more magnificent sight can hardly be imagined. The long lines of soldiers with their splendid uniforms and bristling arms and equipments, the bands playing, and the banners floating proudly out upon the breeze was indeed a sight worthy of the poet's pen or the pencil of the artist.

After crossing the bridge the column pushed on up through the town towards Bolivar, where we camped for a few days. Camp Hill is a small hamlet situated on a hill or circular ridge between the Ferry and Bolivar. It consists of only a few old buildings, which were completely deserted. Passing on through this little town, up a continually ascending road, we soon came in sight of the village of Bolivar, which lies just at the foot of Bolivar Heights, where Colonel Gerry, with the 28th Pennsylvania and the 13th Massachusetts and three companies of the 3rd Wisconsin and a section of a battery, fought and routed a regiment of Ashby's cavalry and a large force of infantry which had come down from Charlestown to disperse Gerry's forces. Bolivar is, or at least was, a neat little town but was at that time nearly deserted, eight families being all that remained.

After remaining at Bolivar for a few days, an advance was made as far as Charlestown, a village about six miles from Bolivar. It was a cold, blustering day in March, and a west wind blew up over the valley like a tornado. Gordon's brigade had the advance of the infantry column, led by the 1st Michigan Cavalry, which dashed into town in gallant style, capturing several of the Rebel pickets whose steeds were not fleet enough to carry them out of the way. In addition to this, several wagon loads of flour were brought in, with quite a number of horses.

At Charlestown our brigade (Gordon's) were quartered in the churches and other public buildings. Charlestown is a place of some note, as it was here that poor old John Brown was imprisoned, tried, and hung. It is a neat, nicely built village (or city) of about three thousand inhabitants, who appear to be universally hostile to our cause, as there were no marks of sympathy exhibited toward us by them. We remained at this place for nearly a week, during which time quite a number of prisoners were brought in and a large quantity of Rebel stores were captured.

While there I visited John Brown's cell, which is a small, damp dungeon furnished with a stove, an old broken down chair, and a small pine table, nearly cut into fragments by those who have visited the cell and have cut off pieces as a relic in memory of the brave old hero. I also visited the spot where he was hung, but scarcely a fragment remains to mark the spot where he ended his sad yet eventful career.

We bade adieu to the Charlestownians and advanced as far as Smithfield, a small burg about six miles from Charlestown. Here we remained for several days, when, after a few unimportant skirmishes with the famous Ashby's cavalry, we made another advance toward the Rebel stronghold Winchester, where it was supposed the enemy were going to "make a stand" and resist our farther progress up the valley.

Banks's corps struck up the Shenandoah Valley (up meaning south and down north), advancing on Winchester, expecting to have Jackson offer battle to his eager troops. Instead, on March 12, just after midnight, the Confederate leader retreated southward, leaving the city open to Federal occupation. Willard vividly describes the surprise of the Union soldiers when they reached Confederate fortifications and found their foes gone.

We arrived to within five miles of the city on the afternoon of the 12th of March/62. Some skirmishing and cannonading occurred in the advance, but no engagement was brought on. The next day, as we supposed, was to be a day of strife and bloodshed. The night preceding it was one of rare beauty; the air was warm and the night was calm and still. The moon shone with unusual lustre, and the stars burned softly in the azure sky above. We were bivouacked in the woods by the road side, and it was no mean sight to see hundreds of camp fires gleaming among the trees and the soldiers gathered around them. This was a new chapter in our experience as soldiers.

Being, as we supposed, on the eve of a great battle, it was natural that a thousand surmises and rumors should be circulated through the camp and a thousand dreams and fancies should haunt the mind of the soldier as he lay down to sleep, perhaps for the last time.

The next morning we were up and going long before the sun had made his appearance. The morning was one of great loveliness, such as a spring in this country always brings with it. Hardly had the sun appeared before we were in motion, moving through woods and over fields towards the city. It was a fine sight on that spring morning to see the long lines of men advancing across the fields, with their sable uniforms and dark, waving plumes, their glittering arms and polished equipments. It was indeed grand.

Skirmishers were sent on in advance to feel the enemy and, if possible, learn their strength and position. Rapidly but firmly they advanced on towards the dark earth works, and it was with no small degree of interest that we watched them as they pushed on, on this dangerous mission expecting every moment to see them fall. Every breath seemed suspended as we saw them near the fortifications, yet no shot had been fired. The silence was mysterious. On went the skirmishers. They approached the work, and for a moment they were lost to sight as they plunged into the ditch. The next we saw them clambering up the embankment and standing within the fortifications; but no enemy was there—they had fled.

One long, loud shout went up, for it was a great, though almost bloodless, victory. The place had been abandoned, and we were masters of the city, the key of the valley, which by nine o'clock we occupied in force.

It is my object only to give an outline sketch of some of the most important events connected with our advance up the valley of the Shenandoah, our retreat, our pilgrimage in the valley of the Rappahannock, etc. To do more than this, to give a history or anything approaching one, would be a work far beyond my present means. In this sketch I shall pass rapidly along, only pausing to mention some important events or to glance at each village or city worthy of note. When the history of this war comes to be written by the future historian, the advance of Banks up the valley of the Shenandoah and his conquest of the entire valley from Harpers Ferry to Harrisonburg, the dividing of his command by the War Department, and his subsequent retreat across the Potomac will form no insignificant chapter in that history.

We entered and took possession of the city of Winchester on the morning of the 13th (March). This was an event which had been looked for with no little interest, not only by the army but by the whole nation. The advance of Banks's army, the capture of this strong hold, and the *occupation* of the valley was an event much to be desired. And when at last the advance was made and the army put in motion, every heart thrilled with emotion. And now that our flag waved in triumph over the Rebel city, it was thought that the lovely valley, so rich, so beautiful, embracing the fairest portion of the old Dominion, would be forever free from Rebel rule. But results proved to the contrary; fate had otherwise decreed.

The valley of the Shenandoah, or the Great Valley of Virginia, embraces some of the finest counties in the state and is a country of surpassing beauty and fertility, or at least *was* in its better days. It is abundantly watered, lying as it does between two ranges of mountains running north and south, and is on an average about twenty-five miles in width. It is quite thickly populated, containing many towns and villages, with here and there a small city. The inhabitants are, as a general thing, civil and courteous and own large farms. The chief production is corn and wheat, for which the soil is well adapted.

The buildings are old fashioned in their model and bear the marks of time and old age. Many of the villages, in fact, are so venerable in appearance, so aged and time worn, that one would fail to discover anything modern about them and would be led to believe that the period of their "beginning" would date back as far at least as the settlement of the country by the "natives." And the "style" of some of them would justify the belief that they were the results of an attempt by the "savages" to imitate their semi-civilized neighbors of Mexico. Some of the villages are, however, very neat in their appearance, the streets straight and clean, and the buildings, though old, look comfortable.

Of this class is the city of Winchester. It contains about four or five thousand inhabitants and is situated in the centre of the valley in the midst of as fine a farming country as the sun ever smiled upon. It has no water privileges but has fine localities for steam works and only needs the enterprise and skill of Northern genius to set them in operation and make Winchester one of the finest inland towns in the "border states."

The valley at this point is fifty miles wide, bordered on the west by the North Mountain Range and on the east by the Shenandoah Mountains, at the foot of which rolls the west Shenandoah on its way to the sea. The city is built in a basin or hollow and is surrounded by a low ridge or range of hills on all sides, commanding an extensive view in every direction. The ridge affords many a strong position, which have been strengthened by the Rebels by digging rifle pits and the throwing up of earth works all along the crest. On the north and east, the direction from which we approached the city, the works assume the dignity of fortifications and are quite formidable.

Fort Jackson is the key to the position and mounted, or at least had mounted, several heavy guns. This point is just one mile from the city and is approached only from the north east over an extensive plain. The city, from its favorable locality, must have been the great mart of trade and, no doubt, in its better days was a lively, attractive business place. But how changed, how sadly changed! For with the birth of the Rebellion the spirit of business died away, and its attractiveness was changed into an appearance of gloom.

The streets, once crowded with a busy, happy throng, now echo to the tread of armed men, and along the paved street where once only the farmer's wagon and light carriage rolled along, the great, heavy army wagons go rumbling by, while cavalry and infantry go rushing along the dusty streets. The clang of arms, the rumbling of wagons, and the tramp of men has drowned the songs of peace, the hum of industry. The church bells are silent, and [the place] where once a happy people met to worship God is now filled by the dead and dying. Where once the prayer and hymn was heard, now echo the groans of the wounded and the mad, wild ravings of the maniac and the poor stricken ones who are *mad* with pain. Starvation has taken the place of plenty, and scenes of misery and death [replace] those of quiet joys. Strife reigns where once peace was king. Where once Sabbath bells rang out their mellow chime, now may be heard the tramp of armed men and the curses and wild rioting of a drunken mob—the reckless soldiery.

Such is now the condition of the once attractive Winchester! The city is one vast house of pain, misery, and death. The country around—the lovely valley, so rich and beautiful, where once broad fields of grain ripened in the sun light—has been changed into a desert, the fields have been trodden down, and acres of grain lie moldering in the dust. Fences have been burned down, and in many places a shapeless mass of charred and blackened ruins alone mark the site of mansions burned and hamlets given to the flames. While all up and down the valley, on the hill sides, by the highways, and in the glens, lonely graves may be found. Such are the evils that this unhappy people have brought upon themselves.

After taking possession of the city, camps were established and the roads to the city strictly guarded. Nothing of importance was found in the city, save a few Negroes who seemed at first to be the only occupants of the place. The doors were closed and the blinds shut.

After a while the people began to show themselves to some extent, as if impelled by curiosity, and looked cautiously out between the shutters, anxious to know what kind of "creatures" the "*Yankees*" *really were*. They evidently supposed that we were real barbarians and that we had come to burn and destroy. But when they came to know us better, and saw how well we did really wish to treat them, they became bold and in some instances treated us with real indignity and impudence. But there were others who, when they came [to see] our object and saw that ours was not a war for plunder or rapine, that we warred not as they had been told against helpless women and children, when by our kind treatment they learned this, they were kind and courteous in return.

The Union grand strategy for the spring of 1862 called for McClellan to attack Richmond with the bulk of the Army of the Potomac by going up the Peninsula, which extends to the city's east. Banks's corps was to head east from the Valley and cover Washington City; other troops in the Valley were to reinforce McClellan. This was a viable plan, probably McClellan's best of the war, and he was filled with confidence. He wrote his wife that he knew that he would win the upcoming struggle.[2] He might well have succeeded except for Stonewall Jackson.

Jackson's assignment was to pin down the Union troops in the Valley and prevent their moving to McClellan's support. On March 22, Banks's 1st Division, led by Gen. Alpheus Williams, left Winchester bound eastward, implementing McClellan's plan, and headed for the gap in the Blue Ridge Mountains near Snickersville. Some 9,000 men of Banks's 2nd Division, under Gen. James Shields, were left at Winchester to hold the town. Jackson soon found out that Union troops were divided and on the move, and he acted quickly and decisively, attacking Shields's force at Kernstown, just south of Winchester, unaware that he would face so many of the enemy. He was repulsed, and Kernstown is generally considered the only battle in this campaign that Jackson lost.

The results of the battle were something else again, however, and he was successful in his object. Williams's men, hearing the gunfire in their rear, were called back to the Valley from their march east. The project of beating Jackson became the focus of the Union Valley command. The city of Washington was left without the cover of troops it had expected, and McClellan received none of the men he had been counting on, just promises that some would be dispatched after any possible threat to Washington was removed, which never happened. Seeds of discord were sown between McClellan and the leadership in Washington, and for some ill-considered reason, the Union's Valley command was fragmented into sectors, losing the benefits of coordinated leadership and making it easier for the fearless Jackson to achieve future victories.

The Confederates withdrew toward the south, with the 3rd Wisconsin and Banks's other men in pursuit.

Our march over the Blue Ridge and return March 22nd. We remained at Winchester until the 22nd of March. While there, quite a number of prisoners were brought in, taken in skirmishes which were an almost everyday occurrence.

Early on the morning of the 22nd, we were astir and ready (per order) to start on a seven days' march. At day light the army was on the move, but we, having the honor of being the rear guard, did not get under way until late in the day, as we were obliged to wait until the army and its almost endless train of wagons had passed us.

In going *up* the valley we traveled *south*; but now the line of march was changed and we were on our way to the mountains in the east. The whole of Banks's corps was on the move save the division under Shields. Our destination was supposed to be Centreville, and our journey was to be over the Blue Ridge, by the way of Snickers Gap. The day was a cold, blustering one of the most uncomfortable kind. All that day we marched slowly onward, over the worst of roads, passing through the little village of Berryville about four o'clock, and at night rested on the banks of the Shenandoah at the foot of the dark old Blue Ridge.

The next morning we resumed our march, crossed the Shenandoah, over which a pontoon had been constructed, and stood beneath the shadow of the grim old mountain. I am an ardent admirer of nature's works; her beauties are to me more grand and pleasing than aught produced by the skill of man. The plains, the mountain, rushing rivers, and the glittering hill, the beautiful earth and the calm blue sky, brilliant with its glittering stars, are more attractive to me than all the transient beauties of art. Yes, I am one of nature's admirers, and it was with a feeling of deep emotion, of admiration and awe, that I stood beneath those huge, dark cliffs, towering way up there in their rugged beauty, their grim, rude forms mirrored in the bosom of the stream beneath.

At an early hour we began the ascent of the mountain pass, up a steep and rugged and *very* winding road, sometimes passing along the brink of a deep gorge, while on the other side loomed up great gray cliffs; again climbing a precipitous ascent or plunging down deep ravines, or through narrow passes, so deep and dark that the sun's rays seldom ever penetrated down to their gloomy depths. At noon we gained the summit of the mountain. Here I witnessed one of the most magnificent sights I ever beheld. Far away to the west lay the valley of the Shenandoah, and the dark blue mountains could be dimly seen in the distance, while long trains of wagons came slowly up the mountain side, and regiment after regiment came gaily through the passes or wound around at the foot of the mountain.

But we halted only for a moment on the summit and then began our descent. We passed down the mountain, and after marching ten or twelve miles, we camped in the woods. This was Sunday the 23rd, the day on which the battle of Kernstown was fought and won by Shields and his brave boys. The next morning we received orders to return to Winchester with all possible haste.

Then began our return march, one of the most fatiguing I ever experienced. We were now twenty-six miles from W., with a mountain to climb and an almost impassable road to travel, were already much exhausted, lame, and foot sore. But the journey was accomplished, and at night we again filed through the streets of Winchester. We bivouacked that night in the woods south of the town. The night was stinging cold, and we had no tent save the starry arch above and no bed save the frosty ground. Supperless, tired and stiff, lame and crippled, we went to bed—and *such* a bed!

The battle field of Kernstown, March 23rd, 1862. When we arrived at Winchester again, we found that bloody work had been going on during our absence. Shields's Division, consisting of Indiana and Ohio troops, had had a battle with the forces under Jackson and had been victorious having, after two hours' hard hand to hand fighting, driven the enemy from the field, who had retreated in hot haste to Strasburg, some eighteen miles distant.

The battle began late on the afternoon on Sunday the 23rd of March and ended at night when the Rebels were completely routed. It was fought about three miles from the city of Winchester in a dense thicket, except the left wing of the Rebel line, which was posted behind a stone wall. The battle began with artillery, but in the afternoon the infantry became engaged, and for a time it raged with the most terrible fury. It was carried on with great energy by both sides, and the issue was for a long time doubtful. Shields had been wounded the night before by an explod-ing shell and could not be present in person to command; but his brave boys had never been beaten, they did not know what it was to be "whipped," and though the 110th Pennsylvania regiment, which was in advance in the line of battle, broke and fled, yet the gallant fellows from Indiana and Ohio pressed bravely on, only laughing at *their* cowardice, and *won* the battle.

The night was a severely cold one, but it passed away at last, and morning, warm, bright, and golden, came. After breakfast, I, with a num-ber of others, took an opportunity of going up to the battle field to see the dead. The "battle field" was a thing *we* had not *then* seen; but since then we have seen them *quite too often*.

When we arrived on the field (the 25th), many of our own dead were yet unburied, and hundreds of Rebel dead lay scattered through the thicket and behind the stone walls and over the fields for miles; and the line of their retreat might be followed by *the dead left behind them*. Never did I see a sight *more horrible*! I had often read of "battle scenes," of the horrors of a field of strife, and had longed to see one and judge for myself. Now I had the desired opportunity. There was the battle field, and there were the dead scattered here and there, just as they had fallen, shot in every conceivable way, limbs shot off, torn away by shot or shell, bones broken, and forms mangled beyond recognition, features distorted with pain, eyes bursting from their sockets or sunken far back in the head, glazed and fixed, staring coldly up to the sky—faces black and white, others covered with blood. Some had died instantly, others had struggled long and fearfully with death, tearing the ground about them with their convulsed hands, as they writhed in the terrible death struggle!

The day was a lovely one, and the sun looked softly down upon that "field of dead" as though it would warm again to life those cold, lifeless forms; but life with them was over, their souls had gone home to God. The ghastly distorted features, the stiffened limbs, and the glazed eyes looking fixed up into the brazen sky gave no token of life, for the soul that had warmed and animated them had fled.

While strolling over the fields, I chanced to discover one that I think had thus far escaped notice. He lay alone in a thicket, where he had evidently crawled away to die. Led by some almost unknown motive, I approached him. He was a very young man, with dark brown, curly hair and features that in life could not but be beautiful as well as intellectual. He was a young Mississippian and might have been an officer, though his uniform did not indicate his rank. I approached him, and while stooping down to see where he was wounded, I saw that he held something in his hand, which I discovered to be a small, gold locket. Curiosity led me to open it. It contained a miniature of a young lady of surpassing beauty. In the back of the case, there was a ringlet of dark hair and a small strip of paper on which was written, "Presented to George by Minnie." I closed the locket and laid it on his breast within his clothes, for I knew he would wish it near his heart. Poor George, poor Minnie! She would never meet him again, until perhaps they meet up there in that better land, where wars never break the peace, for the sound of earthly strife dies away on those happy shores.

We (my friend Dodge and myself), after satisfying ourselves, returned to camp, where we set about preparing for a march. At eight o'clock we were again on our way and, although very lame, marched rapidly on toward Strasburg. It was a hard march, and all night until nearly morning we traveled slowly, painfully on, passing through Kernstown and New-town, and rested at last just in the suburbs of Middletown. All were small villages of but very little importance.

The night was very cold, so cold indeed that the water froze in our canteens. Little sleeping was done that night, but we built large fires, which we hovered around until morning. That cold, dreary night at length passed away, although it seemed that morning would never come. But the longest night *will have its end*, and by and by the cold, gray gleams of light in the east gave proof that morning would certainly come, though we began to suspect that the fierce north wind, which was piping up, had brought with it one of those endless nights so prevalent in the northern latitudes. Yes, morning did come, and such a glorious one. The sky was as blue as the bosom of old Ocean, and as clear and deep. The sun rose, and the air seemed filled with golden sparkles, and the earth, hills, and woods appeared to smile beneath the genial light and warmth. And we, who had been shivering with the cold for hours, hailed the glorious morn with such feelings as they only feel who have watched and waited long and wishfully for the morning. The weary watcher by the death bed, looking longingly for the blessed light of day, would not be more grateful than we when the blessed morning came.

After breakfast, consisting of hard bread and coffee of our own make, we again resumed our march, passing on through Middletown, which is a village of but few inhabitants and is about fifteen miles from Winchester. All these towns, Kernstown, Newtown, Middletown, were found to be filled with Rebels left by Jackson in his hasty retreat. After passing over Cedar Creek, a small stream within two or three miles of Strasburg, we turned off into the woods, where we remained for several days, as it was impossible to advance farther until the bridge over the creek, which had been burned, was repaired. Several regiments were in advance, however, beyond the town, and skirmishing was an almost daily occurrence.

While at this place, we fared very hard, as our teams had been unable to cross the Shenandoah. The pontoon bridge gave way, and they were detained on the other side for several days, thus leaving us without tents or rations, articles quite indispensable to comfort. The weather was what would be termed lovely by those who had a comfortable bed and a shelter from the night air, which was cold and frosty. The days were indeed beautiful, warm, bright, and golden, but being destitute of tents, we were exposed to the keen, frosty night air, with now and then a flurry of snow, which was by no means agreeable. We built shelters with boughs and made ourselves as comfortable as possible, yet many an hour was passed by us shivering with the cold. Seldom have I beheld a more enchanting scene than was presented to one who, standing upon the rocks above the ravine in which we were bivouacked, looked down over the thousands of camp-fires that shone all along for more than half a mile, up and down the ravine. They threw their hard, lurid light up on the surrounding objects, revealing every bush and rock which cast huge shadows about them, which seemed to dance about like a thousand grim phantoms, making the camp appear to be inhabited by the dark, unshapen beings of the infernal regions.

We had been at this place nearly a week, when one afternoon the report was brought that our pickets had been driven in and that the enemy was advancing on us. The alarm was immediately given, the drums beat the "long roll" in every camp, and without giving us time to pack our knapsacks, we were formed in line and were soon off at a double quick to the assistance to those in front. We passed rapidly through Strasburg, expecting every moment to hear the boom of cannon and the crack of rifles. But it was soon discovered that the alarm had been a false one and that no danger of an attack from the enemy need be apprehended. We then went into the woods, where we made preparations for the night. That night the teams came up, which were hailed by us with real delight, as they brought with them the luxury of tents and a fresh supply of food. That night, for the first time for nearly two weeks, we slept beneath the grateful shelter of a tent and enjoyed one entire night of sweet repose.

Banks's men continued to advance up the Valley as the Confederates retreated. On April 1 Jackson's forces withdrew from their camp in such haste that, says Bryant, they left "their dinner cooking over the fire." Union forces next came up against Turner Ashby and his famed Confederate cavalry, and Willard's words of high praise bring into focus exactly how that band earned its reputation. This would not be the last time that Willard would have generous words for his foes, as he was basically a magnanimous man who genuinely liked Southerners.

The campaign seemed a Union triumph. Except for a brief show of force at Mount Jackson, Stonewall offered little resistance, and Banks's corps found itself deep into the Valley, fifty miles south of Winchester.

We remained in the vicinity of Strasburg until the 1st of April, when an advance was made as far as Edenburg, a small town some eighteen miles away. On our way we encountered Ashby and his cavalry and two or three pieces of artillery. A little skirmishing and a few shells cleared the way for our advance. But the brave and daring Ashby and his equally brave followers were continually in our front, skirmishing with our advance and shelling us from every wood or hill where a gun could be posted. Never was a retreat better covered than was that of General Jackson from the valley by Ashby and his cavalry, which were doubtless the best that ever drew a sword in the "Old Dominion."

At what is kown as Narrow Pass, a place where the Shenandoah and a small stream approach so near one another as to allow only a narrow space hardly wide enough for a road betwen them, the Rebels made a stand and effectually resisted our cavalry but were soon compelled to retire before our artillery. After passing the Narrow Pass, we came up on them again near the little village of Woodstock, where they were attempting to burn a bridge, which, fortunately, they were a little too late to do. A shell bursting among them gave them to understand that the Yankees, as they call us, were close upon their heels, an argument, which to them, was conclusive that the climate in that vicinity was too warm for comfort—at least for them.

Woodstock is an old fashioned little village looking rather aged and grim, yet wearing the appearance of comfort and blessings, which the inhabitants doubtless enjoyed in those better days ere the spirit of discordance had assumed the character of a Rebellion and the crimson tide of war had swept up this lovely valley, bearing in its course the elements of ruin and despair. War came and peace departed, and the bright and prosperous days were gone. The contending armies trampled down their fields and consumed the products of their labor. The villages are deserted, for the inhabitants sought refuge in a more peaceful land. Orchards are cut down, and smiling fields are transformed into deserts. The song of the happy husbandman is no longer heard, as he labors in the field or winds his way at night toward his happy, quiet home. The bugle's call, the alarming drum, and the cannon's roar have usurped the songs of peace, and the hum of industry is drowned amid the din of strife. Such are the evils of war, such the curse, the blight that civil strife has brought to this once happy and prosperous land.

From Woodstock to Edenburg the advance was very rapid, yet we were not in time to save the bridge across Rocky Run, a small stream at that place. The Rebels had crossed with all their train and had burned the bridge. They planted their guns on the other side and shelled us as we approached the town. Our batteries were soon in position, and a sharp little artillery duel followed, during which we had one man killed and two or three wounded.

Edenburg is a small but neat village of perhaps two thousand inhabitants, situated on the banks of a little stream that comes rippling down from the mountains, dancing merrily as it goes on its way to join its elder and more sedate sister, the graceful Shenandoah. The village has a fine locality in the midst of a rich and fertile country, over which it commands an extensive view. The bridge being burned, we were delayed until it could be repaired, which occupied over two weeks. During this time we were camped in the woods along the banks of a stream, but at a respectful distance, as we were not anxious to invite Rebel artillery practice upon our camp. Hardly a day passed, however, without more or less cannonading. The next morning after our arrival at Edenburg, we were awakened at a very early hour by the boom of cannon and the screaming of shell, which came in too close proximity to our camp to be agreeable. We would not let this disturb us but went quietly about preparing breakfast, notwithstanding our dangerous visitors.

Our picket line extended along the banks of the stream, as did also that of our Rebel neighbors, and many was the compliment in the shape of minié balls sent across that little stream. At last the bridge was repaired, and long before day light we were up and ready for an advance. The day was just dawning when we began our march, and the rapid firing on the other side of the stream gave proof that the advance had already crossed. Brightly the morning star shone down upon us as we passed through the little village of Edenburg and crossed over the bridge to the dim seen land beyond, wrapped as it was in the cold, gray mist of the early morning.

The Rebel picket fires were still burning brightly as we passed. Their camp fires were burning low, however, for they had gone long since. Passing rapidly forward to within two or three miles of the little village of Mount Jackson, we were brought to a stand by our Rebel neighbors, who had posted a gun or two on a hill in advance and seemed disposed to dispute our farther progress. But a few well-directed shots from our Parrots seemed to suffice to convince them that our course was still "onward" and that we were not to be deterred by trifles. Our arguments were "*weighty*" and seemed quite conclusive, as they immediately limbered up and disappeared beyond the town.

Mount Jackson is a small village or hamlet and is of importance only as it contains several large hospital buildings, which are built after the most improved model, and were fitted up in a very comfortable manner. It is also a strong position, as was Strasburg, which a small force might hold against thousands.

On leaving Mount Jackson, the Rebels burned every thing of value to us that they could not carry with them. Several cars were burned and two locomotives destroyed. On arriving near the town, one brigade (Gordon's) was sent around to the right, while the main force kept straight on. We made a circuit of several miles, fording a branch of the Shenandoah several miles above the town. But whatever the object was, it failed, unless it was to see how fast we could travel over bad, muddy roads. It was late that night before we had accomplished our journey. The road was one of the worst that I ever traveled over—deep mud, rocks, and stumps made up the greatest portion of the road. At last we halted and bivouacked for the night, which was a cold, blustering one.

The next day [April 18] we passed on beyond New Market, a little, dirty, half deserted town about eight miles from Mount Jackson. On our way we were obliged to ford the West, or, as it is sometimes called, the North Shenandoah. The water was very cold and reached nearly to our waists. Passing through New Market, we camped about three miles from the town to wait for the train to come up, as we were and had been for nearly two days without rations. New Market, although it has the term "New" attached, is one of the oldest appearing towns that I ever saw. To discover anything *new* or *modern* about such an apology for a town would be a miracle, a thing at least that *I* utterly failed to accomplish.

About two or three miles from town, we turned into a field to bivouac and passed that night quite pleasantly. But the next day was a stormy one, for a cold, steady rain storm had set in, which we, being minus tents, found not very agreeable. We fixed up temporary shelters as best we could with our rubber blankets and, having brought large quantities of straw from a distant barn, prepared to pass the night as comfortably as possible, the day having been spent in shivering with the cold and wet, huddled together beneath our shelters, which were little better than nothing. But supposing that we would remain there that night at least, we had taken no little amount of pains to fix up as comfortable quarters for the night as could be done under the circumstances. The day passed, and a cold, dreary night came on. We had all lain down, and I had just begun to drop into a sound sleep and feel the influence of that magic power— "balmy sleep, tired nature's sweet restorer," when I was roused by the voice of our orderly as he ordered the men to turn out and prepare for a march immediately. One who has never had experience as a soldier may think to be called up at such a time and under *such* circumstances to perform a long march perhaps a very agreeable affair; but as for me and my folk, we would beg to be excused.

A night march over the Massanutten Mountains, April 20th–21st. We could hardly realize that we were to be turned out on such a night, but such was the case, and we had nothing to do but to obey orders, which we did with as good a grace as could be expected, although there was some scientific swearing done on the occasion. The night was intensely dark, and the rain was still pouring down furiously when we marched back through New Market on our way to the mountains, over which it was our destiny to climb on that dark and dismal night. Slowly and with much difficulty, we made our way over the worst of roads to that dark old mountain. Camp fires burned brightly all along the road, and it seemed as though it would have been a luxury even to have been allowed to *stand* around them that night. Arriving at the foot of the mountain, we began its ascent up a narrow, winding road leading through a difficult pass; but it was so very dark that we could see nothing and only knew that huge rocks were hanging above and around us by their ragged outlines just discernable as they loomed up against the sky.

All the remainder of that dismal night we climbed up that mountain and down the other side into the valley, where we arrived just as the first gleams of morning began to appear in the east. Two companies, G and D, were sent on a short distance to a bridge across the East Shenandoah, where we arrived just in time to save it from being burned. Here on this bridge (it being covered), we made our home for the time being, and a cold home it was, too, during those few stormy days we spent there doing picket duty and guarding it against the destroyers.

The following is as good a description as can be imagined of what it feels like to be on picket.

A night on picket, April 23rd. Never did I pass a more disagreeable night than I did on that of the 23rd of April. I was on picket. The day had been one of wind and storm, of snow and rain. The ground was covered, and the trees bent low beneath their burdens of ice and snow. The night was intensely dark, the storm continued, and it was *very* cold. We were posted about a half mile from the bridge in the edge of a thick pine wood. One who has been on picket, far away—alone—out of sight and hearing of anyone on a dark night—can appreciate the loneliness of the situation; but to one who has had no such experience, it would be impossible. Standing alone that dreary night, the snow and the rain pattering down among the trees and the wind sighing mournfully among the pine boughs over head, the low wailing of the storm as it swept by the impenetrable darkness of the night, the deepening gloom, the utter loneliness, and the known presence of an enemy lurking in the vicinity, makes "*picketing*" at *such* a time and place, on *such* a night, a cheerless task. The picket is supposed to be watching the approach of an enemy, to guard against surprise. He stands alone, waiting, watching, and is startled at every sound that breaks the silence that reigns around him, the crackling of a limb, the moaning of the wind, and even the pattering of the rain drops sounds perhaps like the approach of cautious footsteps. He starts—he listens a moment and then resumes his lonely musings. But perhaps the night is a warm and moonlit one. The stars may burn brightly in the midnight sky, and all nature may be wrapped in a flood of silvery beauty; the picket's situation is a lonely, gloomy one indeed, even then. He listens to every sound and glances frequently out over the moonlit scene around and, perhaps, in the uncertain light of the moon, which always clothes distant objects in a somber light, imagines he sees objects dimly moving, standing, or creeping. He grasps his gun nervously for a moment, perhaps, then discovers the delusion and resumes his thoughts, only to be startled again.

To be a good and trusty picket requires not only watchfulness and vigilance, but courage and coolness. Untold mischief may accrue from the cowardice or excitability of a picket. Often whole regiments have been disturbed or called into line, perhaps by the indiscretion or nervousness of a single man, who has fired his piece at some imaginary enemy, which turns out to be only a stump or bush or perhaps an object of his own excited imagination. Many an innocent hog or cow has been made the victim of fright or nervousness.

While writing of picketing, I am reminded of a very amusing incident which occurred while we were in Winchester. I was on picket one dark, rainy night and had been on post about an hour and a half. Nothing had occurred to break the dull monotony, and I was anxiously waiting for the "next relief," when my attention was distracted by the sound of approaching footfalls—some one was coming up the lane where I was posted. I was sure of it, though I could discern no one, for it *was* dark. On they came, and nearer and more distinct became the sound of footfalls. Soon I thought I could discern several objects dimly through the gloomy darkness, and I could now hear the low sound of voices. They were within hailing distance, and with the usual challenge of "Who comes there?" I cocked my gun and stepped cautiously from behind a tree and looked sharply down the road. I had no sooner given the challenge than they began to scamper away, shouting at the top of their voices, "Niggers, Niggers." I called to them to halt or I would shoot, which they did. I then demanded that one of them should come to me. There was some disputing among them as to which one should come up to where I was. One remarked, "You am de one to go Sam, 'cause you are so black dat he would know you were a

Nig." "Yes," says Sam, "but I am so dogged black dat he could never see dis child's face on so dark a night as dis am, no how." Finally the difficulty was settled by one of them, who declared, "Dis chile am not afraid, no how." When I had called them all up to me, I made them sit down until I was relieved, when I marched them to the station.

The campaign took a turn. Jackson had been threatened by two enemy forces: Banks pursuing him up the Valley and Gen. John C. Fremont coming at him from the west, hoping to link up with Banks. The Confederate general acted to prevent this potentially dangerous juncture, leaving the Valley to take on Fremont. Jackson's move was a success, and on May 8 he scored a victory at McDowell, which prevented Fremont from advancing further. Jackson then returned to the Valley to deal with Banks.

At this point the government's fears for the safety of Washington profoundly affected events in the Valley and on the Peninsula. Gen. Irwin McDowell had been stationed at Fredericksburg to shield the capital, thus denying those men to McClellan, whose plans on the Peninsula had originally counted on them. Shields, who had beaten Jackson at Kernstown, was ordered to separate from Banks's corps and join McDowell in defending Washington City. Thus the capital was now safe, but at what cost? Banks was left alone in the Valley with only 8,000 men, and he had to face one of the greatest generals in American history, Thomas J. Jackson, who had 16,000 men at his disposal. Moreover, Banks and his men, who had suffered no defeat, were ordered to turn around, give up without a contest much of the territory they had gained, and retreat to Strasburg and dig in there. This seemingly useless surrender of ground had a devastating effect on the men, as Willard makes clear.

The Luray Valley is one of great beauty and embraces a fine tract of country lying between the Shenandoah Mountains and the Blue Ridge, extending north and south for many miles. The valley, as near as I was able to learn, is quite thickly settled, and the soil is fertile. We remained there one week, when we were relieved, and on the 26th returned to New Market. It was just sunset, and the view presented was one of surpassing loveliness. To the east lay the Luray Valley, bordered by the dark Blue Ridge, whose summits were still illuminated by the parting rays of the setting sun, though the valley below lay wrapped in the somber shades of twilight. But in the west, the valley of the Shenandoah still glowed in the sun light of that lovely evening.

Far away down below us stretched the great valley, dotted with green fields and blooming orchards, with here and there a white cottage or a lofty farm house and out buildings, while bright, sparkling little streams wind meandering through the green meadows, glittering like silvery threads in the sun light, at last mingling their pure waters with that of the East Shenandoah that winds along at the mountain's foot on its way to the Potomac. The little village of New Market could be plainly seen below, surrounded by innumerable white tents that dotted the green sod for miles, while the village of Mount Jackson could be dimly seen in the distance, as the sun went down and twilight wrapped the valley in its gloomy mantle. Night came slowly, and the shadows deepened as twilight gave place to night, until the valley, with its farm houses and cottages, its emerald fields, its glittering streams and villages, was lost to view.

Passing on down the mountain, arriving at New Market, we bivouacked for the night and the next morning pushed on towards Harrisonburg, where we found the army had gone (the 3rd Regiment was all the force that had been sent out on this expedition). The day was an intensely warm one for the season, and the roads were very dry and dusty. We arrived at Harrisonburg early in the afternoon, where we joined our brigade. Harrisonburg is about eighteen miles from New Market and is only a small "burg" of but little importance. Like almost every town or village through which we passed on our way up the valley, it has every indication of old age. The buildings are time worn, the walls overgrown with moss, and appear to be just ready to tumble down in a mass of shapeless ruins.

Jackson reinforced. The advance of our army was a short distance beyond the village in the immediate vicinity of the Rebel forces, which, it was said, and correctly, too, had been strongly reinforced and were about to attack our advance. But the idea seemed to prevail at the War Department that there was no cause for fear in that direction, that the combined forces of Jackson and Ewell were about to make a descent upon General McDowell on the Rappahannock, and that he was (as he said) in danger of being overpowered, and a road opened to Washington. Hence Shields's Division, the best portion of Banks's Corps, was sent to McDowell. With the lost of Abercrombie's Division, which had been sent to McClellan, the forces under Banks had been reduced to a mere handful, and he was ordered to fall back to Strasburg. Thus terminated our march up the valley, which we had so fondly hoped would terminate only at Richmond. But we were doomed to be disappointed. We had followed Jackson more than a hundred miles, and when we supposed we were about to meet him in battle, we were ordered to retreat!

The retreat began on Monday. Sunday, the troops were all under arms, and that night we lay down in line of battle. All that night the trains were passing to the rear, ambulances and great army wagons went rumbling by, giving proof that something unusual was about to occur; yet all was mystery, and we waited anxiously for the morning. Well the morning came, and as I had feared, but *would not believe*, the retreat began. Bitter indeed was our disappointment when we found that we must turn our backs to the enemy and travel back over the same roads along which we had, only so short a time before, marched so hopefully. We had not then met with a repulse, our moves had been always onward, and it was a bitter pill to retreat!

But such were the orders, and they must be obeyed. Well, we fell back to New Market, where we remained a day and then were sent over the Massanutten Mountain again. In a few days we returned to N.M., and from there we went on to Strasburg, where the army remained until the 24th of May. Strasburg is a small town on the Manassas Gap Rail Road. The valley at this point is very narrow, as the mountain ranges approach quite near together. The country around is rough and wild in the extreme, and the scenery very picturesque. The tall, dark mountains rising proudly up on either side almost darken the valley with their shadows. Just twelve miles east of Strasburg is the little village of Front Royal, where, it will be remembered, the gallant Kenley and his regiment of Marylanders were taken prisoners on the memorable 28th of May, 1862.[3]

Now came the first battle for Willard and his comrades in Company G. General Jackson, hoping to continue operations near Front Royal without molestation from Banks located to the west at Strasburg, ordered the destruction of the Manassas Gap Railroad and the bridges linking the two towns to disrupt Union communications. Willard's company was assigned to guard the north (and eastern) side of a railroad bridge at Buckton Station, midway between the two towns, and a company from the 27th Indiana held the south (and western) side. South of the railroad was a wheat field, and beyond that a stand of woods. Some four hundred of Ashby's cavalry were detailed to destroy the bridge, and on May 23 they acted. From cover in the woods, Ashby launched an attack across the wheat field toward the bridge, taking the Federals by surprise. The two Union companies, though outnumbered, took stock in the face of this charge and assumed position behind the railroad embankment on the north side of the bridge. Their fire stopped the assault and forced a retreat, with the loss of some senior officers dead on the field.[4] The men of the 3rd Wisconsin performed admirably and saw that they could face the enemy and come away victorious.

It was while the main army rested at Strasburg that Co. G (of which I am a member), with four other companies from different regiments, were detailed to guard the rail road from there to Front Royal, a distance of twelve miles. The companies were scattered along the road at different points, with instructions to patrol the road frequently and to guard the bridges, etc.

It so happened that Co. B, 27th Indiana, and Co. G, 3rd Wisconsin, were posted together at a bridge about six miles from Strasburg and one and a half from the White Sulphur Springs. The Indianians occupied the east side of the creek and we the west. The stream was only a small one, in fact being only a creek, and emptied into the Shenandoah. Our camp was a very pleasant one, and the scenery around was interesting. It was situated on the banks of the Shenandoah in the bosom of a wood, at the foot of the grim old Massanutten.

We had been there nearly a week, and the time had passed away quietly. The afternoon of Friday the 23rd was as pleasant a one as ever gladdened the heart of nature. The sky was serene, and the sun shone down on our little encampment in cloudless splendor. The trees were now fully dressed in their summer gear, the birds sang, and the little brook seemed to murmur more sweetly than ever on that afternoon; and save the rippling of the brook and the low murmur of the river, all was hushed and still—quiet as a Sabbath evening.

Little did we dream that afternoon of the fearful storm that was even then gathering around us, a storm that was about to sweep down from among those mountains and drive us, like a helpless ship, a broken and stranded wreck, upon the shores of Maryland.

The silence of our camp was rudely broken, no one suspecting the presence of an enemy until we were startled by the rapid report of firearms and the whistling of bullets through our tents. We were quickly under arms and in line. The attack had been made on the camp of our Indiana neighbors, who were taken completely by surprise, and most of them [were] driven to the river bank, not having time to arm themselves.

The fight at Buckton Station, repulse of the Rebel cavalry under Ashby, and the death of Captain Fletcher and Colonel Sheets. The cavalry, for such was the character of our visitors, were already riding through their camp, yelling like savages. Almost with one accord, our company rushed across the bridge to the assistance of our friends. Our pieces were all loaded, and we poured a volley into their ranks at less than fifty yards. The volley was a fearful one and had the effect of driving them back over the fields at the top of their speed. But a new danger threatened us. They had sent a company around to our left and were galloping toward our camp. This charge had been intended to be made simultaneously with that upon the Indianians, but fortunately was not done. We now recrossed the bridge under a heavy fire and succeeded in repulsing the enemy.

We now had a good position behind the rail road embankment, with the Shenandoah behind us. They seemed designed to make a dash at us in a body across the creek, and for that purpose, the whole force, consisting (as I afterwards learned by one of them) of five companies of Ashby's Cavalry, were drawn off in line behind the woods in order to make a charge. All was still for a few moments, then we could hear the tramp of hoofs and the clang of sabres. Soon they came into view, sweeping around the woods, yelling like very demons, their long sabres flashing in the sun light. We were ready for them, and nearly a hundred rifles rested across the embankment. As they swept down to the banks of the creek, the order was given to fire—then, at the same instant, every gun belched forth its messengers of death, which went crashing through the ranks of the enemy, who disappeared quickly behind the woods.

That discharge told upon their ranks, for our aim was a sure one. Horses and riders tumbled down in confusion, and when the smoke cleared away, we saw nothing but the backs of our enemies and the mass of horses and men that had fallen. The fight was now over, though occasional firing was kept up until dark, when our regiment came up to our rescue. We were never able to ascertain the loss to the enemy, though we knew it was not small. One of them who was taken prisoner near Williamsport told me that their loss in killed and wounded was not less than fifty, and he thought that that number would not cover the actual loss. One captain was found on the bank of the creek the next morning, and the grave of Colonel Sheets was found at Front Royal. A board at his head gave evidence by the inscription upon it that he was killed at Buckton Station.

We lost one killed and four wounded, one of whom died of his wounds. The Indianians lost one killed and eight wounded.

I will give a brief account of an incident which occurred during the fight at Buckton Station. I have reference to the death of Ance Edwards, a member of Co. G. We had crossed the rail road bridge and had driven back the Rebel cavalry that had charged upon the camp of our Indiana neighbors. We were then obliged to fall back across the creek to repel an attack from that direction. This done, our attention was again attracted to the other side of the creek.

One of the Indianians, who had been wounded and was hardly able to walk, was attacked while endeavoring to gain the bridge by two of the Rebel cavalry, who rode up to him with sabres drawn. One of them he unhorsed by a skillful thrust of the bayonet, and he was himself knocked down at the same instant by a blow from the other. He attempted to rise to his feet and was again struck down. He succeeded at last in rising to his knees and held up his hands as if begging for mercy. But the cavalry man seemed lost to every human emotion and, regardless of his helpless victim's cry for quarter, continued to strike the poor fellow with his sabre, which was already dripping with blood. So intent was he upon killing the man that he did not seem to realize his own danger. He had just lifted his gory sabre to give a death blow when the sharp crack of a rifle rang out upon the air, and the weapon dropped to the ground and he threw up his hands, then fell from his horse *dead*. The shot had been fired by Edwards, who had halted on the embankment and had there loaded his piece while the bullets were dropping around him as thick as rain drops. After firing, he turned to descend the embankment, a smile of satisfaction beaming over his handsome face, when he fell dead, shot through the brain. The sun was just rising above the distant mountain the next morning when we gathered around the grave we had dug for him in the quiet glen on the banks of the Shenandoah. The task over, we turned intently and sadly away, leaving him there to sleep alone, where the wild birds of the mountain may come and warble his requiem above his lonely grave.

The death of Edwards moved Willard deeply. He wrote a poem about it, which is included in the appendix.

The outnumbered General Banks, fearing that Jackson would try to cut off his retreat route north and trap him in the Valley, determined to fall back to

Winchester, which he considered a place of safety. This resulted in a footrace between the two sides to see who could get to Winchester first and take the favorable ground. Banks's retreat was dogged by Jackson, whose attacks on the Union rear guard caused panic in Banks's supply train and among some troops, thus endangering the entire force as it fled north. Banks performed heroically in trying to restore order. It was only by the greatest exertions of some brave rear guard units, however, that the Confederates were prevented from rolling up the entire Union column.

The next morning we returned with the regiment to Strasburg, where we found the whole army on the move towards Winchester. This was the 24th of May. Arriving at Strasburg, we passed on through the town on the Winchester road, which we found crowded with army trains and ambulances. We did not know yet what had really occurred, but everything indicated a hasty retreat. At Cedar Creek we passed the "Zouaves de Afrique," who had been left behind to burn the bridge. We passed on without molestation as far as Middleton, where our advance encountered a small force of Rebel infantry and cavalry. After a short struggle the way cleared, and the teams moved on.

But hardly had this been accomplished in front when the booming of cannon in our rear gave proof that a new danger threatened us—that we had been attacked in that direction. Then on came the teams, thundering over the rough pike, with masses of cattle and loose horses which were being driven towards Winchester, with here and there mules, single and in pairs, which had been cut loose from the wagons by their frightened drivers, pell mell, "helter skelter," army wagons, sutler wagons, ambulances, squads of runaway cavalry, etc., etc. all came thundering on in the wildest confusion. A panic seemed almost inevitable throughout the whole train. But our gallant commander, General Banks, rode along among the teamsters and, by threats and entreaties, succeeded in restoring order. The infantry remained perfectly cool and only laughed at their frightened companions. The booming of cannon in the rear still continued, and a strong force was sent back, which succeeded in holding the enemy in check until the train could get out of danger. This, however, was not done until we had lost nearly a hundred wagons and quite a number of prisoners.

We then pushed on to Winchester, where we arrived about nine o'clock. We had not had anything to eat that day and had traveled twenty-six miles. We were very tired and were glad to throw ourselves down upon the damp ground to rest. This was Saturday night, and a more lovely one never followed in the footsteps of day. The sky was perfectly clear, brilliant with myriad bright stars, and the moon never shone with a more soft and gentle light than it did on this occasion.

The enemy ceased to follow us, the firing ended, and all was quiet—so quiet that one could hardly realize that two hostile armies had passed the day in toil and strife. Hundreds of men lay down to rest—

> The bugle sang truce for the night cloud had lowered
> The sentinel star set his watch in the sky,
> And thousands had sunk to the ground over powered
> The weary to sleep and the wounded to die.

All that night after twelve o'clock, skirmishing and picket firing was going on, and we knew that the enemy had followed us closely and the morning would bring on a battle. What a thought! What will the morning bring, how many are to survive the conflict, shall we be over powered? We knew that their force greatly outnumbered our own, and we must either fight or run.

At the battle of Winchester on May 25, Jackson overwhelmed Banks's men, sending them fleeing north. The 3rd Wisconin performed well, holding back the attacking Confederates until it was clear that the regiment would be cut off from the main Union force unless it also withdrew. The whole Federal army, finding itself defeated, fled back to Maryland across the Potomac, which it had crossed so confidently just months earlier.

Stonewall Jackson and the entire Confederacy were elated, as indeed they had every right to be. Jackson's goals had all been more than accomplished. With a force of fewer than 20,000, he had faced Union commanders with some 70,000 men at their disposal, and who had overspread the Shenandoah Valley as far south as Harrisonburg. He had divided, confused, and outwitted his enemy; prevented Union troops from moving eastward to guard Washington or join McClellan (thus helping to ruin McClellan's grand strategy and to save Richmond); and then chased the Yankees out of that area of Virginia altogether.

Well the night—the last one for many of us on earth—passed away, and the Sabbath, calm and peaceful, dawned without a cloud. How lovely, how serenely beautiful it was—too lovely to be marred, so rudely marred, by the cruel work of man mingling in deadly strife.

The sun was not yet up when our pickets were driven in and heavy firing began. A Rebel regiment appeared on the crest of the hill to the west of us but were soon driven back by our cannon. The line of battle was now hastily formed. Our force consisted of seven skeleton regiments, which were drawn up in line at the foot of the ridge from which the Rebels had just been driven. The 2nd Brigade were formed nearly at right angles with us and were on the left behind a wall. The artillery was planted on the little eminences behind us, throwing shell and grape over our heads. The firing began on the left and right, then in the centre, and was kept up for nearly two hours. In the meantime a portion of the city had taken fire from the commissary stores that were being burnt, and huge, dark columns of smoke rose over the city, rolling up, hiding the sun and blackening the sky. Fire and flame leaped up in the air through the smoke like long serpent tongues, flashing out their lurid light with an unearthly gleam. While the city below was on fire, at least forty cannon were roaring on the neighboring hills, spitting fire and smoke and sending their dread messengers of death, screaming demon like through the air, while the incessant roar of musketry along the hill gave evidence that the work of death was being carried on almost hand to hand.

But it was only madness to stand there against such fearful odds. Up from Strasburg, a heavy column of the enemy was rapidly advancing, and the cloud of dust that rose above the woods and the rumbling of artillery in that direction gave token of their near approach, while from the direction of Berryville, another force was advancing on us at the same time. Regiment after regiment appeared in front and far around on the flanks, sweeping down towards the city.

Thus we found ourselves about to be surrounded, with an overwhelming force on all sides, leaving no other alternative but retreat or all be lost. Hence we fell back rapidly through the city, the enemy close upon us, firing and yelling like very fiends, while from almost every window shots were fired by the inhabitants.

After passing through the city, the regiments were formed in line and marched rapidly but in perfect order through to Martinsburg, where we halted for an hour and a half. The inhabitants were very kind to us and gave us bread, milk, and whatever they had on hand to spare. Never will the tired and weary soldiers who passed through that little city on that day forget the kindness of the loyal people of Martinsburg.

After this rest we pushed on towards Williamsport, still thirteen miles distant. It was a long march but was at last accomplished, and that night we lay down to rest upon the banks of the Potomac. The enemy did not press us closely from Martinsburg to the river, for it seems that the main body had taken the road to Harpers Ferry. We had been now two days with hardly a mouthful to eat and traveled a distance of over sixty miles, and some of us had fought in two pitched battles. It can hardly be wondered at that we were glad that Sabbath night when the sun went down and darkness came on to hide us from our cruel pursuers. Never was there a band of men more crippled than we. The next morning (the 26th), we crossed the river and stood once more on the friendly soil of Maryland, while the broad old Potomac rolled between us and our enemies.

There is one coincidence worthy of note. It was on the 26th of February that we crossed the Potomac at Harpers Ferry, and on the 26th of May, just three months later, we crossed the same river at Williamsport. But what a contrast! We crossed at Harpers Ferry with as fine an army corps as ever took the field. With a force of not less than thirty thousand, completely armed and equipped, handsomely uniformed, with banners waving and bands of music playing, with buoyant tread and hearts beating with enthusiasm, the dark, moving mass marched file by file into the hills of the Old Dominion. We went into the valley and marched triumphantly up it for more than a hundred miles. Three months passed by, and on the 26th of May, the broken and shattered remnant of the corps rested in Maryland.

Jackson left the Valley and went to reinforce Lee before Richmond. This gave Union forces an opportunity to return to that portion of Virginia, and Willard's regiment was sent to guard the passages to the Shenandoah.

We remained on the friendly soil of Maryland until the 10th of June, when we again crossed over into Virginia and pushed on to Winchester via Martinsburg and Bunker Hill, the former a handsome, little city about thirteen miles from the river. Bunker Hill is an insignificant village lying at the junction of the Harpers Ferry and Martinsburg Road and is just thirteen miles from Winchester. We arrived at Winchester on the 12th of June, where Co. G was detailed to do provost duty, in which capacity we continued to act until we joined the regiment on the Rappahannock.

While doing duty at Winchester, we had charge of Confederate prisoners, which we were detailed to guard when they were sent to Harrisburg, Pennsylvania. Returning to Winchester, we remained until the 7th of July, when we packed up and started for Front Royal. In the meantime, Jackson had escaped from the valley, in spite of the combined efforts of Fremont and Shields, who had both traveled hard and far to intercept him and would have done so had not McDowell overthrown their plans by not allowing the bridge to be burned across the Shenandoah. Over this bridge, which had been ordered to be burnt by Fremont and the order countermanded by McDowell, the Rebel army succeeded in making its escape. It arrived in Richmond just in time to fall upon the flanks of McClellan's army and contributed not a little to their success and our disastrous retreat to the James River.

Front Royal is a small, dirty town situated on the banks of the Shenandoah, just where the east and west branches mingle in one broad, deep stream. Here the Confederates had made extensive preparations for hospitals, as several large buildings had been erected for that purpose. A burying ground on a little hill a short distance from the town gave token by its many graves of the mortality of the troops who had been stationed there. There were graves filled by the fallen from almost every state in the Confederacy. And there were some also from the North who had come from their distant homes to find here, on the banks of the Shenandoah, a lonely grave. There they lay, men from the North and South who had come to strike at each other's hearts, but now, like brothers, they lay side by side.

From Front Royal we pushed on over into the valley of the Rappahannock, crossed that river at Glen Mills, and marched on to Warrenton, where we remained a few days and then returned to Glen Mills. From there we went to Little Washington, and from thence to Culpeper Courthouse via Sperryville and Woodville. While at Little Washington, the movement of troops gave unmistakable evidence that something of importance was about to occur. All day on the 6th and 7th of August troops were pouring on through Little Washington to Sperryville, where Pope, who was now in command in the valley, was concentrating all his forces in order to meet any advance, either by way of Madison Courthouse or Culpeper. As early as the 7th it was known that the Rebels were advancing towards the Rappahannock and Culpeper. A portion of our cavalry were beyond the Rapidan and slowly retreated before the Rebel force, skirmishing as they retired across the river. A portion of Banks's command had been sent on beyond Culpeper, the remnants of his corps consisting only of two divisions, about eight thousand strong.

It was again Banks versus Jackson, with Jackson outnumbering Banks two to one. Jackson's assignment was to halt the advance of Gen. John Pope's army into Virginia. Banks was then part of Pope's force. He attacked Jackson's men, who were dug in on Cedar Mountain. The attack was a brave one and was having some success before A. P. Hill's men arrived and launched a counterattack. The loss on both sides was severe, and neither side really won the battle. Banks (and Pope, who denied that he had ordered the attack) accomplished nothing to compensate for the losses and retreated to Culpeper, while Jackson barely beat a force half his size and then pulled back as well. One of the regiments making the attack was the 3rd Wisconsin, although Willard and Company G were detached and not in the fight. Willard describes the battle as he watched it unfold from his nearby vantage point.

The Battle of Cedar Mountain. With this little force, Banks advanced boldly on beyond the city to check the advance of Jackson and Ewell. In the meantime, one division under McDowell passed on a few miles beyond the town, and on the night of the 8th, Sigel's corps arrived at Culpeper, where, having traveled all night, they halted to rest. On the afternoon of the 9th, Banks cautiously moved forward towards the Rapidan.

The country around Culpeper resembles a large plain over grown with a stunted growth of oak and pine. The soil is very sandy and dry, and there is no water in some places for miles. On the west of this plain or valley runs the Thoroughfare Mountains, about ten miles distant. Directly in front is Cedar or Slaughter Mountain, and the country is somewhat broken by small hills and ridges. The Rapidan River is about seven or eight miles from Culpeper.

Soon the boom of cannon announced the presence of the enemy. The firing at first was only occasional but gradually increased as the column advanced and new batteries were developed, until the cannonading was almost incessant. The provost guard had been ordered up and were halted just in rear of the batteries. The cannonade continued until 5:00 P.M., when an advance of the infantry commenced. The enemy had several batteries in play, besides three heavy siege guns, which were posted upon the side of Cedar Mountain, directly in front.

Cedar Creek is a small stream some two miles this side of the river. Across this stream, about five o'clock P.M., Banks pushed a portion of his column. The line of battle was formed extending east and west, advancing slowly through the woods and across an open field towards the enemy. Skirmishers were out, of course, consisting of six companies of the Wisconsin 3rd. At last, the position of the enemy being ascertained, the whole line advanced to the attack.

But hardly had they emerged from the woods into an open field when they were greeted by such a volley of musketry, and the artillery poured into them such a deadly shower of grape, that they were compelled to retire; but only to advance again, when they succeeded in driving the enemy before them for some distance. The battle now became general, and the roar of musketry was continual for an hour and a half, when darkness came on and put an end to the struggle. The battle was a desperate one, in many cases hand to hand. The batteries did fearful execution on both sides, and the loss was very heavy. At night, neither party could claim a victory, as neither held the battle field. McDowell came up at night, and the brave but shattered regiments of General Banks's corps were allowed to fall to the rear. They had fought nobly—had done all that brave men could do—had held their ground against an overwhelming force, though the Rebels poured a perfect death harvest into their ranks, sweeping them with grape and canister, thinning out their ranks most fearfully. Hardly an officer escaped without a wound, and some of the very best were killed; when McDowell moved up, hardly an officer was found to command either regiment or company.

Night came on, and the weary fellows retired a short distance and lay down to rest. It was a lovely evening, and the moon shone in all the fullness of its glory. The sky was brilliant with myriad bright stars that seemed to look sadly down upon the field of death. So lustrous was it, indeed, that aspects even at a distance were plainly visible. To the east stretched an extensive plain, while in the west the dark peaks of the Thoroughfare range loomed grimly up against the blue sky. To the south, in the valley where the battle had been fought, a cloud of smoke seemed to hang, resting like a gloomy mantle over that field of death.

All was hushed for a time, and a death like silence seemed to prevail everywhere. Long lines of men might be seen standing motionless as statues, artillery and squads of cavalry were drawn up on the hills around, evidently expecting that something unusual was about to occur, for the very silence seemed ominous. An hour passed and all was yet still and silent as the grave; men conversed in low undertones as if fearful to speak aloud. The deep hush was almost intolerably oppressive.

While thus standing, looking, listening, our attention was attracted by a red signal light, which gleamed far away on a spur of the Thoroughfare Mountains, flashing through space like the eye of a demon. Almost instantly, the crest of Cedar Mountain glowed with a similar light, flashing luridly up against the evening sky. Hardly had the signal appeared up on the summit ere a flame of fire streamed up on its side—then a flash—and the heavy boom of the gun on the mountain side came rolling down into the valley, echoing far away against the distant mountains, dying in feeble echoes as it rolled along in the distance. But the sound had not died away before the deadly messenger—the huge shell—came screaming through the darkness. This seemed to be the signal for a general cannonade, and a most fearful one it was. Every gun at the command of the enemy now opened, throwing their deadly contents into our midst, bursting above and around us, filling the air with flying missiles that screeched like fiends. Hardly five minutes had elapsed before our batteries were in play, and the rapidity of the bursting shells told how fearful was the dreadful work now being carried on. This cannonade lasted nearly an hour, when it gradually died away, until only an occasional boom broke the stillness of the night.

The battle field and its horrors. But the battle field, what of that? What was the condition of the helpless and wounded? No one knew, for neither Confederate nor Federal dare approach the scene of the fatal and deadly conflict. The wounded and dying must be left to themselves, to die or live, to moan and sigh, unaided and uncared for, as the long night dragged slowly and cheerlessly by. Well, the night passed away, and the Sabbath morning dawned clear and bright, as serenely beautiful and glorious as that which dawned on Eden's flowers. For a time, all was hushed and calm as a Sabbath morning in other and more peaceful lands. Then came the boom of a cruel gun, and the hissing shell went screaming angrily through the gold tinted air. Another and another followed, but no reply came from the sullen enemy. At last arrangements were made for the gathering up of the wounded and the burial of those more fortunate—the dead!

What a sad, sad scene presented itself that lovely Sabbath day. The dead, the dying, and the helplessly wounded! What a picture to contemplate—the shattered bone and dissevered limb, the parched lip and fevered brow—pains that drive the eyeballs glaring from their sockets, that make the brain reel and drive the helpless victim to madness. Those who walk the quiet paths of peace, that gather around the fireside and are blessed with all its quiet joys, can have but an imperfect idea of the unspeakable horrors of the battle field. A battle field! The synonym of all that is horrible and cruel, a place where man meets man in deadly encounter, depriving one another of, if not life itself, *that* which robs it of half its charms; changing the brave and perfect man, the image of God, into a helpless victim, a useless thing!

No Sabbath bells chimed out that day. In other and more peaceful lands, where Sabbaths are not robbed of their quiet by the clang of arms or the tread of armies, Sabbaths come and go, unbroken and undisturbed, a happy people wind their way to the house of prayer, and the church bells ring out their solemn but peaceful notes. But how different was it there on that Sabbath day? The sun shone as bright and the sky was as calm and serene above the battle field as where it bends over the most peaceful lands. But how different the scene upon which it smiled. The battle field and the peaceful homes! How different!

All that day the work of bringing in the wounded and burying the dead went on. Many, very many were the graves they dug, and many were the mangled forms placed therein. But the work was not complete, and all the wounded were not brought in until the third day. Many, no doubt, there were who died unknown, unaided, and alone—what a death! To die thus on the battle field, wasting away day by day with no one near to comfort. How slowly the hours of pain and agony must pass, bringing with them no aid, no relief, the cold night and the scorching sun as days and nights come and go, the consuming, burning fever and pain that drives reason from the mind and turns the brain to madness.

But the sad scene ends not here. In the hospitals lie men with their agonizing pains while the life blood trickles silently away, until the life goes out and the suffering soldier finds a lonely grave. While far away in some distant land among the forests of the West, on the green slopes of New England, or in the cottage by the sea, loved ones, lonely broken hearted ones, are sighing sadly for their beloved soldier, suffering or dead, who they never more may see. Verily, war is a curse.

On Monday an advance was made to the Rapidan, but the enemy was not there; he had gone. Banks's shattered and broken column fell back to the city, while Sigel and McDowell held their position along the banks of the Rapidan.

McClellan's huge force was in the process of changing its base of operations by sea from the Virginia Peninsula to the area between Washington and Richmond, where it planned to meet up with Pope. During this enormous and time-consuming move, it was effectively taken out of action. This presented an opportunity for the Confederates, a fact not lost on Robert E. Lee. He determined to attack Pope while one of his armies was, as it were, at sea and before the two forces could combine against him. Pope realized that he was in an exposed position and that his ability to pull back to Washington was threatened, so he ordered a retreat across to the north side of the Rappahannock River. The two sides now faced each other across that river.

The second Bull Run campaign followed. Pope was known as an obnoxious braggart and proved to be incompetent as well. Facing Lee, Jackson, and Longstreet, all acting together, was way beyond him—as it was beyond most generals—and he suffered a particularly humiliating defeat. He was so discredited that he was transferred to Minnesota, out of the war altogether. There he fell to blaming others for the defeat, but he was too far out of the picture to matter. Banks's corps, including the 3rd Wisconsin, did not take part in the fighting. It had been assigned the task of guarding the army's supplies and the railroads and bridges used for transporting them. From the perspective of the men of Banks's corps, confusion surrounded them and the Rebels seemed to be everywhere. By the end of the campaign, Willard, like most other Union soldiers, was angry at the abysmal leadership.

All remained quiet until the 16th, when, as unexpected as it was sudden, a retreat was ordered. On the evening of the same day we found ourselves on our way to the Rappahannock. All that night the trains were passing to the rear, rolling on through the city. But little progress was made that night, owing to the crowded condition of the roads, and though we were on our feet all night, we were hardly out of the city when morning came. We reached and crossed the Rappahannock on the afternoon of the 17th, where we bivouacked for the night. Every one who has read of the doings of General Pope, whatever may be his other faults, cannot but admire the skill and the promptness which he manifested in conducting this retreat.

Arriving at the Rappahannock Station, the troops were drawn up in line of battle, but we, being provost guard, went a little farther back, where we bivouacked. A few days after, we were again ordered to join our regiment, which we were glad to do, as provost duty is not the most agreeable duty in the world. While on the river, Banks's corps was held in reserve, only marching here and there as the occasion required. Not a day passed for over two weeks that we did not hear cannonading, and some, too, which was very brisk and interesting.

One very foggy morning, while we were lying at one of the fords, where all had been silent the day previous, we were roused rather suddenly by a most deafening crash and a roar, as though the whole forests were crashing down, and a score of shells came hissing and tearing through the woods most furiously. This was rather a rude salutation that Sabbath morning, and we scrambled to our feet, hardly comprehending what had occurred. The first impression seemed to be that an earthquake or something of the kind had occurred or that the grim old forest was tumbling down about our ears, and it was not a little amusing to see the men just awakened from a sound sleep, scrambling to their feet, looking curiously around or glancing up among the trees as if ready to dodge any stray limb that might tumble down in that vicinity. Hardly had we had time to think before another thundering discharge shook the ground and gave us to understand that the enemy, at least, was awake. The Rebels had planted a couple of batteries during the night and were shelling our batteries most merrily. But our gunners were up and doing, and having been able, by the flashes of their guns, to get the range of them, let go a volley or two in return.

This sport was kept up for half an hour, when, very fortunately, the fog cleared away and revealed large masses of enemy infantry moving rapidly down towards the ford. Other batteries were quickly in position, and such a furious storm of grape and canister swept their ranks as they pushed on through the open field that they soon broke and fled back to the woods beyond.

A few days after, one brigade was sent over the river to reconnoiter, when suddenly the Rebels opened on them from an ambush. After a few rounds the brigade broke and fled back across the river in confusion. But one of the cleverest affairs that occurred was the trap that Sigel, the brave, fiery, and sagacious little Dutchman, set for the Rebels. The Rebels had, unbeknown (as they supposed), constructed a bridge during the night on which they intended to cross early in the morning. Sigel was aware of their designs and let them work on undisturbed but in the meantime prepared to receive them in due form. The bridge being completed, they came cautiously down early in the morning and began to cross. One whole brigade was already over, and still they continued to press forward. At the given time Sigel opened on them with his concealed batteries and tore their bridge to atoms in a moment. The Confederates found themselves in a trap and surrendered without firing a gun. Nearly two thousand prisoners were taken.

Having marched up and down the Rappahannock for more than two weeks, we at last arrived at Warrenton. In the meantime, the Rebel cavalry had made one of their bold raids around to our rear and burned quite a number of Pope's wagons, killing and wounding a few unarmed teamsters and sick soldiers and doing some damage to the rail road track, when they were fortunately dispersed by the timely approach of General Kearney.

When we arrived at Warrenton, it was ascertained that a large portion of the Rebel force had gone completely around us and that Hooker and Kearney were fighting them at Manassas. The whole army then fell back from the river and made its way rapidly towards Bull Run. Here the army operations were, and still are, a mystery to me, and I do not believe that there is a general, not even Pope himself, that can elucidate them. Battles were fought when least expected, portions of the army were separated from the rest, and all communication cut off until Pope fled with his army in confusion towards Washington.

Banks's corps was left to guard the rear, but the enemy whom Pope was retreating before were apparently on every side. Banks was nearly surrounded and cut off at Bristoe Station and made a narrow escape by a rapid march of about eighteen miles around to the right, over almost impassable roads. That was a hard march, one that I never wish to do over again. We finally arrived at the far famed Bull Run on the 31st of August, where we were drawn up in line of battle. The Rebels were outwitted, as they had thought to bag Banks and his entire command between Bristoe Station and Bull Run, but Banks had been in too many tight places and was too sharp to be caught in such a trap.

Everything seemed to be in confusion. Regiments, brigades, and divisions marched here and there, the object or destination unknown to their commanders, the boom of cannon was heard on almost every side, and no one knew at what moment the enemy would appear in our immediate vicinity. Pope was evidently out generaled and most completely bewildered, and finally fled to Alexandria and crept behind the guns of the fortifications for protection.

We had hardly crossed Bull Run Bridge when the Rebel cavalry came sweeping down upon us like the wind but did not follow us across, retiring after exchanging a few shots, evidently deeming it advisable to get out of range of our rifles. After a scanty supper, we were glad to lie down upon the rocks to rest. Dark, heavy clouds swept across the sky, rolling up in sombre banks against the mountains, which stretched far away to the north like a great wall of mist until, as they grew dimmer and fainter, they lost themselves in the distance. It was a gloomy afternoon, but not darker or more gloomy than the thoughts that passed through our minds as we hurried on towards that famed but fatal locality where many brave men have laid down their lives in defense of liberty and their dear native land—Bull Run! Oh, how many sad memories cling around that name! The battles fought and lost, the many graves, and the bitter memories render that name an incentive to do and dare to every loyal heart.

Bull Run and Manassas did not appear to me as I had supposed they would. It had but little of that wild, rough, hilly appearance that fancy had painted it with. On the contrary, it is a very level country and, in fact, is almost what might be called a plain, and would be one were it not broken in places by a small hill or ridge, covered here and there by woods and bushes. Looking to the north in the direction of Alexandria, one sees nothing but a forest, almost unbroken, stretching on towards the Potomac. To the east the country is more open, stretching far away like a plain, until broken by the distant mountains just seen along the horizon, looking like a long line of blue mist, rising and falling like the waves of the ocean. To the south, beyond Manassas, the country slopes off as far as one can see in one vast plain of an almost barren waste of sterile, sandy fields, while to the west the Thoroughfare Mountains loom up in grand sublimity against the sky. Thoroughfare Gap is about ten or twelve miles from Manassas.

Between Manassas and Bull Run, a distance of three or four miles, the country is covered at intervals with woods, which at the scene of the memorable battles of Bull Run fought on the 21st of July/61 and August 30th, become dense and heavy in places. Bull Run itself is only a small stream or creek, which was so shallow that it could be crossed on the rocks without wetting one's feet. The banks are in some spots quite high and steep. From the top of one of these little bluffs, I had a good view of this famous battle field and the surrounding country. The scene of strife still bears the marks of fearful carnage that had raged there. Dead horses, broken down and upset gun carriages, and army wagons and ambulances were scattered around in confusion, while many, very many newly made graves told the sad tale of death and carnage.

Just at night the clouds cleared away, and the sun shone calmly and softly down on us at parting as it went slowly down behind the dark blue wall of mountains, wreathing their lofty brows with a circle of gorgeous sun light. Although the day had been a gloomy one, the night was extremely beautiful. The last day of summer had passed, and this, the last of its many glorious evenings, was far spent when we, or at least I, fell asleep. Sweetly the stars burned in the sky that night. The encampment was wrapped in silence for sleep, balmy sleep.

"Tired," nature's sweet restorer, had sealed many a weary soldier's eyes in repose and wafted his spirit away into the blissful regions of dreamland. But as for me, I could not stay asleep. As I lay there among the rocks, looking up into the broad expanse of blue, brilliant with its myriads of bright, lustrous stars, I could not but think of the "evenings of long ago," resembling this in their sublime beauty, evenings of other and better times. . . .

The next day (Monday, the 1st of September) dawned warm and bright, and we were up and astir long before sunrise. Little did we comprehend the real condition of affairs. We were aware that battles had been fought, it was true; but the result we knew nothing about. Hardly a day had passed but what we had heard the booming of cannon, and a thousand rumors had been in circulation. But still we were completely in the dark as to what had occurred outside of our own little circle. Little did we dream, however, that our army had been beaten in every engagement and was already hurrying towards Washington. But such was the case.

On the afternoon of the 1st, we again formed in line and marched on towards Centreville. Here we found a large part of Pope's army scattered over the hills, swarming around the fortifications or straggling about the country in the wildest confusion. Good heavens! What a condition for an army to be in when in the presence of the enemy—no order, no system. But thus it was and had been. Generals had fought without knowing who was to support them on the right or left—what *generalship*! Who can wonder that our army was beaten at Bull Run when such a general as *Pope* or *McDowell* had the leadership. Pope and McDowell fought the battle of Bull Run, and though their forces far outnumbered that of the enemy, yet they were defeated. Pope the *blockhead* and McDowell the *traitor*.

Passing through Centreville, we marched rapidly towards Alexandria. We halted after marching about four miles, when we set down to rest for a few moments (as we supposed); but our halt was much longer than was agreeable.

The Battle of September the 1st, the death of Generals Kearney and Stevens. The afternoon wore away and we began to think of supper, when we were startled by the report of a cannon just over a little ridge and to the west of us. This was followed by another and another in quick succession. In a few moments the rattle of musketry was heard, and we knew that a battle was being fought, and as it was only a short distance from us, we expected every moment to be sent to take part in it. The battle began just before sunset and continued until after dark. In the meantime a violent storm of thunder and rain came up, which at times completely drowned the sound of strife going on around us.

The afternoon had been a fine one, with hardly a cloud to mar the serenity of the sky, until just at night, when dark, heavy masses of clouds came rolling up from the west, shutting in the sun and spreading over the whole heavens. It was a sublime scene to look upon as those great, black clouds came sweeping over the sky, to watch the forked lightning as it leaped from cloud to cloud or forged its way towards earth, and to hear the thunder as it came, crash after crash, dying away in the distance, echoing through the woods or reverberating among the far off hills. In the meantime, the air grew dark and the rain came down in perfect torrents. Night soon came on, dark and dreary; still the battle and the storm went on. At times we could hear the boom of the cannon, while the rattle of musketry came faintly to our ears through the storm. Darkness, deep and impenetrable, wrapped woods, hills, and fields in its folds. The violence of the storm had abated, yet it still rained and it was very cold. For hours we stood there, guns in hand, impatiently waiting for orders. We were not allowed to make a fire, and being wet to the skin and having no blankets, we had no other alternative than to stand and shiver. The battle lasted until about eight o'clock, when the enemy withdrew. It was at this battle that the brave and noble Kearney was killed, together with General Stevens. The ground where we were was covered with water, but notwithstanding this, many of the men, overcome with fatigue, threw themselves upon the ground and slept.

The night was a cold and cheerless one, one of the most uncomfortable that I ever experienced. We were glad when the cold, gray glimmerings of light in the east gave token of the approaching morning, which came at last; and after a scanty breakfast we again resumed our march towards Alexandria, where we arrived about twelve o'clock at night. We were delayed several hours on the way, and once, when within a few miles of Alexandria, we were ordered back to Fairfax Station. A battle, or at least an engagement of some kind, was going on there, as we could hear the booming of cannon in rapid succession. When we had nearly reached the Station, we (i.e., our brigade) were ordered back to Alexandria again. As I have said, we reached there about midnight. There we lay down to rest (or rather shiver with the cold) until morning, when we traveled on towards Washington.

We were aware by *this time* that our army had been defeated in every battle of any importance, that it had met only with disasters and was already crowding over to the friendly shores of Maryland. We had been beaten, but the fault was not with the soldiers. There was no lack of courage or willingness to fight on their part. All were willing, yes *anxious* to meet the enemy. The blame rested, and will ever rest, with those in command. A thousand new made graves, a nation's disgrace, and the voice of an enraged people swelling up from the bosoms of New England and sweeping in thunder tones over the great North West demanded a change and the reinstatement to the command of the Grand Army of the gallant young general who had led our victorious army at Williamsburg and Yorktown. And in justice to the soldiers, the people, and McClellan, it was done. Though it was with sad hearts that we again found ourselves compelled to turn our backs upon Virginia and retreat into Maryland, yet we were not discouraged, for with McClellan to command, we were sure of success.

The beaten Federals fell back into the defenses of Washington. On September 4, flush with victory, the confident Army of Northern Virginia crossed the Potomac into Maryland. Lee saw many benefits to a move north. Politically, he hoped to rouse Maryland to the Confederate cause, scare the North and embolden antiwar Copperheads, embarrass the Lincoln administration, relieve Virginia from the constant battering of war, and gain credibility with foreign nations. Militarily, he wanted to maintain the initiative, draw Union troops away from other areas where the Confederacy was being pressed (such as the Western theater), and force the Army of the Potomac out of its defenses around Washington and inflict on it another—perhaps conclusive—defeat. It is certainly quite possible that if he had won at Antietam and remained strong enough to continue the campaign northward, antiwar sentiment in the frightened North might have forced an end to the war on Southern terms. That was how high the stakes were.

History calls the battle of Antietam a draw—even, to some, a tactical Confederate triumph—and in a strict military sense, this may be so. Yet politically, the foiling of Lee's grand designs constituted an important victory. Certainly, Lincoln saw it that way and used it as the springboard for the Emancipation Proclamation. Once this was issued, the war's aim became the freeing of slaves, and this perceived shift of focus guaranteed that the European powers would never come to the rescue of the Confederacy. Those commentators who say that Lincoln was grasping at straws in calling Antietam a sufficent victory to justify issuing the proclamation are underestimating its achievements. Moreover, there is a sense in which it was a military triumph as well. Willard was an honest man and had no trouble calling a defeat a defeat. Yet he considered Antietam the resurrection of the Army of the Potomac from a band of demoralized rabble to an effective fighting force, a stunning development just weeks after the devastating loss at second Bull Run. Conversely, the Confederates went into the battle flush with victories and sure of another. At battle's end, they had lost more than 13,000 irreplaceable men and returned to Virginia having accomplished virtually nothing.

McClellan was solely in command of the Army of the Potomac. The unsuccessful Banks was gone, replaced by Gen. Joseph Mansfield. With the 3rd Wisconsin present for action, the momentous campaign began.

We crossed the river at Georgetown Wednesday the 3rd and passed on out into the country in the direction of Rockville about five miles, where we came up with our wagons, which was the first we had seen of them since we left Culpeper on the 16th of August. Here also we received our mail. On the night of the 3rd we slept under shelter of a tent and enjoyed the luxury of a blanket. The next day we were mustered for pay, and after dinner we again took up our line of march, passing on through Rockville towards Darnstown.

The Confederates had, it seemed, crossed the Potomac and advanced into Maryland, taking possession of several towns and cities, and among the rest was Frederick, which is in every way a loyal town and contains as good and warm hearted people as any city in existence. The Rebels' visit, however, was a short one, and the town was soon again in our possession.

We bivouacked about half a mile from Frederick City on the afternoon of the 13th. We forded the river just below Frederick Junction, the water being only about three feet deep (the Monocacy). All the afternoon as we approached the city, we could hear cannonading in the direction of Crampton's Pass and Sugar Loaf Mountain, and also in the direction of Catoctin, a mountain on the west of the city and about seven miles from it. When we arrived at Frederick we could see the smoke of the cannons on the top and at the foot of the mountain, the former being the Rebel batteries, the latter being ours.

I was on guard duty that night. It was about eleven o'clock, and I had been pacing to and fro along my long, lonely "beat," thinking of old times and the many changes that had so unexpectedly occurred, when I was startled from my reverie by the cry of "fire, fire," and the loud ringing of the alarm bells. Looking towards the city I soon saw the cause of the alarm; dark, heavy masses of smoke were rolling up against the sky, and soon the "thousand tongues" of the "Fire Demon" were lapping the air in every direction.

Huge columns of fire and smoke reddened the sky, lighting up the whole city with a lurid glare that gave everything a wild, unearthly appearance. The cry of "fire" rolled along the streets, and the alarm bells rang out their call, filling the night air with the most terrible and dismal sounds. The old jail had been set on fire by its inmates and, in spite of the most gigantic efforts, was burned to the ground. The building was a very ancient one, having been built during the reign of George III prior to the Revolution. There are many appalling sights and scenes, but to me there is nothing so terrifying as a fire in a city. To be startled at the dead hour of night by that cry, the most horrible of all cries, "fire, fire" ringing in one's ears, shouted by a thousand voices, the hoarse deep voices of men, the shrill screams of women, and the frantic cries of children, mingling with the ringing of bells and the hurrying tramp of the excited throng, is dreadful.

The next day (Sunday the 14th), we passed through the city, meeting many old friends, who came out to shake hands with us and bid us good by and "God speed" on our dangerous mission. Late in the afternoon heavy cannonading was heard behind Catoctin Mountain, which we crossed over, down into the Middletown Valley and on to the foot of South Mountain, now famous for the bloody battle fought upon its side and summit, over which the Rebels were driven with the most terrible slaughter on both sides. The Rebels attempted to hold the mountain pass (Turner's) but were driven through it at the point of the bayonet. It was here that Gibbons's brigade won undying honors and covered themselves with glory. The laurels they won can never fade, for they will ever be remembered with pride by their countrymen and especially by the people of Wisconsin. They fought at Gainesville, Thoroughfare Gap, Bull Run, South Mountain, and Antietam, winning by their great bravery and endurance the name of the "Iron Brigade," given them by McClellan, who said they were as brave and good soldiers as any army in the world could boast of. It is composed of the 2nd, 6th, and 7th Wisconsin and 14th Indiana.

It is interesting to see that the Iron Brigade's fame was already established and its nickname generally recognized when Willard wrote this about the unit just a few months after Antietam. As a Wisconsin man, he was proud enough of their accomplishments to describe them here, yet he seems not at all envious, even though the 3rd Wisconsin, one of the Union army's most reliable battle units, never received the same level of recognition.

Willard's regiment did not take part in the battle of South Mountain on September 14, when Union forces seized a major pass separating them from the Confederates, who were spread on the other side of the mountains. Instead, the 3rd Wisconsin caught glimpses of the battle as it unfolded. Afterward, the men marched through the debris field of the battle and then on to Sharpsburg. On the night of September 16, they slept right on the edge of what would the next morning become the battlefield of Antietam. For many, it was their last night on earth.

The Battle of South Mountain. The battle of South Mountain was fought late in the afternoon and evening of Sunday the 14th. It resulted in the complete rout of the Rebels, who made a stand at the foot of the mountain but after a desperate struggle retreated up the side, fighting as they went, our brave fellows following and driving them slowly upward. They attempted to hold the pass, which was narrow. The Rebels crowded the pass in dense masses all along, while their cannon bristled on every eminence, showering down a perfect storm of shot and shell upon our men. But so resistless was their advance that as well might they have attempted to stay the rising of the tide as those brave, determined men who came rushing up the mountain, closing on the Rebels on almost every side, who, after a short but most bloody struggle, broke and fled through the pass into the plains below in the wildest confusion.

It is said that in that pass at South Mountain, where the fight was indeed terrific, the dead of both sides lay in heaps, or scattered thickly over the ground, lying side by side. The fight here was hand to hand, foot to foot, and is said to be one of the most desperate battles ever fought.

It was a Sabbath afternoon, that on which we climbed the Catoctin, from the summit of which we could watch the progress of the battle on the mountain side beyond. It was a beautiful scene which met the view which ever way one looked. To the east was the valley in which Frederick is situated. This valley is a lovely one, covered with fine fields, dotted with large, white farm houses with the clusters of out buildings. The fields were (though the grain had been gathered) still green and the orchards laden with fruit. Frederick City could be seen below, its many spires glittering in the light as the sun itself went down behind the gray old South Mountain, just glancing down into the valleys as if to see if all was well. Middletown Valley lies between Catoctin and South Mountain and is about five miles across. In the centre of this valley is the little but lovely village of Middletown. This is the most beautiful valley I ever saw—so rich, so green, so attractive.

From the top of Catoctin, we watched the progress of the battle as it went on that Sabbath evening. We could hear the booming of cannon and could see the cloud of white smoke as it rose at the foot of the mountain, and as it ascended higher and higher, we knew our boys were driving the enemy from the position. But the sun went down behind the mountain, and twilight soon deepened into night, wrapping mountain, village, and plain in its gloomy mantle. A few shots were fired after the day had closed, and then all was still. Thus closed that Sabbath day when—

Night let her curtain fall,
And pinned it with a star.

We passed on down the rugged sides of Catoctin through the Middletown Valley, over the foot of South Mountain, where we bivouacked for the night. Traces of the battle were visible on every side. All along the road and in the fields, old knapsacks, blankets, guns, and cartridge boxes were strewn, while scores of dead and wounded men and new made graves were scattered all along the wayside. The next day we passed over South Mountain and through the neat village of Boonesboro. Boonesboro is a small village on the Hagerstown and Harpers Ferry Pike and is the place where we took dinner after our first march in Maryland. Little did we think at that time that we should ever meet the Rebels in that vicinity. We halted in this little village a short time, but long enough to be convinced that the inhabitants were "Union." We passed on a few miles beyond the town, where we halted for the night. Some shelling was done during the afternoon but no fighting occurred.

On Tuesday we were in order of battle all day, but at night we (Mansfield's corps) moved over to the right across Antietam Creek. This move was a slow and cautious one, as we were very near the enemy's lines. No one was allowed to speak above his breath; every gun was loaded, and we were prepared for any emergency. We halted at last in an open field with a wood in front of us and formed in line of battle. Silently and quietly we lay down that night, and but few words were spoken as we lay there beneath the calm sky waiting for the developments of the morrow. The evening and the night were indeed beautiful. Sweetly and softly the stars shone in the great field of blue, and the fair faced moon seemed to look sadly down as if in sorrowful contemplation of the horrors that the dawn would inevitably bring.

The next day was a historic one that vies with Gettysburg for consideration as the turning point of the war. The 3rd Wisconsin played a prominent role.

McClellan had a promising battle plan, intending to attack both Confederate flanks at the same time with his numerically superior force. Unfortunately, the plan misfired, and during the course of the daylong struggle, Union troops launched uncoordinated sequential attacks on Lee's left, right, and center, with no one attack supporting the other. The Confederates responded with vigorous counterattacks. Fighting was unusually ferocious, as neither side held anything back, and casualties were staggering.

When substantial armies contend over a large amount of terrain, it is frequently the case that the battle actually becomes a series of smaller, separate, localized conflicts. So it was at Antietam, where names were given to the engagements that made up the battle, names that still resonate after more than a century: Burnside's Bridge, Bloody Lane, the Dunker Church, and the Cornfield. The 3rd Wisconsin was placed at the right of the Union position and would fight in the cornfield.

Hooker's I Corps was originally deployed in and behind some woods north of David Miller's farmhouse, and Mansfield's XII Corps, which included Willard's regiment, was about a mile north of Hooker. Just south of the house was a field full of tall corn almost ready to harvest, east of which were more woods. Straight south of the cornfield was a clearing, and to its southwest were woods that skirted the clearing and ran northward up its west side. The Dunker Church was located where the southern point of the clearing met these west wood. The Confederate line stretched from the woods west of the clearing, southwest of the cornfield, across the southern portion of the clearing, then northeast over to the east woods, east of the cornfield. Their advance forces were as far north as the cornfield.

Hooker initiated the contest by attacking Confederate positions in the east woods and also charging into the cornfield. The Confederates fiercely contested the ground but gave way at both points, while Union cannon raked them in the corn. Then Jackson brought up Lawton's division and hit Hooker with a counterattack, pushing him back through the cornfield. Hooker responded by bringing in his reserve units and succeeded in forcing back Jackson's spent forces. At this crucial moment, Hood's Texans entered the cornfield and threw Hooker's men back through it. By now, with so many dead, wounded, and missing, Hooker's corps was worn out. Mansfield's XII Corps was called upon to stem the Rebel advance, which had reached the northern edge of the cornfield.

Mansfield assigned Gordon's brigade, with the 3rd Wisconsin, to move through the north woods and take up a position just east of the Miller farmhouse and north of the cornfield, supporting an artillery battery that was already there. It arrived just in time to meet the Confederates emerging from the cornfield. The seesaw aspect of the battle continued, with the 3rd Wisconsin first stopping the oncoming Southerners, then advancing into the cornfield, then retreating in the face of fresh enemy troops. The regiment both inflicted and took terrible casualties that September morning, one of whom was the twenty-one-year-old Van Willard.

September 17th—Battle of Antietam. The night's quiet was broken by picket firing, which was often sharp and rapid. Early, almost before daybreak the next morning, we were awakened by the rattle of musketry and the roar of artillery.

The morning was a calm one but not bright, and the sun shone dimly down through the sombre haze which hung over hill and dale. The sky seemed veiled with a dull, leaden hued hazy vapor which wrapped everything in its folds. To the west, far away, might be seen the blue peaks of Elk Ridge, while South Mountain loomed grimly up in the east, its summit encircled with wreaths of clouds. But we had little time for observation as the continual roar of musketry, the boom of cannon, and the screaming of shells gave token that the work of death had already begun. We were soon in motion, forming in squares by regiments and brigades, divisions and corps, ready for action.

An hour and a half passed away, and still the battle went on with uninterrupted fury. The roar of musketry was incessant, and the cannons boomed with the most terrific of violence, seeming almost to shake the very earth. Hooker's men were at work, and well did they do their duty that day. As the storm of death swept around them, they fought on, pressing upon the enemy, who slowly gave way, contesting the ground foot by foot, rod by rod. The Rebel line retreated through the woods, across a large cornfield, while Hooker and his brave fellows followed close in pursuit.

The field was bordered on the west by a forest, in which the retreating enemy disappeared. Hooker's men were much exhausted, and their ranks had been fearfully thinned. Thousands of them had fallen, and the ground was thickly strewn with the dead and wounded of his gallant men. Besides, their ammunition was gone, and worse than all, their brave and noble commander, "Glorious Fighting Joe," was wounded. The Rebels disappeared in the forest, but fresh troops were there, and from out [of] the bosom of those gloomy woods there came a volley, and such a terrible one, that it smote our line, already so much weakened, with such resistless violence that it halted, wavered, and as volley followed volley, it bent, it broke, and the men fell back in confusion across the field. They were brave fellows that had fought nobly; they had done all that brave men could do but had been over powered by fresh troops.

But Mansfield was there, and his men came into line at the double quick, and with cheers that wakened the echoes for miles. Hooker's men formed quickly in our rear. We were in line of battle, and again the fire and smoke rolled up along our line. We poured volley after volley into the Rebel columns as they came sweeping up to within half musket range, firing and cheering as they came. Then, as they halted or seemed to waver for a moment, came the order to "fix bayonets." It was done, and in a moment the sharp ringing of steel died away—then *Charge!* rang out along the line, and down into the corn swept that long, dark line with lowered bayonets that flashed and gleamed angrily in the sun light. It must have been a sight stirring and grand to see, that line of men with their glittering arms, dark uniforms, and black plumes, as they rushed in to meet the enemy in deadly encounter—a hand to hand conflict. The Rebel line stood firm for a moment, but as we came, the clash of steel rang out sharply for an instant, and they broke and fled.

We followed them to the woods, where, as had been the case with Hooker's men, they were again reinforced, and after a sharp and desperate struggle, we were compelled to yield the field again. We fell back slowly, fighting as we went. In the meantime, Sumner's corps had arrived on the ground. French was there, and Richardson's—"Fighting Dick's"—division came dashing into the field.

I had, by this time, received my wound in the thigh and was compelled to leave the field. It is useless to dwell upon the details of the battle. Suffice it to say that Sumner gathered off the shattered remnants of Hooker's and Mansfield's corps, one of the commanders wounded and the other dead, and made a charge upon the enemy, driving them back across the field—now covered with the wounded, the dead, and the dying—and took possession of the woods beyond, from which our forces were not again driven. Burnside's, on the left, stormed and carried the heights of Sharpsburg after one of the fiercest contests of the war. The Rebels were driven back at every point, and as night, as if in mercy, came on to put an end to the fearful strife, we were left the undisputed masters of the field. The loss on both sides could not have been less than fifty thousand in killed and wounded.[5]

After being wounded, I limped away to one of the hospitals, but so great was the crowd of wounded already there that I thought I would hobble on as far as I could. I went on until I came to a stream of water, where I drank, and filling my pail (a small tin one which I had carried for nearly half a year), I went into the woods and washed and bandaged my wound. Then, fortunately, an ambulance came along, I got aboard and was taken to the church at Keedysville. It and all the other public buildings were converted into hospitals, as was also the case at Sharpsburg, Boonesboro, Middletown, and all the other towns between the battle field and Frederick City. I remained until Sunday the 21st, when I was taken to F. C., where I remained until November the 10th, when I arrived at this place, Philadelphia, Pennsylvania.

Only six of the company to which I belong escaped; all the rest, nineteen in number, were either killed or wounded. The regiment suffered badly. Out of about four hundred, only one hundred and eight could be mustered the next morning. We were in a very exposed position, and our ranks were swept by a perfect storm of shot, shell, and minié balls.

It was a most desperate struggle, one of the greatest on record, one that carries the mind back to the bloody fields of other times, when the great Napoleon led his grand armies over the plains of Italy and fought his great battles beneath the shadows of the pyramids, and at Austerlitz and Wagram, or when he swept along the stormy banks of the Inn. It

was indeed a great battle and also a great victory, one that will not be soon
forgotten.

The battle, too, was fought by an army that only a few days before was
flying in confusion, almost in terror, before the same enemy, which now,
reinforced and flushed with success, stood before it on the banks of the
Antietam. For days and weeks we had known nothing but defeat and disaster. Disasters on the Rapidan, disasters along the banks of the Rappahannock and on the plains of Manassas, disasters at Bull Run, at Thoroughfare
Gap, and at Fairfax—in fact, disasters every where. We had no confidence
in our leader, Pope, he had proved himself incompetent; McDowell we
dared not trust; and when we fell back to Alexandria, the army, if army it
might be called, was most thoroughly demoralized. But mark the change,
see how quickly, as if by magic, a confused and shapeless mass of demoralized men assumed the splendid and great proportions of a magnificent
army, one capable of coping with the gigantic and vaunting one under
General Lee, flushed with victory and confident of success as they were.
No wonder that the whole world was astonished at the result, for it beheld
only, as it supposed, a shattered and disheartened rabble going out to meet
a powerful, well organized, and boasting army, and looked only for a
renewed and more terrible defeat on the side of the Union army.

What was the cause of this wonderful change, what potent charm of
magic has been cast over the disheartened army of the Union? What is it
that has brought light out of darkness, order out of chaos, success out of
disaster and misfortune? See yonder chieftain as he proudly rides among
his men, who cheer him joyously, wildly on every side—that is not Pope
or McDowell, but it is the noble hero, the deeply loved commander, the
Glorious McClellan, restored again to the command of the Grand Army.
That is the answer, that is what inspires the heart anew, that is what gives
fresh courage to the disheartened and lifts the drooping head. It was that
which gave a disheartened and dispirited soldiery new confidence. It was
that that won for the cause of the Union the battles of South Mountain
and Antietam, and sent the boasting hordes under Lee, Jackson,
Longstreet, and Hill back beaten across the Potomac and saved the capital
and perhaps the Union.

But he has been again removed, and we await the result with painful
interest. We are confident that it was not for any fault of his but to satisfy
and hush the clamor of a certain class of men at the North. The reason is
doubtless what some pretend to be a political necessity. But whatever the

cause may be, I believe it was an act of injustice to one that we soldiers so much respect, and who has such substantial claims upon the gratitude of a people whose country he has doubtless saved from almost certain ruin.

Willard finishes Book Two with a compelling analysis of what it will take to win the war. There is little doubt that he wrote this plea for unity as a response to Copperhead sentiments in the North.

There seems to be a partisan strife at the North, a political element at work which is doing more to sustain and prolong this Rebellion than the armies of the South and may yet be the overthrow of our government. Could we have but a united people, an undivided Congress, an intelligent and thorough going Cabinet, and competent and trust worthy generals, the work of ending this horrible war would be speedy and effectual. But with a divided people and incompetent leaders we must ever fail—our cause is hopeless.

Whatever may be the result of this war, whether treason is to triumph and the cause of liberty is to be stricken and die, and the glorious Union with its thousands of manifold God given blessings is to be lost, or whether it is to be again restored with all its blessings unimpaired, remains with the people of the North to determine. They hold their destiny under their own control; the knife that is to sever the sacred bonds of union, if they are to be severed, is in their own hand, for by a hearty and united effort we must most assuredly succeed.

Shall the bonds of union be broken? Shall the American republic be no more? Shall "Liberty's Tree" wither and die, shall the struggle of our forefathers be all in vain, shall the lives they lost and the blood they spilled be wasted, shall their dearest hopes be blasted, shall our glorious Union be dissolved? Break this Union in twain, and like a stranded wreck, it will be dashed to fragments. Greece and Imperial Rome are our precedents. Once great and powerful empires, they ruled the world; but they were wrecked upon the same rock which lies before us. They have passed away and are known only in history. Greece and Rome are no more, and if we allow this Union to be dissolved, their fate will be our own.

Van Willard fought under this very flag, which was used by the 3rd Wisconsin in the early days of the war. COURTESY THE WISCONSIN VETERANS MUSEUM.

Capt. Stephan Lieurance of Co. G was also an acquaintance of Willard's. COURTESY THE STATE HISTORICAL SOCIETY OF WISCONSIN.

Col. William Hawley of the 3rd Wisconsin. COURTESY THE STATE HISTORICAL SOCIETY OF WISCONSIN.

Gen. Thomas Ruger, longtime commander of the 3rd Wisconsin. COURTESY THE STATE HISTORICAL SOCIETY OF WISCONSIN.

The 3rd Wisconsin at Antietam, as sketched by A. R. Waud. COURTESY THE LIBRARY OF CONGRESS.

The Chancellor house at Chancellorsville, May 1, 1863. This is the scene as Willard would have seen it, drawn by Edwin Forbes. COURTESY THE LIBRARY OF CONGRESS.

Reunion of the 3rd Wisconsin Volunteer Infantry Association, 1903. Courtesy Michael W. T. Howe.

The fourth man from the left is Dr. Lee Willard, Van Willard's son and only child. Lee Willard died childless in 1929, so Van Willard has no direct descendents.

BOOK THREE

A Book Without a Name
by Van R. Willard
Co. G,
3rd Regiment
Wisconsin Volunteers

Swiftly the current of life bears us on
And the bright days of youth hurry by,
And ere we're aware they're vanished and gone
And we approach the cold grave to lay down and die.

Almost 5,000 men died at Antietam, and 20,000 were wounded. Thousands of the wounds were serious enough to require treatment at a hospital as close to the battlefield as possible. For many, including Willard, that place was the military hospital at Frederick, fifteen miles from Antietam and the nearest major hospital to the field of conflict. The scene there must have been horrific, with unimaginable pain, suffering, and death all around. The severity of Willard's wound dictated a lengthy convalescence, one that he found almost intolerable. When, in November, he had a chance to be transferred to another hospital (where presumably there would be a much smaller percentage of desperate cases), he jumped at it. He starts with a clear description of his life in the ward at Frederick.

>─┼─◂▸─○─◂▸─┼─◂

I am a member of Co. G, 3rd Wisconsin Volunteer Regiment. I was wounded at the battle of Antietam and sent to the general hospital at Frederick City, Maryland. I remained there until the 9th of November, when I was sent on to this place (Philadelphia). I had been there nearly two months and had grown most heartily sick of life in those gloomy abodes.

Of all horrible and lonely places, I think a military hospital the worst—shut up in a narrow, sombre ward, with narrow beds and curtained windows, bare walls, and in fact, everything wearing a cheerless, gloomy aspect of a sick room. There the sufferer lies in his bed, unable, perhaps, to help himself, as hour after hour passes away and long and weary days and sleepless nights come and go, bringing with them no change—no amusement—nothing to cheer or enliven the long hours—nothing to break the dull monotony of hospital life.

It is horrible indeed to be there in those narrow wards, deprived almost of the light of day, with no companions save the sober attendants, the sick, the dying, and the dead. The knife and the saw do their work, and death, too, is not an infrequent visitor, and the dead house is never without an occupant. The groans, the screams, the death struggle, and the ravings of the delirious, are the sights and sounds and the events connected with all our army hospitals. The Ward, the Dead House, and the Grave.

The horrors of the battle field are indeed dark and appalling, but not darker are they or more appalling than are those of the hospital, where the life blood trickles slowly away, where strong men waste away day by day and droop and die. The inmate of the hospital soon grows weary of such a life and longs and sighs for more active scenes. Even the toilsome march, the hardships and exposures of camp life, or the dangers of the battle field are preferable to *such* a life. Anywhere, sighs the soldier, but a hospital.

I had been in the Frederick hospital nearly two months when one afternoon the surgeon came through the wards to ascertain who were able to be sent away to another hospital. My name among the rest was taken, for I was anxious to do something or go somewhere—any thing for a change. So I prepared for the journey. We were to go—where was the question. To Baltimore said some, others said Washington, while not a few predicted that Philadelphia was to be the destination. As for myself, I cared little where we were to go. Any where would suit me, any thing.

The night before our departure was a cold and stormy one. An old northwester was in progress. The wind blew, rushing down the old Catoctin Hills and sweeping up the valley, driving the snow before it in a manner plainly indicating the rude habits to which it had been given up in the frosty, windy, frozen regions of the North. Bright, sunny Maryland is not subject to such storms, especially at that season of the year, and with the first shrill blast from old Storm King's trumpet disappeared the tender Marylanders to seek a more genial atmosphere around their firesides. The night and the storm passed away and morning came; but still, great, heavy, dark masses of clouds hung around the sky looking cold. By and by the clouds grew thin, and here and there patches of blue sky could be seen, looking bluer and clearer by contrast with the dark clouds around. And the sun, too, glorious old Sol, who always smiles upon us whenever he can, glanced ever and anon down through the rifted clouds, scattering showers of golden light and warmth upon the snow covered earth, as if to remind us that when the clouds cleared away, he would bless us with ten or twelve hours of his royal presence.

That Sabbath morning was a pleasant one, notwithstanding the wintry aspect of every thing around. The bells were ringing for church when we got aboard the cars, and I listened to their solemn but musical notes, as they chimed out over the goodly city, with something of the feeling of one who is about to leave his native village and hears perhaps the chime of the village bell for the last time. We were soon in motion, and the chime of bells was lost in the sound of rolling wheels, and as we moved swiftly away, city, church, and lofty spires were all lost to view in the distance.

Just before we started, a wounded soldier, one of the heroes of South Mountain, was put aboard the car. He was very pale and emaciated looking, more dead than alive, and was unable to move or help himself. His father was with him; he had come from Baltimore to see his son and had at last got permission to take him home with him. "He will die if he remains here," said the surgeon. "He may live to reach home, better die there than here." Yes, he was being taken home to die. He could not live, the surgeon had pronounced his wound fatal and his case hopeless; they were taking him home to die.

"Thank you," said he as I wrapped my blanket around him to make him more comfortable, "I will not forget your kindness when I am dead." "I hope not," said I, "but I trust you are not going to die very soon." He shook his head and, as a sad smile played for a moment over his pale, ghastly features, remarked in a low tone, "You would cheer me up, stranger, and make me believe that I am not to die, but I assure you that I am, and I am ready and willing to go; only I wish to die at home among my friends and be buried in the grave yard by the side of my mother." What a sweet wish, what a holy resignation. Willing to die, only that he might be buried by the side of his mother! What a noble youth, what a brave, true heart he must have had. But I will leave them there—the gray-haired old man, his father, holding the head of his dying boy, who only wishes to be buried by the side of his mother.

In the hospital, now and then the death of a soldier is announced, or perhaps only spoken of by those in his ward. And, in fact, so little attention is paid to the death of a soldier that sometimes the occurrence is not known at all. Generally, the soldiers show their respect for their dead brother in arms by forming an escort and following him to the grave while a death march is played on the drum and fife, and the whole procession, escort, soldiers, and others who follow in the train, march slowly and sadly to the grave, stepping to the tune of the march. Arriving at the grave, the usual ceremony is performed, or if no clergyman is present, a short prayer is offered up for the dead or perhaps a few words are said by some one chosen for the purpose, and then a salute is fired over the grave, when all return, marching to the time of some lively tune. Thus the soldier dies here, alone among strangers, is buried and then forgotten. Forgotten? Ah, no, not forgotten. Although he dies in a hospital far from home, among strangers in a strange land, his grave a lonely one with no costly monument to mark his resting place, and few, perhaps none, go there to plant flowers or water them with tears, yet he is not forgotten. No, his loss is mourned by those who cannot forget. In some cottage upon the sunny slopes and hill sides of New England, or amid the forests or prairies of the

West, fond parents, those near and dear, remember him and shed tears, bitter tears, to his memory.

Yes, to die thus in a hospital in a distant city, to be buried alone where no kindred foot comes to press the sod around the grave, is indeed hard. But when we go to the battle field where death, the Grim Reaper, has gathered his sheaves on the "crimson plain," and see the manner in which the dead are buried there, the heart will grow sick and we turn sadly away, wondering why there is such a thing as war, where men are slaughtered by thousands and the image of God defaced and marred.

It was late when we arrived in the city of Baltimore. I had no opportunity of viewing the city as I would like to have done. We were detained at every station along the road, and it was nine o'clock when we arrived in the city. We were invited out of the cars to partake of refreshments at the eating saloon. This we were very willing to do, as we were weary, cold, and hungry. The supper was a good one, and I am inclined to think that we did ample justice to it at least. Many, *very* many were the cups of coffee and slices of bread and butter and pieces of meat that disappeared from those tables that night. Supper over, we again got aboard the cars and, bidding the good city and the better people "good by," were soon on our way to the City of Brotherly Love.

The ride from Baltimore was more rapid, though we were so often detained that we did not arrive in Philadelphia until early morning. In fact, the sky had already begun to glow with the crimson light of the rising sun, and the morning star was high up above the hills, when we disembarked from the cars in this, the Quaker city of the old Keystone State. We were brought over to the Citizens' Volunteer Hospital,[1] where we partook of an excellent breakfast, such a one as the good folks of Philadelphia know how to prepare and hungry soldiers know so well how to do justice to. The Volunteer Hospital is a fine affair and is conducted in a manner that does indeed speak well for the kind hearted and patriotic citizens of this glorious loyal city.

About noon, having had a good long rest, we were taken in ambulances, whirled away to different parts of the city, and distributed among the various hospitals. I, with a large number of others, was brought to this place—the Summit House—where I now am.

The Summit House derives its name from the building in which it was first begun, which was formerly a public house, and is situated on the Philadelphia and Darby Road, about four miles from the city and one from Darby.[2] The little village of Kingsessing is just to the west of us and is an old, ancient burg resembling not a little some of the time worn and time scarred "burgs" to be met with in the "Old Dominion" and not infrequently in Maryland. The people in this vicinity, however, are of the very best kind, being mostly of the William Penn or "good old Quaker" stock.

But I have wandered from the Summit House, which has become as familiar, if not as dear, as the "old house at home" to me. It is a square, old fashioned structure located upon a small rise of ground and commands a fine view of the country around. It is nearly surrounded by a fine farming country, interspersed with fields and woods and meadows, and dotted with many white, pretty, little cottages and farm houses with their groups or clusters of out buildings, resembling in every way the farms and houses in Virginia or Maryland.

Virginia—resemble the farms in Virginia! That is a mistake—they *once did*, but not now. War in Virginia has done its fearful work. Buildings are marred or perhaps completely demolished, fences for miles are burned down, and fields of grain are trodden. Old land marks are obliterated, and the whole face of the country has been changed. War has left its withering, blighting touch upon every thing. Even the people have been changed. One seldom meets nowadays on the "Sacred Soil" one of the real FFVs, the social, genial companion, the warm friend, or the proud but courteous gentlemen of former days. No, poor old Virginia, the "Mother of Presidents," marred and disfigured by the cruel ravages of war, does not *now* resemble grand old Pennsylvania with her peaceful homes, old but *quiet* villages, her rich fields, well filled granaries and her happy, contented people.

From the front of the Summit House one has a fine view, a scene embracing both land and water, the former dotted with white, peaceful appearing habitations in which dwell some of the warmest Quaker hearts in existence. Beyond these fields is the Delaware River, covered with crafts of every kind and model, from the great white steamers that go plowing through the waves down to the little white winged schooners that glide up and down, dotting the river for miles.

Way over across the bay yonder is the great city of Philadelphia, looming so grandly up over the water, its glittering domes, lofty steeples, and huge piles of brick and mortar reflected in its placid bosom.

A few days ago was Thanksgiving Day, and we celebrated it in a right royal manner. The ladies in this vicinity (God bless their noble hearts) proposed to give the soldiers in this hospital a Thanksgiving dinner and have a celebration in the afternoon, with music by a band, which was to be in attendance, and music too by the children—by the children, only that would be a little new, something like old times really. But that was not all the ladies were going to do on the occasion; they were going to present a large and splendid banner to the hospital. We were a little incredulous in regard to the matter, but it turned out that all our incredulity was unfounded.

Well, Thanksgiving Day came, bright and glorious as a summer's day. The air was warm and the sky clear, blue, and serene. The very loveliness of the day was enough to fill every heart with gratitude to *Him* who "doeth all things well" and make it a day of thanksgiving and praise. No snow had yet fallen, the fields (many of them) were still green, and the grand old oaks still flushed in the glory of a wealth of crimson leaves. The forenoon passed with the continual arrival of ladies coming in carriages and cars, and gentlemen, too, bringing baskets, bundles, etc., containing something for the table. But the ladies always brought with them something besides eatables, something more cheering even, a smiling face. The smiling face of woman! What can be more cheering, what more potent charm can there be to dispel the gloom that gathers around the heart than a cheerful smiling face.

The dinner drum was at last beaten and we went into dinner, and *such a dinner*—turkeys, chickens, cakes, pies, and a thousand other articles too numerous to mention. After dinner, we assembled in the front yard to listen to some remarks by some gentlemen who were to address us, among which was the Honorable Mr. Kelley of this city. While the crowd was coming together, the band played several fine pieces, and everything presented quite a lively appearance. When all had gathered around the stand or platform on which the surgeons and speakers sat, the children, some fifty in number, began to sing, and their little voices joined in harmony, making music sweet as that "that breathes where angel spirits are." It reminded one of those dear days, when a child, he sat in the Sunday School and sang with the rest those little songs he never can forget, songs he learned ere cares and sorrows had weighed down his spirits or shaded his brow with sadness.

Oh the bright, the golden days of childhood—the balmy days of youth. How quick they hurry by, bearing us on to the unknown future, and almost before we are aware, youth is gone and we are growing old. The laughs and songs of childhood die away or are drowned amid the hum and bustle of busy life. See yonder laughing child as he dances in the sun light or prattles to the birds and flowers. How glorious, how beautiful!

A few years hurry on in their swift course, and the child becomes a man—
a youth. Again time waves his magic wand and youth departs, the hair
grows gray and the bright eye dims, the heart is burdened with care. The
rippling laugh of childhood hardly dies away before it is changed to the
sterner tones of early manhood; and these hardly are altered ere they die
away in the feeble accents of old age. The cradle and childhood's joys—
manhood, its temptations and disappointments; old age and the grave,
death and its unknown land—all follow one another so quickly that one
condition is hardly begun ere it is over and the other begins.

But I have wandered far from the Thanksgiving scene of which I was
speaking a while ago. After the youthful band had sung a few pretty and
very appropriate songs, the speaking began. A prayer was first offered up to
Him who said, "let there be light," then a few eloquent but brief remarks
were made by the man chosen by the ladies to present the banner to the
surgeon, which was done in a very graceful manner. But this whole affair
can be of but little interest to anyone, and so with many thanks to the
noble ladies of Kingsessing, I will dismiss the subject.

The Starry Flag of Liberty

> Dear, dear Columbia we'll stand by thee yet
> Though dark is the prospect before thee today,
> Thy glory, thy grandeur we cannot forget
> And the stars of thy greatness can never decay.

> Columbia, Columbia, great land of the West
> Where the day star of freedom shines ever on high,
> Home of the weary, down-trodden, oppressed
> We'll not forsake thee when dangers are nigh.

> Bright is thy banner,
> Flag of the free,
> Glorious emblem of sweet liberty,
> Starry banner of the free.

> Hail to Columbia, land of the brave
> Temple of freedom, shrine of the free,
> Onward, ever onward thy banners wave
> Onward, right onward to bright victory.

Kings cannot govern us, or traitors dissever
The bright bond of Union, brotherhood's tie,
One *Banner*, one *People*, one *Country* forever
For these will we *perish*, for these we will *die*.

Bright is thy banner,
Flag of the free,
Glorious emblem of sweet liberty,
Starry banner of the free.

Willard took a sight-seeing trip into Philadelphia with a friend from the Irish Brigade. They visited Independence Hall, and from Willard's description, it appears that the shrine looked very different then. Today the building in which the Declaration of Independence was signed has been restored to its original appearance to the fullest extent possible. Willard and his friend saw the place filled with memorabilia, including the Liberty Bell, and lined with portraits of the founding fathers and other heroes. These included the first Union officer to be killed in the Civil War, Elmer E. Ellsworth.

The City of Philadelphia, Pennsylvania, November 25th. One bright, warm day not long since, I obtained a "pass" and paid a visit to the city in company with my friend Baker, a jolly son of the Emerald Isle, a fine fellow, and a good soldier. John (i.e., Baker) had seen not a little service, having fought in nearly all the battles on the Peninsula and at Antietam, where he was wounded. He belonged to the Irish Brigade, and that is enough to convince anyone that he knew what it was to hear bullets whistle and [that he] could interpret the scream of a shell. Well, John and I got a pass, and hailing one of the passenger rail way cars, we jumped aboard and [were] soon on our way to the city. The rate of speed was not quite as rapid as that of the "iron horse," but though the distance is nearly four miles, we were but little over half an hour in making the journey.

At the foot of Market Street we got out and soon found ourselves in the midst of the city. The streets were thronged, as are the streets of all cities, and it was with no little difficulty that we "cripples" made [our] way through the crowds that continually pressed around us. One who is unaccustomed to city scenes and city life would wonder, were he to stand on some corner and watch the endless, ever shifting throng, as they hurry on in one continuous train, where all the people could be going to.

But the only object of interest to me (for I hate a crowd and crowded streets) was the old "Independence Hall," where the Declaration of Independence was signed. The hall is only a small, square room, not exceeding in size more than thirty by forty feet. The whole building, in fact, is one of not very ample dimensions. There around the venerable hall hang the portraits of the "signers," with that of many other noble men of those troublesome days. Of course, the first face we seek is that of immortal Washington. There he hangs among the many faces, more serenely majestic, more God like, the noblest of the noble. Among the many pictures that cover the wall is that of the brave and gallant Colonel Ellsworth, one of the first, even in the pride of his youth and the glory of his manhood, to offer up his life in defense of those principles which they whose pictured faces surround him fought and struggled to establish. There are many objects of curiosity grouped in that old hall. Among the rest is the old bell which was first rung in the city when the declaration was signed. There is also a piece of the pew which Washington used to sit in when he attended Christ's Church here. It is a simple, fine bench with a back to it and was once perhaps adorned with a coat of paint. It is kept not only as a relic but a curiosity. But why should it be considered a curiosity? It is not a curious fact that Washington sat in a plain pew and attended a humble church, even though he was the greatest or at least *one* of the greatest men the world ever knew.

Having viewed all the curiosities in this venerable structure, we passed out through the park to Market Street and again mingled in the throng of passers by, and with no small amount of dodging and twisting, elbowing and pushing, we made our way to the Darby Road, got aboard one of the cars, and were soon on our way back to the Summit House, where we arrived just in time not to lose our bread and tea.

Summit House, December 14th. The morning has been one of sweet and quiet beauty, with no rude sounds to mar the holy calm, and the sun shines down through the thin, white clouds with a subdued golden lustre, while the rude winds of winter seem to sleep. Today is the blessed Sabbath, and the bell on the little village church yonder has been ringing out its solemn but musical notes this morning, bidding the villagers to come to the house of prayer. The hour for worship has arrived, and I can see from my window the happy throng, as one after another steps out from their quiet homes to wind their way to church.

The young, the old, the rich and the poor, the well clothed and those whose garments are worn and tattered, the silvery haired old man clasping his cane with trembling hands and the bright, light hearted little child whose feet patter up on the pavement like rain drops, all winding their way up to the house of God. The church on yonder hill, the ringing of the Sabbath bell, and this bright, golden Sabbath morn bring back to mind the memory of other times and other scenes, and I seem to hear again the chiming of the church bell in my native village, far away in the distant land of the West. In imagination, I mingle again in the happy throng and hear the laughs, the voices, and the songs of bygone days ringing in my ears with a sweet yet mournful melody. Ah memory, how faithfully thou bringest back to me those scenes.

Sunday afternoon. This afternoon, the usual quiet which prevails here has been broken by the arrival of a large crowd of sick and wounded soldiers, mostly from the hospitals of Washington, Alexandria, and Georgetown. The number which has arrived today is said to be about three hundred, for whom ample preparations have been made. Many of the poor fellows look wan and pale, having been confined so long in the hospital, for it does indeed take the color from the cheek and the light from the eye to be thus confined in a sick room for so many weary days. It is a sad sight to see so many men crippled and broken down with disease. Look at those poor fellows as they go swinging along on their crutches, or those with an empty coat sleeve hanging at their side—they have lost a limb—better perhaps to have lost their lives.

But there are many other invalids here besides those who have been wounded in battle—men once strong and active who have lost their health by exposure. See yonder pale, haggard looking man with the dark eye and white, sad face; watch him as he moves slowly about; listen to that low, dry cough; and see how red the hectic spot on his white cheek glows sometimes. That man has got the consumption, and relentless death has written on his cheek and brow in characters too plain to be mistaken— "This is my victim." The open grave lies before him almost at his feet, and he looks down into its damp, narrow depths, so silent and cheerless and cold!

But over there is another one, a victim to *one* at *least* of the ills that flesh is heir to. See those blue, pinched up features, those misshapen limbs, that stiff ungainly walk, that face all awry with rheumatic pains. Of course, he has the rheumatism brought on by exposure.

But I have seen, not infrequently, patients suffering with a disease which I have never seen in the calendar. For instance, there is that silly looking chap who staggers about as though his legs were continually refusing to obey his body, or at least refusing to sustain its weight. What is the matter with him? Why, I should say he was troubled with "weak-leggedness," or in other words he is slightly under the influence of intoxicating drinks, or perhaps he is inebriated, or to speak plainly, the fellow is drunk. Such fellows usually find lodgings in the "black hole."

On December 13 Union troops commanded by Ambrose Burnside crossed the Potomac River and attacked heavily entrenched Confederate positions around Fredericksburg. The 3rd Wisconsin did not take part. The entire country—including the soldiers at the Summit House—waited anxiously for news from the front, but as it arrived piecemeal it became clear that the Army of the Potomac had suffered a disaster. Willard, like all Northerners, was deeply affected by this tragedy. President Lincoln feared that the Union was "now on the brink of destruction," and Sen. William P. Fessenden of Maine summed up the feeling of the nation when he said, "I am heartsick."

A thousand rumors have been in circulation here today. It is said that Dame Rumor has a thousand tongues, and I am inclined to believe that she has. "They say" is one of the very greatest busy-bodies in existence. "They say" says a great many things and tells us many a tale. "They say" is one of the first minions (if not the very first) of Dame Rumor and is an indispensable personage to the success of "granny gossip." Well, rumor has had a great many agents at work today, busy circulating all manner of reports in regard to events on the Rappahannock.

It is said that our glorious army has met with a serious repulse, that in attempting to drive the Rebels from behind their breast works that we were driven back in confusion to the river, that a second attempt proved alike unsuccessful and that many of our field and general officers have been killed or wounded. One of Dame Rumor's tongues says that brave old General Sumner was among the killed, while another of the thousand tongues says it was not so. But however it may be, I will venture to say at least that there has been as many as one gun fired today and that a few have been hurt.

The silence and torpid inactivity which has so long pervaded our ranks, and the "all quiet," at last have been broken, and the roar of 170 cannon betokens the fact that the work of death has actually begun. Ten thousand shells were thrown into the city of Fredericksburg in one day, and the old and almost venerable city, around which clings so many hallowed associations that link the present with the past, has been almost reduced to ashes. Charred and blackened masses of smoldering ruins alone mark the site of once proud old mansions and happy, peaceful homes.

Fredericksburg, with its beautiful surroundings, is known to us and to every true American heart as the early home of our own great Washington. There, in the now ruined city and its vicinity, George, who it is said never uttered a falsehood and is reported to have said, "Father, I cannot lie, it was I who cut it with my hatchet," spent many of his boyhood days. Here, too, is the Washington farm and, more than all, the grave of Washington's mother. The name Fredericksburg awakens within the heart historic memories and reminiscences of the days in which the good Washington, the Lees, and the Fitzhughs lived and labored for their country—the same country which now their traitorous sons would ruin and destroy.

This Virginia, once so proud, so loyal and true, and so prosperous and happy withal, the native state of the father of his country—the state that Washington loved and was so proud to call his own, the home of the Randolphs and the immortal Jefferson—the state which bears the title of Mother of Presidents, is now made the battle field on which is being fought the battles of the Union and of human liberty and human rights. And this same Virginia, vile with treason and red with patriot blood, stands first and foremost in the Rebel ranks, clutching the assassin's knife with which to stab at the heart of the country Washington loved, struggling fiercely for the country's overthrow.

Could Washington return today and look over the barren fields, desolate homes and towns sacked and cities burned in his loved Virginia, and know that her people were disloyal and untrue and had brought all this ruin upon themselves by their treason—ah, how his great, noble heart would fill with sadness. Yes, the venerable old city has been well nigh laid in ashes, and the hallowed grave of Washington's mother shakes with the jar of Union cannon. We wait the result—the terrible issue—with breathless anxiety, and can only pray God give us the victory.

Although it is true that Old Winter has really begun his reign, yet as I look out there on the bare ground and over to the still-green fields yonder by the river, I can see but little that would indicate that such is really the case. Everything resembles the appearance of spring more than autumn or winter—the sky is ever changing, the mists hanging like a canopy above the moist earth, wrapping fields, wood, river, and hills in its foggy folds. The weather, too, is very warm and mild, the atmosphere is soft and humid, such as April brings. This must be a very remarkable season, or else winters here in the old Keystone State are much different, that is as far

as the weather is concerned, from those we used to have up in the Badger
State. Winter there, I will venture to say, is reigning in all the severity of
storms, snow, and ice. I should like to spend a few days up there in that
cold, healthy region, where storms come with a fury that makes them
really sublime. I always did enjoy a real north west snow storm. The
weather here is by no means disagreeable, the mild sunshine is not
unpleasant, yet I miss the cold, clear, bright, frosty mornings. I had rather
spend a winter in those cold, frosty latitudes, where winter comes with a
power that makes itself felt, than in those climates where it is neither winter nor summer, where it is cold one day and warm the next.

I miss also the merry chime of sleigh bells and the quick tramp of hoofs
on the hard beaten road. Ah! I hear it now—the soul stirring music of hoof
and bells and the merry, ringing laugh of gay, frolicking youths. What could
there be more charming to a soldier, especially one who has been shut up
for months in a gloomy hospital, than to spend some of those clear, bright,
frosty evenings in taking a sleigh ride. I always enjoyed a sleigh ride by
moon light. There is indeed a charm in a bright, cold, moonlit winter
evening, a fast horse, a sleigh and bells, and a companion to keep one warm
and scold him should he be so careless as to run over a log or stump, and
upset the sleigh and precipitate himself and the fair one into the snow. Yes,
give me the winter in the North West, where one can have sleighing to his
heart's content. I wish for no better or sweeter music than that when hoofs
keep time with music chime, and all is fair and bright.

Monday, December 15th. The news from the Army of the
Potomac is but little different from that we received yesterday. The army
has crossed the river and has gained a footing on the other side. And
though we have only come within range of the enemy's guns, we have
gained a great advantage. Still, the enemy is massed in great force behind
their works, and it will, or perhaps *has*, cost many a precious life to dislodge them. We read of two attempts to drive the Rebels from their
works, which were unsuccessful.

But there is one instance of which we read that awakens within the
most indifferent heart the most unbounded admiration. An attempt was
made on the morning of the 11th to lay the pontoon bridges, one below
and the other directly in front of the city. No sooner had the work been
begun on the latter bridge than the Rebel sharp shooters began to pick off
the workmen, who were compelled to abandon the work. The bombard-
ment now began, but though a half thousand of shell and round shot were

sent every three moments into the city, and the river banks were swept by a perfect storm of grape and canister, yet the sharp shooters could not be driven from their hiding places and continued to pop away whenever they could see a man to shoot at. Volunteers were then called for to go over the river in pontoon boats and drive the obdurate rascals from the town. No sooner had the call been made than hundreds of noble fellows stepped out saying they were willing to go, and they went, and right nobly did they accomplish their glorious but dangerous mission. The Rebels were routed, many of them killed and a large number captured. These gallant fellows were from the 7th Michigan. Brave sons of the West, right nobly have you maintained your reputation. No better or braver act could have been performed. All glory to the 7th Michigan.

While Willard waited for news, he pondered about life, death, and what really happens afterward.

Change, it is said, is one of the laws of nature. Every thing is undergoing a continual change, so the wise ones say. This is undoubtedly the case, at least it is so with the weather, for within the last ten hours quite a change has taken place. The golden sun and the serene sky of yesterday has been superseded by clouds and storms today. Yesterday nature smiled with more than usual serenity, and the sun shone with unwonted lustre. Today the sky is overcast with clouds laden with rain and snow. Well, such is life, clouds today, a serene sky tomorrow. Sunshine and storms, light and darkness. As night follows day, so sorrows follow in the train of all our joys. Despair is lightened by hope, yet hope is often lost in despair, as the sky is obscured by clouds. Hope comes to the despairing heart, struggling through the gloom to lighten and cheer, like sunshine breaking through the rifted clouds on a cloudy day. The longest night will have its end, and the darkest clouds will pass away; the deepest sorrow will subside, and the saddest heart will have its cheerful moments. The most sorrowing are not always sad.

As the years are made up of bright and stormy days—as the day is composed of light and darkness—so is life composed of joys and sorrows, of hopes and disappointments. But beyond all, like the lustrous sun and the serene sky above the clouds and darkness, there is a land, where it is said, there are no clouds or storms and where sorrows do not find an entrance and pain and death are strangers. Up there in that land, hopes do not wither and die, and hearts do not languish. So we are taught to believe.

Yet who can say that there is not sorrow in Heaven, that tears are not shed by angels, and that there are no regrets, no disappointments beyond the grave? Is it true that there are but two conditions, a Heaven or a Hell—the one a land of perfect bliss—the other of endless woe? After death, shall we never know regret or feel the pang of sorrow? Shall we never think of the bright, dear hopes that have vanished, or shall we be forever condemned to hopeless despair? Shall we forget all our dear old associations, shall memory die? Will we never think of the past—the days of the long ago? Can the past be all forgotten?

The past with all its varied joys and sorrows, its hopes, its bitter disappointments and its vain regrets, its clouds, its sunshine and shades, its childhood's scenes and youthful joys, mingled though they be with regrets and sighs, still is dear. There are, it is true, many things that pass from the mind forever, that do not return at memory's call. But they were events that did not make an impression on the heart or ones so slight as soon to be obliterated. There are events we can *never* forget—there are faces the memory of which will live enshrined in the heart forever. No, we cannot forget the history of the past, and we would not if we could; for it forms a part of our existence. It may indeed cause us sorrow to look back over the past after the lapse of years, for the interval is filled with the graves of many old and dear friends. It may awaken within the heart some sad memories, memories that long have slumbered. How often these old bygone scenes come back to life again and fill the heart. The dear old associations and companionships of other days—associates we never more may meet—again we hear their voices and songs and ramble amid old familiar haunts. Where are those associates now, do they ever think of me now? Such are the thoughts of every one as he wanders on through the mazy labyrinth of this life. Yes, as we look back over the past, there are many memories that awaken, that fill the heart with sadness, regrets, and remorse and bring the tears unbidden to the eye. But there are other recollections that afford us real pleasure.

Does the soul live after death? Is there an existence beyond the grave? If a man die, shall he live again? If so, then, too, will *memory* live, and while it still exists, we cannot forget the past. Who will say that this is not the case, for otherwise there would be no existence after death, or at least no individuality. Then, if the soul lives, the memory cannot die; hence there can be no perpetual Heaven or endless Hell.

Evening the 16th. This morning the weather had changed from fair to foul, and the serene sky and golden sunshine had been superseded by a storm, the first intimation of which was a sudden dash of rain on the roof. A few scattering drops at first, and then it came down with a dash and a roar, a perfect volley of rain drops. It did not rain long, however, but settled down into a fine, steady, drizzling storm and continued until about noon, when the cloudy canopy became light and thin, and in a short time spots of clear, blue sky could be seen through the rifted clouds, through which the sun light came in flashes of gold. Long before night these patches of blue had grown to great fields, and before sunset the clouds were all chased away, leaving the sky bluer and brighter by contrast. This evening the stars are twinkling clear and lustrously, but there is no moon and it is quite dark. The wind is high and howls around the old Summit House, moaning and sighing so mournfully that one might almost imagine that fiends had come to howl a death dirge tonight.

The news from Fredericksburg is but meager. The paper tells us that a crossing has been effected and that the city—what there is left of it—is in our possession, that our pickets are fully a mile from the town, and that two desperate attempts were made by Sumner to drive the enemy from their works but were unsuccessful; but that Franklin had driven the enemy for over a mile. Our troops, it is said, have fought well and have behaved nobly. The fire of the enemy is described as most terrific, being concentrated upon our columns as they pushed up the hill on their way to storm the works. Death must have reaped a terrible harvest, as it is said the dead lay in heaps and windrows all up and down the hill side. Before this, doubtless, the great battle has been fought and perhaps the fate of the Rebellion is sealed, the conscript legions driven from their hiding places. Or it may be that the cause of the Union has received another check and our army defeated. God forbid that it should be so.

The wind continues to blow and the night has become a dark and tedious one, but I will hope for a fair morning, a clear sun, and good news from the front.

Wednesday morning, 17th. The storm of yesterday has passed away, leaving hardly a trace to show that such an event had occurred. Not a single cloud of all that vast troop that swept scowlingly across the sky remains to mar the beauty of the broad, blue field that bends so serenely over head today. The face of the sky looks clearer and bluer this morning than ever, as though it has been washed by the storm and painted over anew.

There is something indeed charming in a clear sky and golden sunshine after a storm. It teaches that though the sky may be dark above us, the horizon may be overshadowed by clouds, and all may seem cheerless, all these sombre clouds will pass away, and the sky will be clear again. Life is dark enough, but it is not half so dark as some would seem to believe. It is only those who are continually looking downward that do not see the sun light.

Just before sunrise a heavy mist hung over the river like a curtain, but when the sun rose the mist rolled away, slowly dissolving in the sun light, rising up in wreaths and little clouds of white, bespangled with dots of red and blue and gold as the sun shone through it, reflecting all the colors of the rainbow. In a few moments, the river, sparkling in all its usual beauty, was revealed, dotted with many white winged little vessels that were gliding up and down as if by enchantment. Thus, as the sun light dissolves the mist and lifts it from over the river and valley, so does hope light up the human heart and dissipates the gloomy clouds that overshadow it.

While I am thus musing over and admiring the beauties of nature that smile around me this morning, thousands of brave fellows are struggling, or perhaps dying, on the field of battle, and the same sun and the same cloudless sky that bends so serenely over us is darkened by the smoke of battle.

The last intelligence from the scene of action upon which all eyes are fixed as if by mesmeric power left our army still the masters of the city, but having failed in driving the enemy from their works, and resting on their arms waiting to begin the strife anew. The most desperate fighting occurred on Saturday, when French and Howard stormed the enemy's works and, after repeated efforts and most reckless daring and courage, were compelled to retire. What a picture was here presented as those brave fellows rushed over the plain, up the hill towards the Rebel strong hold. Below them is the deep and rapid river over which they have just crossed, and upon its banks the dark and smoking ruins of the city, standing out in striking contrast to the light, sparkling waters below.

Before and about them was the enemy's works—their rifle pits, redoubts, and breast works bristling with cannons, while their infantry lay in thousands behind stone walls running along at the foot of the hills and upon its sides. The long, solid column rushed on in line of battle with fixed bayonets and bright arms flashing in the sun, banners flying, and cheers echoing far and near. Not a gun was fired by the enemy until the storming party had advanced to within rifle range of their works. Then, with a crash and a roar that shook the very hills, the Rebel batteries opened, and a perfect tornado of iron hail swept through their ranks and hundreds of men went down, never to rise again. Still they rushed on, and again and again those murderous guns belched upon them showers of shot and shell;

but not until they had encountered and received the concentrated fire of thousands of rifles and scores of heavy batteries did they waver, and when the order was given to fall back, it was done in splendid order.

Another column moves quickly to their support—the line is formed, and with a cheer, they rush upon the enemy's works again. Again the hill tops are wreathed with flame and smoke and the walls are fringed with fire, while the solid earth rocks beneath the concussion of the Rebel guns. Great gaps are cut through the advancing line, legs and arms and mangled forms are thrown into the air, and the fields and slopes are heaped with the dead. The fire is said to have been most terrible, and that the storming party suffered a loss in killed and wounded unparalleled in any other battle of the war, or at least by any engagement of the same duration. More than a hundred cannon, it is said, were thundering from the Rebel works at one time, with a prolonged echoing sound that went reverberating far away among the distant hills. The line pushed bravely on, but the concentrated fire of infantry and artillery and the storm of grape and canister that swept their ranks with a perfect death harvest was so terrific that the centre was thrown into confusion, and after a long, desperate, and bloody struggle, they were forced back.

Night, in the meantime, came on, and darkness threw her mantle over the bloody scene. The night was a clear one, and the stars burned brightly in the wintry sky. Our men slept on their arms on the battle field. A correspondent of the *Philadelphia Inquirer*[3] writes as follows: "The whole day (Saturday) has been marked by the most brilliant fighting; but the grandest battle scene was after dark, as the clear star light rendered the battle lines more distinct than the smoky light of day; for the lines were fringed with fire, while the deeper and more prolonged flashes and lurid lights of the many heavier guns painted a most vivid scene on the dark blue sky."

Franklin seems to have met with better success and to have driven the Rebels some distance, but not without a terrible loss. The impression seems to prevail that the Rebel force does not amount to more than eighty thousand and that Burnside has men enough and ample means to drive them from their works, and that victory is almost sure. This may be so; I hope it is, yet I hope that our generals will not be deceived. Today's paper will, I think, settle the question. Yesterday's paper gave no new or additional news. The press is silent, or nearly so, and what is said is so meager, so unsatisfactory and restrained, that one is led to believe that they were almost afraid to tell the whole truth and give the real facts as they are. This silence is quite oppressive, it does not augur well; for three days we have had but little news. If we have met with a disaster, if it is ascertained that the Rebel works cannot be carried by storm without a too great loss of life, why not say so at once and, if it is necessary, return to this side of the Rappahannock.

Evening, 17th. Since morning a great change has occurred in the weather, and the sky, which was then as clear and blue as any summer sky, is now darkened by clouds. A little snow has already fallen, and there are indications of a considerable storm. One would not have supposed that the serene sky of this morning could have been covered by such dark, scowling clouds so soon, yet we know that a clear sky is not always a surety of fair weather, but that the highest sky is often covered with clouds within an hour.

We see every day human life mirrored in the works of nature. Yonder fields and leafless wood, once so green, so beautiful; but how changed, how cheerless, how barren they look this wintry evening, when we remember how beautiful and green they were only a short time ago! The bright hopes and joys wither like those leaves that are blown about by the winds of winter and at last are buried beneath its snows. And those sweet, little flowers, too, that grew down there in the glen by the murmuring little brook, in the meadows, and on the hill side, they, too, have withered in the chilling blasts.

> Summer went and Winter came
> With his destroying breath,
> And the flowers withered one by one
> And slept the sleep of death.

Yes, we see life in the death and existence of the flowers and the leaves, and we see it mirrored in the sky. Leaves fall and decay, and the fairest flowers wither and die. But do the flowers pass forever from existence—will they never live again—is there nothing left of them? Yes, when the winter passes and the snow disappears from the hill sides, and the sun and the gentle breath of spring comes to warm them back to life, they will spring up anew, as fair and lovely as before.

This morning's paper puts a very different face on affairs at Fredericksburg. Yesterday the army was on the other side of the Rappahannock, today they are back again, having evacuated the town. This is rather sudden and proves that the attempt to drive the enemy from their works on Saturday was not only a failure but a disaster of no small account. We have lost heavily and have gained nothing in any way, except it be the knowledge of the enemy's strength and our own weakness.

The Rebels must have been not a little surprised when they awoke the next morning and found that the Yankees had gone. The evacuation, it is said, was conducted "skillfully," with the loss of not a single gun and very few men.

What is to be done next is beyond conjecture. An advance on Richmond by another route may be the next movement, or perhaps the army will now go into winter quarters or may pick their flints[4] and try again.

Willard, who exhibits a good understanding of military science and history, here discusses the historic difficulties of crossing bodies of water and taking bridges. There is no evidence that he ever went to a military academy, and he did not enter college until after the war. He must have been a prodigious reader.

Such things have been done. In the year 1809, Napoleon crossed the Danube at the island of Lobau. It was a daring action but resulted in the repulse and defeat of the French army at Assem, which compelled Napoleon, as great and invincible a warrior as he, to retreat and recross the river. He was by no means discouraged but recruited his army, built new bridges, and was soon ready for another crossing. He did not know what it was to be discouraged. His motto was "try again" and his watchword "perseverance." After his defeat at Assem, he applied himself to the tasks with redoubled energy and renewed determination, and the result was that when he crossed the Danube the second time, he was successful and won the battle of Wagram. May we not hope that, should our Burnside undertake a second crossing, he may, like the great French warrior, meet with success and future history bear the record of another Wagram.

In the history of every war, we read of famous passages in the very face of the enemy. At the Granicus, Alexander was met by a large army of the Persians who attempted to prevent him from crossing; but Alexander, though opposed by an army much superior to his own in point of numbers, was not to be frightened. At the head of a small, select army of Greeks and Macedonians, he plunged into the stream and completely routed the enemy. But in those days the use of artillery was unknown, and heavy batteries were not planted so as to sweep the crossings with a perfect storm of iron hail. In these modern times, war has been reduced to a real science, and a river is a most formidable barrier, especially when its banks are bristling with cannon. A crossing is attended with no common danger and is a task requiring skill and courage. And when the crossing has been effected, there is not only danger of defeat but of almost ruinous disaster, for unless the bridges were strong and ample, the loss of life would be terrible and the effect on the troops would be to dishearten and demoralize.

In 1812 the French army, after being repulsed, attempted to retreat across the Berezina over inadequate bridges. The result was fearfully fatal, and did more to discourage and demoralize the French army than any other event that had occurred. It seemed to be the finishing stroke to a perfect hail storm of disasters. Small streams often play no small part in grand tactics. When the Allied army moved upon Sebastopol, the Russians chose their positions on the banks of the Alma, where they fought in September 1854. The tributaries of the Danube, the Iser, the Iller, and the Inn, and even the Lech, have been of no insignificant value in every campaign along that great river. At Marengo, we read how the tornado of battle swept along the banks of the Farraro and Bormida, and how even the brook Fontanone ran red with the blood of those who attempted to cross. In reading of Waterloo, one can hardly fail to discover how the little foggy, mazy streams in Belgium dictated the movements of that great battle.

The little creek along which the battle of Antietam was fought on the 17th of September proved an almost impassable barrier to the Union army, and it was not without the most terrible slaughter that the bridge was carried and the hill gained beyond. Could this position have been carried earlier in the day, a victory would not only have been gained but the retreat of the Rebel army would have been prevented, for their right wing would have been turned and a large force thrown between them and the Potomac. The Chickahominy was relied on by the Rebels as being a barrier sufficiently strong to prevent McClellan from reinforcing Casey's division from the main army, which had not yet crossed the river, but nevertheless the crossing was effected and the battle of Fair Oaks was fought. The Potomac, the Blackwater, the James, the Rappahannock, the Hatchie, and the Shenandoah in America, the Danube, the Sulferino, the Tanaro, the Iser, the Inn, the Granicus, and the classic Rhine in Europe, plus many others that could be mentioned, have been important in many battles. Yes, rivers have always had more or less to do with every campaign, and always will.

Even at this moment, when the future of the Union was in question, Willard predicts that the Civil War will ultimately result in the rise of America as a first-rate power.

Whatever may be the result of this war, there will be one thing that we shall learn, and that is our own strength, and it will teach Europe that America, though divided she may be, is not a weak or even a second rate power. Our army has indeed met with a repulse, and our loss has been most terrible, yet there is no cause to despair, but we should struggle on and hope on to the bitter end. We know little as yet what the real history of the siege of Fredericksburg has been. Imagination paints many unreal pictures and

> Imagination frames events unknown
> In wild, fantastic shapes of hideous ruin
> And what its fears create.

Thursday, December 18th. The weather today has been very fair and warm, notwithstanding the portents of a storm last night. Nothing has occurred today here at the Summit House to mar its quiet, or rather the quiet of the inmates. Last night the patients, those that were able, gathered in the dining hall, as it had been given out that a concert would be given by some lady or ladies for the amusement of the soldiers. But we were doomed to be disappointed, as the said lady or ladies did not make their appearance. We had some singing, nevertheless, although it was not very musical or charming.

This is a clear, cold evening. The stars glitter up yonder in the clear, blue fields of ether with their usual wintry brightness. Notwithstanding the dreary reign of the Winter King, there is much of beauty in earth and sky. We all love the beautiful. That love is of celestial origin, the offspring of the love for the good and true. The myriad faces of earthly beauty that spring up in the humblest pathway of human life are visible symbols of the infinite, ineffable beauty of diviner spheres. How affluent is the exuberant earth in revelations of loveliness! They burst into life beneath our feet in—

> The bright mosaics that with storied beauty
> The floor of Nature's temple tessellate.

They beat the air with iris tinted pinions above our heads—stretch out enchanting vistas before our eyes—dance on the crest of the impetuous waterfall—slumber upon the bosom of the tranquil stream—gaze at their own image in the mirror of the glassy lake—look down from the effulgent

stars—unfurl their orient-hued banners at the waving of Aurora's hand—
shoot their meteoric lights before wondering eyes—start into life whenever nature lifts her scepter, an undisputed sovereign—arch the prismatic
bow in the blue canopy above. They sparkle in every quivering dew drop
and pulsate through the great artery of all creation. And day and night,
these glorious witnesses of beauty's all pervading existence are chanting in
chorus—

"Love the beautiful, for those immortal fountains from whence all
purity descends are beauty's wellsprings!"

And the poet lifts his voice to echo the universal hymn and sings—

> Thus has Beauty sent from Heaven
> The lovely ministress of Truth and Good
> In this dark world; for Truth and Good are one,
> And Beauty dwells in them and they in her,
> With like participation.
>
> Wherefore, then, oh sons of earth,
> Would ye dissolve the tie?
> Yes, Beauty embellishes all, pervades all,
> And dwells in all, and all in it.

There are other beauties aside from that of nature's works around us,
other beauties than that which beams from yon clear sky or sparkles from
those lustrous orbs that makes the night so beautiful. There is a beauty in
the human form, animated as it is by a spark of that life emanating from
Him who giveth light and life to all. Beauty radiates from the human face
when the light of a pure heart shines through it. It beams from the
sparkling eye—glows on the cheek of health—dances around the mouth
of innocence.

Sunday, December the 21st. Another week has come and gone,
and another Sabbath has come to bless the earth, bringing with it that rest
and quiet so dear to every Christian mind. The Sabbath has been a day of
rest, and all nations have revered and respected it in some way or another.
The same day perhaps may not have been observed, and observation of it
may have differed widely, yet a Sabbath has existed from all time and
among all nations. This day, bells ring out their mellow notes on this and
other Christian lands, far away on distant shores, among the islands of the

sea. In formerly heathen lands, the light of the Christian religion has penetrated, and those who in years gone by knelt in humble and blind adoration at the foot of the imaginary deities made of wood and stone, and kept their Sabbaths in a barbarous way, now wind their way to the house of God, there to be warmed and awakened to a higher and nobler life and taught to worship Him who said, "There is no other God than Me," who proclaimed that "there should be light" and caused the sun to shine.

Religion is an element of our nature. It springs up within the heart spontaneously even from childhood. Every nation or people, whether Christian or savage, have some form of religious worship. The simple heathen as well as the enlightened Christian feels that there is that which rules and governs which surpasses his comprehension. He feels that there is a God, sees God in every thing, acknowledges Him in all around, feels Him in his own heart, and worships Him according to his best *idea* of worship.

The Christian has his form of worship and the heathen has his, and though it may be in a simpler way, yet it is as sincere. The one, it is true, worships God according to the more enlightened forms of higher intelligence, the other pays his tribute of devotion to an imaginary being of wood or stone. This he calls his God and is as earnest in his devotions as the one who worships at the Christian's altar. Yes, there is religion in every heart, although it may be smothered by habit and evil associations.

Religion was once abolished all through France, or at least the forms of it were done away with. The churches were closed and the bells hung mute and silent in the towers, for their mellow voice was no longer heard calling the people to the house of prayer. The Sabbath came and went unobserved, uncared for, and unheeded by at least a portion of the people. No religious gatherings occurred, for they were not allowed. Yet the people, especially those in the rural districts, longed to hear again the chime of the church bells and to see the church doors open on the Sabbath morn, and the assembling of the congregation in their old, familiar places of worship. They felt the want of religious worship and sighed for its return. "It is," said Napoleon, "absolutely indispensable to have a religion for the people," and he restored the church to them. Napoleon, whatever may be said of him, interested himself in the cause of the church, although opposed by nearly all his generals and the statesmen around him. He saw the wants of the people in this respect, and actuated by a lofty motive, he sought to relieve them. He was the first consul then, just in the beginning of his career, and no act of his life reflects so much credit on him as the effort he made to restore the right of worship to the people. Amid all the glory of his conquests and the splendor of his achievements, there is no brighter spot—no nobler act than that by which the church doors were opened and religion was again allowed to shine, to comfort, and to cheer.

Napoleon, although a tyrant, a despot, and a warrior, still possessed a religious nature—he was a Christian, though not a devotee. "My religion," said he to Monge the sage, "is very simple. I look at the universe, so vast, so complex, so magnificent, and I say to myself that it cannot be the work of chance, but that of an unknown, omnipotent being as superior to the finest machines of human invention in his works as the universe is superior to the simplest works of man." Man wishes to know, respecting himself and his future destiny, a crowd of secrets which the universe does not disclose. "We must allow," he continued, "religion to inform him of that which he feels the need of knowing." One day, when the subject of religion and the restoration of the church was being discussed in the Council of State, Napoleon said, "Last evening I was walking alone in the woods amid the solitudes of nature. The tones of a church bell in the distance fell upon my ear. Involuntarily, I felt deep emotion, so powerful is the influence of early habits and associations. I said to myself, if I feel thus, what must be the impression on the popular mind?" Great indeed was the rejoicing of the people when the "Concordat," as it was called, was announced to the public, for by it the churches were again opened, and the bells rung out their mellow notes as in other times. The peasantry longed for the return of religion, and when Napoleon restored it to them, he won their hearts forever.

Man sees God in every thing around him. He catches His smile as it beams from the serene sky that bends above him, from the flowers that bloom along his pathway, from the glittering orbs that smile down upon him from above, from the leafy forests and the green meadows, from the bosom of the placid lake and the sparkling hill, from the lofty mountain and the flowery plain. He feels God in all the workings of nature, he feels Him in the gentle zephyrs that fan his dusky cheek and cool his heated brow, and in the fierce tornado that rends the giant oak. He feels Him in the summer's warmth and the winter's cold, and in the throbbings of his own heart as it swells with emotions of joy or sadness. He hears Him, too, in the many voices in which nature speaks—in the sighing of the gentle

wind and the crash of the tempest, in the low murmur of the little brooklet, the boom of the cataract, and the roar of the mighty deep, in the songs
of birds and the wailings of the storm and the thunder crash.

In speaking of religion, I do not speak of it as a devotee of any form
or particular church. I belong to none and believe in none in particular—a
friend to all, a devotee to none. Religion, I hold, consists not in any
prescribed form of worship, not in words but deeds, in pure motives and
noble thoughts, in aspirations for a higher and nobler existence. He who
feeds the hungry, befriends the friendless, and makes the sad hearted
rejoice will merit a higher reward and receive a brighter crown than he
who kneels for hours at the foot of the gilded altar; for his has been a life
of good deeds, while that of the other has been one of long prayers and
empty professions. The church of the present day is sadly corrupt, differ-
ing widely from that of its primitive existence. Arrogant aristocracy has
crept within its walls, and its shadow falls darkly upon its altars. Brotherly
equality in the sight of heaven seems to have been abolished and religion
itself has been almost smothered by the pride and extravagance of its pro-
fessors and devotees. Pride seems to have taken the place of simplicity—
arrogance that of religion.

Across the river from yonder city, the voice of a score of bells comes
tonight, and a throng of worshipers at their bidding wind their way to the
magnificent temples of worship. Along the same street pass the rich, the
poor, the man of untold wealth and the penniless beggar; the one
enveloped in rich broadcloth and warm furs, the other shivering in beg-
garly rags. See the poor, perishing supplicant as she stretches out her thin,
white hand and begs a pittance with which to purchase a mouthful of
bread for her famishing child. But the man of wealth passes on, heeding
her not, only to remark that "such creatures should be horse whipped to
their homes or sent to the house of correction."

See yonder temple so brilliantly illuminated with its many chandeliers,
thronged with a congregation of the most wealthy. How richly decorated
it is, how costly are all its adornments, how embellished are its walls. What
a splendid pulpit, what a magnificent carpet, what a lofty dome, and what
a gigantic structure is that church, how brilliant the gems that sparkle
upon the persons of those children of fortune there assembled! But the
light from those golden chandeliers, as it flashes out upon the night, rests
upon another object and a face far different from those within; for it falls
like a mockery upon the pale, haggard face of the poor beggar.

And while the Christians worship within, the rude, chill winds of winter rudely whistle through her tattered garments, the snow gathers on her pale brow, and the tears turn to ice as they fall. Hark, how softly the music of the Christian voices and deep toned organ within arises from that Christian assembly and echoes out on the wintry air. How brightly the light spreads over the congregation, how warm, how happy, how beautiful seems every thing within; but the light falls upon another form, the music on other ears. A mortal being, a fellow creature, lies dying of hunger and cold almost beneath the shade of the holy Christian altar, and her groans and cries mingle with the hymns of the "Christian Worshipers." Thus it is all through the Christian world; thousands this winter night are wandering, homeless and friendless, while millions of dollars are spent in adorning the churches.

Sorrow originates with ourselves and emanates from our own hearts. Many there are who will tell us that sorrows are sent upon us by Deity, that they are acts of Providence. They will exclaim when smitten by some sudden calamity—"What have *I* done that God should send this upon *me*?" Just as though God, after having made and peopled this great universe and adjusted every thing so wisely, had failed to make the wrongdoer his own punisher. Sin is unnatural and never fails to bring with it its punishment. The fruits of evil doings, of foolish acts and hasty words are regrets or sorrows. These come not as a direct dispensation of Providence. When we thrust our hand into the fire, we feel pain. Who will say that that pain is measured out to us by the hand of Divinity or that it was an act of Providence? Thus it is with all our mental pain; it is the legitimate offspring of our own doings. If those who are continually complaining and charging God with having sent afflictions upon them would look down into their own hearts, they would see the real cause of all their sorrows.

See yonder impatient man as he bustles about fretting, scolding, and finding fault with every one he comes in contact with. Nothing goes right with him, he is in trouble always. He is unhappy and makes everyone else the same. Why is this; are all his sorrows and troubles the acts of Providence? Or are they the results of his own fretful disposition, a disposition he has failed to cultivate, a temper that enslaves and masters him and continually makes him miserable? But some "special Providence" man would say, if he should happen to read what I have just written, that I "was an infidel—that I did not believe in an overruling Providence." Such is not the case, far from it. I believe in God and His overruling power, but I do not believe in such a thing as "special Providence." If we have committed a sin or crime, the very act itself will bring, sooner or later, its own retribution, and it would not be just to inflict a double punishment.

But perhaps some would inquire "where do those sorrows originate that are not the result of sin, sorrows derived from events beyond our control?" Such sorrows, although not having the origin within ourselves, cannot be the special dispensations of God. God is the author of all things and has made laws by which all things are governed. These laws are perfect and infallible. They are natural, and to break them is to sin against nature. We often hear it said, when a person meets with some great affliction, that it was a chastisement sent from Heaven. An infant dies, perhaps, or some other one who was near and dear. It will then be said, "God sent it as a chastisement." Just as though man was not born to die and that all sooner or later were not doomed to pass the portals of death, to enter the grave. How absurd to call that a punishment or an act of Special Providence, which is only the fulfillment of one of nature's laws. All must die—life cannot always last—mortality *must* have ascent. This would be the same, or nearly so, were there no crimes committed. Death is natural—it is an established law, not a special act.

The subject of Special Providence is one that affords a wide field for thought. Does God rule by special act and by direct intervention (so to speak) or does He rule by laws, fixed and unalterable, laws that have existed from the beginning? Does He send afflictions upon us or are they the sting of wounded nature? As for me, I cannot believe that God interferes directly with our worldly affairs. It is with man as it is with all the other works of nature. He is governed by natural laws, and all his joys and sorrows are but the fulfillment of those laws.

Go out into nature's gardens and walk through the labyrinths of beauty that are every where spread out before us. Behold the leafy forests, the green earth, the flowers, the babbling brooks, and the golden sunshine. Is there not harmony in all? When the leaves withered and fell from yonder trees, did not the grass fade and the flowers die? And did not the birds, who in the summer hours warbled their notes in those bowers, when winter came, fly away to a sunnier clime? Do not the seasons bring with them their varied changes, and are they not governed by natural laws?

See yonder sun, how bright, how glorious. And yonder sky, how grandly sublime, and with what serene beauty and grandeur does it bend over head today. Is it not natural—is it an act of Special Providence? Has

God withheld the clouds today, has He folded them away in some far off region, has He added a new lustre to the sun and a new beauty to the sky? No, the sun shines today and the sky bends above us just as it has done ever since the world began. And it will continue to do so, until perhaps the laws that now exist shall by their workings bring others into existence. And they in their turn will bring out others, and as one bears upon the other, and change after change occurs, the whole face of nature may be changed.

Watch the flowers as they grow, the manner in which they spring into existence—their life and death. How natural, how beautiful! Thus it is with man. He lives, he dies as nature has ordained he should. Calamities befall him, misfortunes overtake him, and sorrows gather around him and darken his pathway, yet all is natural. Those sorrows spring from the heart—they are not from above. His social sky may be darkened and the sun may refuse to shine, but these sorrows are not from above; like the clouds that gather in the sky, they come from the earth—they go up but never down. But enough of theology. I am not a theologian.

Sorrows are not always the ministers of ill. They often bring us good, and when they have passed away, we are happier than before—happier by contrast, just as the sky always looks brightest after a storm. Sorrow enables us to appreciate real happiness, therefore is necessary to our enjoyment. Were we never *unhappy*, we should hardly know when we were happy or when we ought to be; the pang of sorrow only adds to the thrill of pleasure, and disappointments to hopes, when realized. The darkness of the night only serves to make the day more beautiful. The clouds that swept across the sky yesterday make it appear more beautiful today. The heat of the summer teaches us to appreciate the mellow lustre, the cool air, and subdued sunshine of autumn, with its crisped leaves and withered flowers. winter, with its clouds and storms and driving snows, its piercing air and scowling skies, is necessary, and by its severity we are taught how much to prize the spring with its balmy air, its warmth and freshness.

Thus it is with us while journeying onward through this life of shades and sunshine. The very sorrows which gather around us, that fill the soul with darkness and for the time make life almost unbearable, fit us for the enjoyment of the blessings of life and make us more capable of enjoying them. "Sweet are the usages of adversity," sung the poet, and so they are; for they school and educate us. The man who has no sorrows or trials will have but a poor capacity for the enjoyment of life's blessings. If we were never hungry, we would not know the pleasure of eating. Were we always happy, we would not be mortal.

Christmas Eve. This is Christmas Eve, the time above all others that everybody should be merry. All over the Christian world tonight, merry-making is going on, and in spite of the sad condition of our country, the people generally will be happy—or at least merry. Families and people of all classes—the rich, the poor—the old, the young—in village and in city, and in the country, too, are gathering in social, happy throngs tonight, and the laugh of thoughtless joy will resound every where.

And well may the world rejoice over the return of this holiday; for it was the advent of the Christian era, when Bethlehem's star arose over Galilee and a voice from Heaven proclaimed "Peace on earth and good will to man." Nearly two thousand years ago the first gleamings of the Christian religion began to tinge the ancient sky and break through the dark clouds that had so long overshadowed the world. And what a glorious dawning! The light of the Christian religion, which was then but a spark struggling with difficulty through the darkness, has grown to be a great illumination, shining its resplendent light abroad over the whole world. It, like the morning, dawned in the east, traveling rapidly to the west, until it had encircled the universe with a belt of glory, throwing over all the lustre of the "Son of Righteousness."

Six thousand years ago, we are told, the earth was wrapped in darkness and all was void. The dark earth hung aloft, swinging through space, until the voice of Deity broke the silence and then—"Let there be light," when lo! the glorious sun burst forth, the dark sky was radiant with splendor, and the earth was filled with light. Years in their quick course sped on, and again the earth was darkened, but with a moral gloom; for darkness entered the heart of man, and he grew blind with sin. Ignorance, superstition, and oppression covered all the land. Goodness seemed a stranger, and God had been forgotten, His covenants broken and His sanctuaries thrown down, and religion seemed nearly to have been smothered beneath the ruins of the altar. Amid this gloomy darkness, again there came the voice of Deity echoing through the portals of the benighted world, the Star of Bethlehem arose above Judea's hills, and the lowly shepherds hailed the coming dawn as the advent of a new born day—a day that should continue to brighten until the whole world shall be absorbed in its glory.

The day has come and its light has magnified, spreading far, illuminating all lands and climes, and has entered into the heart of man, driving out the darkness of superstition, elevating us to a higher plain of manhood, and teaching us to worship God in a nobler way. Not two thousand years have yet passed since first the light of the Christian religion dawned upon the darkened world, but how great the work it has wrought—how magnificent the change it has accomplished—how glorious it has made the world—how happy it has rendered mankind.

Christmas at the Summit House. This is Christmas Day, and a fair one it has been, too. Old Sol seemed to wish to show us how brightly he could shine today, or perhaps, as this is the anniversary day of the birth of that Son who rivals even him in brightness, he has put on his brightest apparel and pours out his golden favors with a true royal hand.

The day has been passed very pleasantly here. A Christmas dinner was gotten up by the ladies for us, and everything was done that *could* be done to make us happy. The people of this vicinity seem never to grow weary in doing acts of kindness. The long tables of the great dining hall, usually so barren and destitute of even the most common fare, were today loaded with all the luxuries of life. And instead of the rough, surly fellows who usually threw us our crust of bread and gave us our cup of water, we were waited on by the fairest young ladies of the village. Many a stern, brave heart was filled with gratitude, and from many a manly bosom went up the prayer—"*May God bless the ladies.*"

Such acts of kindness are not confined to the ladies of this vicinity alone. It is the same all over the land. Wherever a soldier lies wasting away with disease or languishing in pain, there will woman be, and her soft, white hand will press his brow, her gentle voice and the sunshine of her presence will make him forget his pain, his loneliness, and his sorrows. The kindness of the ladies—their many acts of patriotic devotion—will not be forgotten.

Many a scarred soldier will return to his home or the battle field bearing within his heart memories of kind deeds that cannot be effaced. Their praise will be spoken around the camp fires and bivouacs of the whole Union army. One would hardly think that he was in a hospital today, so differently does every thing appear from the usual dull, unbroken monotony that prevails here. The voice of woman, the songs and laughter of children broke the silence, and their presence was like sunshine amid the gloom. But after all, one cannot forget that he is far from home and those he loves, and many a heart filled with sadness as thoughts of the absent, far off ones awakened, and memories came back of other times when we sat down to Christmas dinners with the dear loved ones at home.

After dinner we had music, both instrumental and vocal, and all were as happy as a soldier in a hospital could be; and soldiers will be happy if such a thing is possible.

Willard's time for philosophizing was over, as he had recuperated enough from his wound to be sent back to his unit. Although he wrote two more books during the war, he never returned to the lines of thought he pursued at the Summit House. He left for the front just after Christmas. Along the way, he paints a harsh picture of the various convalescent camps that recovering soldiers were forced to endure on their way back to their units.

Soldiers Retreat, Washington; December, Monday the 29th.
After a restless night, I find myself in what is known as the Soldier's Retreat. Having nearly recovered from my wound, I with a number of others was sent on to this place, from which all that are able will be sent to their regiments, the others to the Convalescent Camp.

We left the Summit House on Saturday morning and were taken to the provost marshal's office where we were kept until two o'clock the next morning. Then we were "escorted" by a score of armed soldiers to the depot, and in a few moments were aboard of the cars and on our way for Baltimore, where we arrived just after sunrise. Being too late for the morning train, we were obliged to "lay up" until nearly noon. In the meantime we were conducted to the rooms of the Relief Society, where we were treated to a good breakfast, after which we went out on the street and had a stroll through the city.

Baltimore is one of the neatest looking cities in America. The streets are straight and clean, and the buildings, mostly of brick, are large and fine looking. It being a Sabbath morning, the city was wrapped in a profound quiet. But very few persons were to be seen on the street, and an almost oppressive silence seemed to be the order of the day. Here and there a solitary individual might be seen strolling leisurely along the pavement. But at last the silence was broken by the chime of a solitary church bell in a distant part of the city. Soon another joined in the solemn but melodious music, then another and another joined their voices, until the whole city rang. In a short time, the streets, which just before had been so desolate and lonely, were thronged with a crowd of people on their way to church. I have seldom seen such a change; it seemed almost the work of magic. Men, women, and scores of little children came along the pavement. I stood in a door way and watched the crowd as it hurried by, but the faces were all strange to me, none were there that I had ever seen before, and though in the midst of a crowd, I felt that I was alone. I am naturally perhaps a little given to lonely feelings, but it is very seldom that I have felt more lonely than I did that Sabbath morning. For a long time I remained

there, until at last the shrill scream of the locomotive gave me to understand that it was time to get aboard of the cars again.

I hurried to the depot and sprang upon the platform just as the train
was moving away. As we swept on over the country, I watched the beautiful
city as it rapidly disappeared, growing dimmer and fainter until at last its
white monuments, tall spires, and glittering domes were lost in the blue
dim distance. A half hour's ride brought us to the Relay House, a fine, large
building among the rocks and hills, with a small village to the south of it.

The country between Baltimore and the Relay House is open and
mostly level, with here and there a low, wave like hill, the whole sparsely
covered with timber and resembling in many respects the beautiful prairie
openings of southern Wisconsin. Around the Relay House the country is
quite rough and broken. However, between Baltimore and Washington it
is generally level, well settled, and the farms apparently well cultivated.
The buildings are large and built after the old mansion like style so prevalent in Maryland and some parts of Virginia, especially among the wealthy.
Our ride through to Washington was a very pleasant one, for the weather
was mild and warm, and we were all in good spirits. It was about the middle of the afternoon when we arrived here at the "Retreat," where we
were fed, roomed, etc.

The "Retreat" is not one of the most agreeable places in the world, by
a long ways. We were first shown into the eating room, which is a large,
long room with tables running the whole length and is calculated to be
large enough for two thousand men to eat at a time. The fare is none of
the best, being only a slice of bread, a piece of cold meat, and a cup of
coffee. After supper we were shown to our sleeping apartments. These
consisted of large rooms, the only furniture of which was a stove placed in
the centre of the room—not a chair or a bench or bed—nothing but the
bare floor. Into one of those rooms we were told to go and make ourselves
as comfortable as possible, and we did. But to make oneself comfortable in
such a place was impossible. The room was cold, dark, and dismal. We had
been joined at the Retreat by a large crowd of convalescents, many of
whom were not the most sober men in Washington. I never shall forget
last night; I never wish to pass another like it.

Night came on, and the Retreat was as dark as any prison, for there
were no lights to be had, and we were obliged to grope in the dark. Finding a vacant corner, I spread my rubber on the floor and wrapped my
blanket around me and lay down—not to sleep, I did not expect that, for

one might as well have attempted to sleep in *Pandemonium*. As I have said, some of the men were *drunk* and were cursing and raving as drunken men always will, while another crowd, being a little jolly also, were singing and laughing. Another party was playing cards by the light of the stove, the door of which was open, and the fire within cast its dim, uncertain light around, half revealing their rude forms and rough features as they hovered over their cards, casting on the floor and wall their dark, unearthly shadows that flitted and danced in the sombre fire light like grim, misshapen spectres of phantom land. At the same time, in another part of the room, a few religious persons were singing hymns and praying. One of them undertook to say a few words to the crowd, but his voice was drowned amid the most horrible curses, oaths, and screams of the drunken rabble.

A row or fight occurred, first between two—then others joined in, until a dozen drunken and half-drunken men were yelling, swearing, and fighting there in the dark. It was only quelled by the interference of the guard. In the next room adjoining was a dead soldier, a man that had died last night. This seemed to make not the slightest difference, but only made the horrible revelry seem more hellish. The poor fellow is lying there yet, just as he died. His was a very sudden death—almost without a moment's warning. A few moments before, he was walking about, apparently as well as any man. He was seen to fall, was brought in there, and in less than ten minutes was dead! I am accustomed to death bed scenes, I have seen many a man die and have watched with them alone during their last hours. I have seen many, *very* many dead men in hospitals and on the battle field. Yet I could not but feel sad as I looked down upon that man lying there, who only a few moments before was seemingly in the full enjoyment of health and strength.

Thus it is with Death—he is with us always, ever by our side. He walks with us by day and lays down by our side at night. His ghostly, ghastly, grim, and horrid form casts its spectral shadows over our pathway, and a death's head is continually grinning before us. The grave ever lies open at our feet. The voice of death laughs at us from the air—stings us from the earth—stares at us from the decaying flowers—mocks at us from the dying sun light—is seen in the withering form—burns on the cheek of beauty where the hectic flush of the consumptive glows—flits before us in the sun light—dances in the moon light—and in fact is our constant companion. Its shadow is ever by our side.

With the war going badly and seeming interminable, the Lincoln Administration came under attack from all sides. Some thought that the president was weak and not doing nearly enough; others considered the losses unacceptable and faulted him for not concentrating on a negotiated peace. Many people today would be surprised to know how few out-and-out public supporters Lincoln really had. It is therefore particularly interesting that Willard here expresses his trust in Lincoln as well as support for his Emancipation Proclamation.

Camp Convalescent; Wednesday, December the 31st. Once more I find myself on the "Sacred Soil" of the "Old Dominion," yet so close am I to Uncle Samuel's dominion that even from this hill on which my tent is pitched, I can see the great dome of the "White House" where "Honest Old Uncle Abe" carries on—or at least presides over—the "'fairs of state." Speaking of "Old Abe" reminds me that this is the last day of grace given the rebellious children of the South in which to lay down their arms and quit their naughty tricks. "If you don't do it," says Uncle Abe, "I'll take away yer Niggers and make ye do yer work yerself." God bless you, Abraham! The theme of reflection now is, with those who ever reflect on anything, the president's "Emancipation Proclamation." Will he carry it out—or will he revoke it? I have heard it said by many that they believed the president would withdraw his proclamation. I cannot think so; I have too much faith in him to think so. Should he be so weak, so puerile as to withdraw it now, the sneers of the whole world would rise about him like a whirlwind.

On Monday last, we were escorted to this place, where we were left to provide for ourselves as best we could. We were first marched to the colonel's (Belknap) head quarters, where the roll was called. We were then conducted to our respective encampments, then to our "wards" or "streets" and *then* to our tents. Each state's soldiers are quartered by themselves. The Eastern, Middle, and Western states have their encampments separate. The camp of the Western troops is very small in comparison with that of those from the East; the proportion cannot be less than twenty to one.

We are quartered in tents such as could be used nowhere except here, for they would be condemned for army use. But *anything* seems to be considered good enough for the convalescents. A few of the tents are good, but the major part of them are old and begrimed, and many of them are tattered and torn. We are furnished with a fair amount of rations, but nothing else—not even a stove, a plate, or a cup. Yet all of these things, to a greater or less degree, are to be found in every tent. Soldiers have a wonderful faculty of providing for themselves when such a thing becomes necessary.

The Eastern boys are much better provided for than we are, but what the boys of the West lack in being cared for, they make up in natural sagacity and self reliance, much to the discomfiture of the New Yorkers and Pennsylvanians. I have often heard it said that the boys from the West would live where Eastern men would die. This camp contains about five thousand men, is located among the hills or ridges known as Arlington Heights, and is about four miles from Washington and three from Alexandria. It is in a pleasant place, and wood and water is near by.

New Year's Day, January the 1st, 1863. Once more we find ourselves at the beginning of a new year. The old one went and the new one came, dawning with a clear sky and a bright sun. The day has been a pleasant one, though the wind was high and strong.

It is New Year's night, and the stars shine brightly in the New Year's sky. Once more, after another twelve months of dangers and toil, the new year comes and is hailed by joyful hearts all over the wide world. Good by to the old year, and welcome to the new.

Last night the soldiers bade the old year good by in a very soldier like manner. Wishing, I suppose, to pay the old year a proper tribute as he, like an old soldier, was about to take his departance from "time to eternity," and having no better way, they resorted to the following manner of paying their respects. Though it seemed that no prearranged plan had been adopted, and every one seemed to act on his own responsibility, about eight o'clock a gun was fired, then another and another, until one would have supposed that quite a battle was in progress. Every man that had a gun or could borrow one was out and popping away as fast as he could load and fire. The firing increased until there was one continual rattle of musketry.

Orders were sent to the street sergeants to put a stop to the firing, but blaze—blaze—pop—pop went the guns. "Cease firing," screamed the sergeant but bang-bang went the guns. Bullets whistled and the men shouted until the whole encampment was in a perfect uproar. But at last the firing died away, and the old year was allowed to depart in peace.

The night was a lustrous one, for the sky was cloudless, and the moon and stars out in the wintry sky seemed to look sadly down upon earth, as if bidding the old year a sad "good by." The morning dawned bright and golden, and the day has been warm and beautiful. This day has been observed all over the Christian world—even by the soldier, though far from home he may be, in the camps and on the battle field, far away in the west, along the old Potomac and by the seaside. No rich repast, no bounteous table has been prepared for him, no feasting, no family gathering or social circle, no music save the crackling of the camp fires, no familiar voice or friendly hand to greet him, alone or among strangers. Yet he feels that this has been the beginning of a new year, and he has observed it in his own quiet way, even in his loneliness. Many a soldier's heart has thrilled with emotion as his thoughts traveled back, wandering over the scenes of by gone years, of happier times and brighter days. Many a moist eye has been turned homeward today, looking sadly across the misty old Potomac and over the barren and deserted fields of the Old Dominion.

Willard saw emancipation as a turning point in American history, as indeed it proved to be. He greeted the epochal event both in prose and with poetry.

With the New Year begins a new era in the history of America. *Slavery*—the curse which has so long darkened our fair land and been upheld and sustained by the arm of the government has today been declared *abolished*. The slave, so long bound in cruel chains, is to be forever *free*.

The Dawn of Freedom

Lo! The morning star appearing
Above yon mountain's brow,
The watcher's heart so lonely, cheering
For morning dawneth on us now.

Awake ye bondsmen and ye slaves
Awake ye now, down trodden race,
See Freedom's banner proudly wave
As freedom's dawn draws on apace.

Lo! New Year's morn with rosy wing
With golden beauty now unfurled,
Light, beauty, and warmth to bring
To a dark, benighted world.

The morn is coming not afar
When the bondsman shall be free,
And slavery shall no longer mar
Our dear land of liberty.

Hark! Hear the shouts that rise on high
As freedom's host march on amain,
The tyrant slavery now shall die
The slave no more shall clank his chain.

Bondsmen, now the hour has come
Arise, awaken, and be free,
Arise in every cabin home
From shore to shore, from sea to sea.

Why should you live in slavery's thrall
Hear ye the voice that says, "be free,"
Better never live at all
Than be bound in slavery

The Song of the Slave

Bondsmen awaken
    Slumber no more,
See the bright skies
    That bend over thee.

Thy dark days of thraldom
    Forever are o'er,
The Nation has said it
    The Negro is free!

Lift up your heads
    And see the bright token,
The bright dawn of freedom
    Liberty's reign.

The chains that have bound thee
        Soon shall be broken,
Shake off your fetters
        Burst every chain.

Wake the glad anthem,
        Let it ring to the sea,
Freedom has triumphed
        And we're free, we're free.

Dark sons of Africa
        Bondsman and slave
Children of slavery
        (Worse than the grave).

Heard ye the voice
        Of the nation that spoke?
Then awaken, awaken
        Cast off the vile yoke.

Spring to your feet
        And burst every thong,
Proclaim yourselves free
        And join in the song.

Wake the glad anthem,
        Let it ring to the sea,
Freedom has triumphed
        And we're free, we're free.

See the bright morning
        As it sweeps to the west,
And gilds every hill top
        And dark mountain's crest.

Thus shall the dawning
        Of Liberty be,
As from ocean to ocean
        It sweeps to the sea.

The slave at his toil
    Will catch the sweet sound,
And the chains that have bound him
    Will fall to the ground.

And with rapturous joy
    Will he join in the song,
The chorus of *Freedom*
    So deep and so strong.

Wake the glad anthem,
    Let it ring to the sea,
Freedom has triumphed
    And we're free, we're free.

Alexandria, Virginia. I obtained a pass a day or two ago and took a walk down to the far famed city of Alexandria. It is about three miles from here and is built on a low piece of land on the banks of the Potomac. The city is filthy and old, looking as do most of the cities and towns of the Old Dominion, grim and time worn. It is built mostly of red bricks, many of which have grown green with old age. It was in this city where the brave, young Colonel Ellsworth was shot by a man, or rather a fiend, by the name of Jackson at the Marshal House. The Marshal House is now used as a hospital, and from the same flagstaff from which Ellsworth tore the Rebel banner now waves the stars and stripes. There does not appear to be many people in the city, and a great majority of what there are, are Negroes. Drunken soldiers are, however, abundant.

Arlington Heights consists of three distinct circles, or rather semicircles, of low hills, all of which are crowned with forts. This, before the blight of war came upon it, must have been a fine section of country; but ah! how barren, how desolate now. It is *very* sad to look over a portion of country so interesting as this has been, so sacred as it is, and see the ruin that meets the eye at every turn, the fenceless and barren fields, deserted homes, and the graves of the ancient and noble dead trodden beneath the feet of the careless stranger. War does indeed scatter blight and ruin abroad with an unsparing hand.

While on my way home from Alexandria, as I was passing an old, ruined, and, as I supposed, deserted house, I saw a pale, white face looking out at the window. The face was very wan, the eyes were large, dark, and sad, and seemed to reflect the light only of a cheerless soul. I never shall forget that face so white, with its expression of deep seated sorrow. There is but little either interesting or beautiful about the city of Alexandria. The broad old Potomac sweeps proudly and scornfully by, dotted here and there with the white winged vessels that glide up and down, to and from the capital. Washington can be seen from the heights near Alexandria, as it is only about eight miles distant.

Willard ends Book Three with a tribute to his fellow soldiers from the West who had died for the cause.

The Western Dead

The dead, the dead, the Western dead
Are found in every vale and glen,
Where Freedom's hosts have fought and bled
Their country to defend.

Where e'er the blood of battle poured
On hill or mountain side,
There waved the gleaming Western sword
With crimson deeply dyed.

Amid the far off Western wilds
And by the ocean's stormy flood,
And where Mississippi sweetly smiles
And on Murfreesboro's field of blood.

On South Mountain's ragged crest
By Potomac's misty side,
Have the Heroes of the West
Bravely fought and nobly died.

Sleep, brave Heroes, in your graves
On the crimson field of battle,
There the storm of conflicts rave
And the thunders hoarsely rattle.

No nobler graves were ever made
No braver men have fought and died,
No truer words were ever said—
"They were our country's pride."

Sleep on then, dream no more
Of scenes of blood, of death and strife,
The country's fate no more deplore,
Thou hast yielded up thy life.

Sadly will we think of thee
But proudly of thy victories tell,
And our song shall ever be
Thou hast done thy duty well.

BOOK FOUR

Campaigning in Pennsylvania, Maryland, and Virginia and Scenes in Camp and on the March

Van R. Willard, Company G, 3rd Wisconsin Volunteers

There's a voice on the wind like the Spirit's low cry
'Tis the muster roll sounding, who shall reply?
Not those whose wan faces are turned to the sky
Where they fell in the deadly affray.

Wartrace, Tennessee. After the battle of Antietam, the regiment went into camp in Pleasant Valley in Maryland, near Maryland Heights. It numbered at that time but little over one hundred men for duty, as over two hundred had been cut down at Antietam, and those wounded at Cedar Mountain had not yet returned from the hospitals. While encamped at the "Heights" the regiment, with others, cut down the timber on the top and sides of the mountains, built forts, linking them together by long lines of breast works and rifle pits, making the place almost invulnerable. The regiment did not remain there long, however, but was sent back to Antietam Creek and went into camp near Antietam Forge, where it built fortifications also. Here it remained until about the 10th of December, when it was ordered to Fairfax Court House, but remained there only eight or ten days, when it was ordered to move on towards Falmouth.

In the meantime, the great battle, or rather, the great sacrifice, at Fredericksburg had been made and Burnside had lost. The march to Stafford Court House was a hard one, the roads were very bad, almost impassable, the weather cold, wet, and dismal. On the march the regiment passed through Dumfries, or, rather, halted for the night near what is known as Dumfries' Landing, the site of what was once a town or "burg" of some kind; but as it, whatever it was, had long since died with old age, there was nothing to mark the spot save a mass of moldering ruins, a few old tottering buildings, and a score of tall, black chimneys. Such ruins may be found all through the Old Dominion—old towns long since deserted, inhabited alone by bats and owls—places of loathsome decay and desolation. From Dumfries' Landing the regiment went to Stafford Court House, where it remained until the 27th of April/63. After the death of General Mansfield, who was killed at Antietam, our corps (the 12th) was commanded by General Slocum.

Having been wounded, I was not with the regiment after the battle of Antietam until after it had gone into camp at Stafford. After recovering from my wound, I was sent from the hospital at Philadelphia to the Convalescent Camp, Virginia. This Convalescent Camp is a good institution in some respects and a bad one in others, as it gives an opportunity for many who are well and able to do duty to remain away from their regiments and for some to speculate off the government. Yet it is necessary that there should be such a place to send those coming from the hospitals to, previous to sending them to their regiments.

Here in this camp are collected all those who have been sick or wounded, and as fast as is expedient, they are forwarded on. In that camp may be found men from every regiment and state represented in the Army of the Potomac. There are some that suppose that those in that camp are those who shirk from duty, that stay there by pretending to be unwell for the purpose of remaining behind, that they may idle away their time in a comfortable camp while others are doing their duty at the front. Such is not the case, though many do so, it is true; but you will find many there who are faithful soldiers, men who do not shirk from duty or danger.

At first this camp was located on one of those bleak, barren hills that form the celebrated Arlington Heights. It was near Alexandria in a bleak, open country near the river. The tents were mostly old and tattered, and but few of them were furnished with stoves or any means of keeping them comfortable. While the camp was there during the cold weather, the poor fellows suffered very much from their exposure to the cold. They had to carry their wood nearly a mile, and then it was only brush when they got it. The men were not half clothed or fed. It was a shame and reproach on the government that men who had suffered every thing, almost, should be left there to suffer as they did in that camp. Some actually died in their tents, and many lost their health. Indeed, nearly as many were sent back from there to the hospitals as was sent on to their regiments.

Three men were sent to the hospital from one tent, the fourth and last one chose to remain, although unwell, rather than go back to those dreary wards in the hospital. He was very anxious to go to his regiment, but poor fellow, he was doomed never to see it again. He went into his tent one night and, wrapping himself in his blanket, lay down to sleep—he slept never to awaken in this world again. The night was cold and stormy and the wintry wind swept furiously around those bleak heights, drifting the snow through his ragged tent, half burying him in his bed—such a bed—a single blanket and the frozen earth. When he was found in the morning, he was dead and cold as the snow that had frozen to ice on his brow. That was not the only instance of death from exposure and ill treatment in that camp.

At last, however, the attention of the government was called to the subject by Wilson of Massachusetts,[1] the best friend the soldier has, one who has done more for them than any other one man. The camp was then moved to a better locality, and steps were at once taken towards erecting barracks.

I came to the new Convalescent Camp about the first of January, and
though it was a miserable place, it was much better than the old camp, and
after the barracks were completed, it was quite comfortable. I remained
there until the 9th of March, when I was sent to Camp Distribution,
where those from the various corps are collected together and finally sent
to their respective regiments. This camp was within a mile of Alexandria.
This is a miserable camp, where hundreds of men are sent to shiver with
the cold until nearly dead from exposure, and then sent where they ought
to have gone weeks before. I was fortunate enough, however, to be
obliged to remain only two days in that camp.

*Willard's journey back to his regiment was an interesting one, offering views of
the Potomac jammed with craft, Mount Vernon, and the military depot at Aquia
Creek Landing, through which passed the myriad men and equipment on the way
to the front in Virginia.*

On the morning of the 11th, those belonging to the 11th and 12th
Corps left Camp Distribution and got on board the steamer *Wilson Small*
to go down the Potomac to Aquia Creek. The day was warm and bright,
though in mid-winter. We were on board at an early hour and in a short
time were gliding down the smooth waters of the grand old Potomac. The
scene from the deck of the steamer was one of extreme loveliness. The
weather was warm and fair, the sky serene and cloudless, save now and
then a bank of thin, white vapor that floated gracefully across it.

The river was covered with boats of every kind, from the little skiff of
the fruit vendors to the huge barques that lay proudly on the water, their
hulks looming high up above the tugs that went dashing up and down. It
was a fine scene from the deck of the steamer, looking back as we swept
down the stream—the river itself, broad and deep, flowing slowly and
smoothly on to the sea; the many ships with their white sails and steamers
with their banners of smoke; the city wrapped in haze with its tall steeples
and spires; and behind it, dark and grand loomed up the heights of Arlington, crowned with forts and battlements, while far away up the river dimly
seen in the distance was the Capitol with its great, white dome glittering
in the sun light.

Soon after leaving Alexandria, we came in sight of Mount Vernon. I
must confess that my expectations were somewhat over drawn. There was
nothing of that grandeur of scenery that I had expected to see in the

vicinity of the Mount Vernon estate. A small eminence covered with trees and a modest, plain, old fashioned house was all that could be seen from the river.

The ride down the Potomac was a slow but pleasant one. About four o'clock we landed at Aquia Creek Landing. At this place one of the first battles was fought or, rather, the first naval affair of the war. I think that there never was a town there, as no traces of any thing of the kind can be found; at least I could not see any. Yet it was quite a town then, that is, a military one; a number of buildings had been erected and a good landing constructed. The country in that vicinity is very rough, consisting of rock hills and bluffs, all covered by a heavy forest. Aquia Creek is about seventy miles from Washington and fifteen from Fredericksburg. It is a small stream, but as the river sets back up it for eight or ten miles, it is navigable for small steamers for about ten miles.

A rail road runs from Aquia to Falmouth and did run through to Richmond. We got on board of another steamer, the *Osceola*, and went up Aquia Creek to Pope's Landing, which brought us within six miles of Stafford Court House. The country up this creek is rocky and bluffy, crowned by a forest of cedars, and the encampments along the bank among the rocks, with the groups of soldiers and white tents reflecting in the stream, gave a peculiar charm to the scenery.

Bivouac in the Wilderness. It was almost dark when we landed. We still had six miles to travel and that, too, over an unknown road. But we started for the regiment (Ed Moran[2] and I), determined to go as far as we could, hoping to reach camp that night. The road was very bad, one of those dreadful corduroys—a road made of logs, many of which were out of place, leaving deep holes into which the unwary traveler tumbles up to his hips in mud and mire and finds himself almost unable to extricate himself. Such, at least, was my experience that night, for it was very dark, and I often found myself plunging into some pool of mud or brought to a stand by running off the track against a stump or a tree. My friend Moran was not more fortunate, as I often heard him praying in an old style (a style not uncommon among soldiers) and picking himself up, now and then, after having lain down in a very awkward manner and not a very comfortable position.

We at last came to the conclusion that we had better bivouac for the night. We did so, building a bed of limbs to keep us out of the wet. We were in the midst of a wilderness, a pine forest. We rolled ourselves up in our blankets and slept as soundly as though we had been in a feather bed. The night was extremely dark, the wind blew, moaning dolefully among the pine boughs, and worse than all, it began to snow toward morning and increased to a furious storm that howled and roared through those dismal forests most furiously. In the morning, we found in addition to our woolen blankets, we had one of snow. Those who have had no experience in camping out may think it strange that one could sleep under such circumstances, and it is; but the soldier becomes so accustomed to such things that he can adapt himself to any emergency.

In the morning we resumed our search for the regiment, which we found at last, quartered on a pleasant hill side about a half a mile from Stafford. The first one I saw was my friend Lenard, who came out to meet us. It was snowing still when we got into camp. I found the boys well, especially those of Co. G. None were sick and all were in good spirits, full of fun and good nature. The camp at Stafford was in a fine, dry locality on a pleasant hill side, with everything convenient except wood, which had to be brought from the woods some distance from camp.

The country around Stafford is generally very level with some slight, wave like undulations. The soil is sandy and of a poor quality. The timber is principally pine of a second growth. The inhabitants are very poor, as the men have all gone into the Southern army and the Negroes have, nearly all of them, run away; though it is not an uncommon thing to find the slaves living in their master's house, that individual having gone to parts unknown.

The buildings in this portion of the Old Dominion are hardly worthy of the name of house, that is, the most of them. While there are a few large and fine old mansions, the homes in former times of wealthy landowners, there are hundreds of small hovels, the homes of the laboring poor, the "low white trash" of Dixie. The buildings are, two thirds of them, log concerns, almost ready to tumble down with old age and rottenness.

The farms are not half cultivated and never were. The fences are old and broken down. There seems to have been but little energy or industry; every thing wears the almost unbroken appearance of stagnation and decay. No thrifty farmers with well cultivated farms and well filled garners, no white school houses by the way side, no new and thriving towns. In fact, there is nothing new, everything wears that same appearance of unbroken monotony. One who has never been in a Southern state can hardly imagine how very different things are there from what they are in our own states in the North.

The soil and climate is by far the best in the South—the North is cold and bleak. Wintry storms and barren rocks are against the North, while warmth and sunshine, a mild and healthful climate, a rich and fruitful soil are all in favor of the South. But the people lack the spirit and enterprise so characteristic of those of the North. The institutions of the Southerners are wrong; they have those that they ought not to have, and have not got those without which no people can be great and free.

The institution of slavery has been their bane, it has rested on them like a curse and deadened all their energies. The slave owner depends on his slave for support; their labor is his meat. The slave, robbed of all his rights and made to labor for another's advantage, learns to hate his master and will not work for his interest more than he can help. He slights his work and takes no interest in it. But it is only a small proportion of the population of the South that owns slaves; the rest are poor whites, too poor to own slaves and too indolent to work. Indeed, to work is considered a disgrace. It is below the dignity of a white man to work, they think. Yet they must either work or starve, and so the white laborer is put on a par with the Negro slave and is thought no more of. The non-slaveholding portions of the South are destitute; the institution of slavery keeps them down.

The slaves themselves are as well informed in regard to most things as their proud and haughty masters. Beneath a dull and seemingly stupid appearance, the Negro slave often hides a cunning and quick witted nature. The slave can tell you more about the country than the generality of the whites. They know the distance from one place to another much better. There were but few slaves or whites in the vicinity of Stafford at that time.

But there is another reason for the backwardness of the South: their neglect of the free school system. They do not educate; they allow their children to grow up in ignorance. Schools are hardly known. I have not seen half a dozen school houses since we came into Dixie. Public schools do not exist there; very few of the people of the South can either read or write. Books are strangers to all save a few of the most wealthy. Newspapers are not abundant, the people know but little of what is going on outside of their own county. They know or care nothing about politics;

they are led blindly by their masters. A few wealthy slave owners rule, and the masses bow humbly to their will—the few dictate and the people obey.

Such is the condition of the South, and it is no wonder that New England, notwithstanding her rocks and barren hills, is far in advance. The people of New England are educated, industrious, and endowed with a spirit of enterprise. Their manners, their nature, and their institutions are all different, and they are far ahead in everything, notwithstanding the South has the advantage of soil and climate. But what are bright skies, a healthful climate, and a prolific soil without intellectual and moral culture?

While the system of Negro slavery exists in the South, as long as a single slave is bound in servitude, the South can never keep pace with the North. While the foot print of a single slave is imprinted on its soil, while a single shadow falls, it will be a curse to them, for its presence is a spell of evil. Slavery in time must die; it cannot live in America. The South may madly cling to it, yet it will be wrested from them. The march of progression and civilization is ever onward. It cannot stand still, and may it ever move onward until our country is freed from this curse forever.

While we were encamped at Stafford, the armies were resting, for with the battle of Fredericksburg, the campaign closed and the weary soldiers were allowed some peace. The thunder of battle had died away along the shores of the Potomac and the Rappahannock.

Willard and his compatriots were pleased to have a chance to see Abraham Lincoln. Many men and women of his generation would cherish a fleeting glimpse of or brief meeting with Lincoln their whole lives, telling stories about it to their children and grandchildren.

We had several reviews, one of which was by the president. It was a grand affair. The day was a bright, warm one in early Spring. The review ground was a large field or, rather, plain, on one side of which is a small hill, from the top of which a fine view could be had of every thing below. The whole corps was there; the divisions, brigades, and regiments were put into position; the batteries were planted; the banners were out; and every thing was in readiness for the president. We were kept waiting some time, but at last the clattering of hoofs up the road and the boom of cannon heralded his approach. Having [ridden] along the lines, he took his place on the little eminence, and the columns were put in motion and passed him in review. It must have been a fine sight, those long columns of men dressed in black and blue, with polished arms and glittering accouterments, marching in line and sweeping on past him, moving all at the same time. We were all glad to see the president.

While in camp the most rigid discipline was kept up—drills were resumed, and weekly and monthly inspections occurred regularly. We lived well. No army was ever clothed or fed better. We had a great deal of picket duty to do, and that, with our inspections and drills, took up about all of our time. But soldiers will grow tired of camp life and inactivity, and so it was with us. The same routine of duty grew irksome. The dull, unbroken monotony of camp life began to make us wish for a change.

The winter was not a severe one, yet the weather, though not cold, was unpleasant. Very little snow falls in Virginia, and it is never very cold in comparison to Wisconsin. Sometimes I almost wished for one of those winter storms, a real old northwester; but it was well that no such storms occurred and that the weather is generally mild. Well, the long, dull winter came to an end at last.

Spring came and the bleak rain storms became less frequent, and by and by, little green blades of grass and flower buds began to make their appearance among the dry leaves. At last the earliest spring flowers began to dot the brown hill sides, and birds, whose notes spoke of a warmer clime, were present, cheering nature with their songs.

We began to expect and look for active service, to a summer of hardships. We knew that hard work was to be done, that long marches were to be made and hard battles to be fought. The future lay before us darkened by toil and danger. We had heard much said in regard to peace, but to us, peace was far in the distance, and our only way to it seemed to lay almost, as it were, through "the valley of the shadow of death," dotted with graves and red with blood. It was not without feelings of dread that we looked forward to that summer campaign, yet it must be, and we would not shrink from it. We had had not a little experience in the hardships and dangers of war. Cedar Mountain, Antietam, and Pope's retreat had not been forgotten. But we did not make ourselves unhappy by anticipating the future; soldiers never do.

With the summer came the Chancellorsville campaign. More than 130,000 Union troops were on the north bank of the Rappahannock River and Lee's 60,000-strong Army of Northern Virginia faced them from the south bank. Although vastly outnumbered, the Confederates were riding the crest of numerous impressive victories, were full of confidence, and still occupied the position over which the inept Burnside had sacrificed so many men.

Joseph Hooker, newly appointed to succeed Burnside, was an aggressive general, and he was looking for an opportunity to prove himself against Lee. He developed an attack plan that is generally considered excellent. He would take most of his army up the Rappahannock River away from the strong Confederate defenses at Fredericksburg, cross at the upriver point, then cross the smaller Rapidan River to the south. He would then hit Lee's army on its left flank from the rear and roll it up, thus trapping Lee by the river and coming between him and Richmond. Meanwhile, the other segment of Hooker's large army would make a demonstration against the Confederate lines at Fredericksburg, holding the enemy there to prevent their moving upriver to contest the major crossing.

In the face of this threat, Lee took a gamble that proved to be brilliant, though had it failed, it would have seemed merely reckless. He divided his outnumbered army, leaving a small portion to defend Fredericksburg and taking the rest north to attack Hooker's principal contingent. This carried with it two risks: It gave him fewer men with which to face Hooker to the north, increasing the possibility of defeat there, and it might have led to the Fredericksburg garrison being overwhelmed and his right flank being rolled up.

On April 26 in the momentous year of 1863, Hooker gave orders for his army to move, which Willard's regiment, in the lead, did the next day. In high spirits, the men crossed the Rappahannock and Rapidan Rivers and arrived at Chancellorsville on April 30.

Well, the order came at last for us to prepare for a move, eight days' rations were issued to us and all our extra clothing turned in; in fact, every thing was put in readiness for a march. Several days passed, however, before the order to move came, but it came at last, and the camp was alive with preparations. All was activity until late that night, the night of the 26th. It was quite late before the camp was quiet, and when at last all was still, it was nearly morning. It was hardly light before we were called up again. After a scanty breakfast, we were ordered into line and at an early hour were under motion.

It was a morning fitting to the occasion. A dense fog prevailed, settling darkly down into the little valleys and ravines, growing lighter where it rested on the hill tops. It gave every thing a strange, weird, unearthly appearance. As we looked around us from our hill side encampments, watching the waves of mist go floating by, we (at least I) could see in the dim, uncertain appearance of every thing around a representation, as it were, of what was before us.

We were soon moving away, as we supposed, from our camp for ever. It seemed almost like leaving home; indeed, it had been our home, the only one the soldier has. But, of course, it must be, and no one seemed sad but marched away cheerfully as though it had not been to endure the greatest of hardships and to brave the most appalling danger. We knew that we were going out to meet a brave and desperate enemy, but *that* enemy was the enemy to our own *dear native land*, the enemy of all that had made our own states so much the superior of those *they* came to represent, the enemy of freedom and human progress every where. We knew that we were going to fight, that some of us would probably fall; the soldier thinks but very little of such things. It is his duty to go forward, and he is willing to take his chance with the others.

The column got fairly under way about eight o'clock and moved slowly forward, halting now and then while the pioneers repaired the road or built a bridge. The weather had been quite dry, yet the roads were in a very bad condition. The country roads in Virginia are the worst that I ever saw; there seems to be no end—or rather bottom—to the mud. The pike roads are of the very best kind, but the country roads are horrible. Our march that day was not a very long or hard one, as we only marched about ten miles.

The load we carried was none of the lightest, consisting of a gun and accouterments, sixty rounds of ammunition, our clothing and blankets, and eight days' rations, all weighing not less than fifty pounds. Notwithstanding their burdens, the men were cheerful, bearing up under their heavy loads and overcoming difficulties bravely, and pushing forward with the determination of keeping up. We halted for the night in the woods near Harwood Church.

A camp at night presents a scene of peculiar beauty and interest. Hundreds of fires are burning, around which groups of soldiers gather, seeming to dance like blue devils in the fire light, while thousands of white tents are gleaming among the trees. Around these camp fires, groups of soldiers gather to smoke and chat, talking of old times—the grand old times of the long, long ago. The soldier, however long he may have been in the service or however hardened he may be, does not forget the past. He cannot, it will come to him in memory at all times, it walks with him as he paces his lonely beat and will sit down with him at his camp fire, mingling in his thoughts by day and his dreams by night. The past is all the soldier has; the present is not his own, and the future lies darkly before him. He loves not to look forward, for his pathway lies across a crimson plain, gleaming with whitening bones and dotted with graves. The past, with its wealth of varied joys and sorrows, its hopes and bitter disappointments, are all that is left for him to think and dream of. He looks fondly back and lives again amid the scenes and joys of other and better years. Such dreams cheer him often in his most lonely hours.

We were up early in the morning, a little after sunrise, and resumed our march towards the Rappahannock. At Harwood Church the road forks, one branch running a little to the North to Rappahannock Station, the other straight on to Kelley's Ford. We took the latter. Harwood Church is one of those old fashioned structures which one often meets when traveling through the Old Dominion. It stands alone—no other building near—in a little grove by the wayside. The old church was a fine one, with its galleries and broad aisles, high pulpit, and sounding board. However, it has been deserted and is fast passing into decay. It has been sadly marred, its seats broken down and its walls disfigured and defaced. Rude characters and pictures of horses and men were drawn on the walls. One drawing, near the pulpit, exhibited more than ordinary skill. The picture represented a cavalry charge and was well executed. The drawings were mostly nothing but caricatures drawn by ruthless hands that scruple not at acts however low, even to the marring of a church or trampling of a grave.

Near the church, in an inclosure walled in by a stone fence, is the cemetery where the dead for many years have found a resting place. Some of the inscriptions on the stones date back as far as 1700. The place has been much neglected since the war, and weeds have taken the place of flowers. The wall has partly tumbled down, and horses and cattle have trampled on the graves. Several dozen new graves have been dug there—soldiers' graves! Federal and Confederate sleep there side by side in that deserted grave yard. The country around is very thinly settled. It stands there, that old church, alone in the midst of the tombs of the dead, a prey to the hands of the ruthless.

After passing Harwood Church, we came into a wild, half cultivated country very sparsely settled, and what few old buildings there were being inhabited by the slaves—"as Massa had run away."

Crossing the Rappahannock. That night (the 28th), we reached the banks of the Rappahannock at Kelley's Ford, and early on the morning of the 29th, we crossed to the south bank. A part of the 11th Corps had already crossed and were encamped about a mile from the river in the woods. The 11th Corps, was a fine, large corps numbering not less than twenty thousand and was commanded by General Howard. Many of the regiments in that corps were new ones, mostly all composed of Germans.

It was a warm morning, that of the 29th, one of spring's bright, lustrous mornings such as come but once a year. After crossing the river, we took the advance, passing on through the woods past the 11th Corps. We (the 3rd Wisconsin) were deployed as skirmishers on the right of the road, the old 27th Indiana on the left. We had gone but a little distance before we were fired at by the Rebel pickets. Some slight skirmishing took place, but none of any importance until we arrived on the banks of the Rapidan. Quite a number of prisoners were taken on the way, however, by our cavalry, which cut off some pickets and videttes.

All that day we pushed forward through the woods and brush, over rocks and logs, which made it almost impossible to keep ahead of the column moving along the road, the flanks of which we were out to cover. The road was a crooked one, and when the head of the column turned to the right or left, those on the extremes of the skirmish line would have to travel very fast to keep up their position in the line. The distance from the Rappahannock to the Rapidan the way we went was about fourteen miles. This distance we in the skirmish line had to travel through brush, up steep rock hills, through muddy fields, over fences, through marshes and swamps, at the same time carrying our heavy knapsacks and being ready for an engagement at any moment.

Such kind of marching is very hard, but where there is danger ahead and one is expecting to meet the enemy, see guns flashing from the trees and bushes before him, and hear a bullet or perhaps a dozen of them go hissing by, or take effect in his person, under such circumstances skirmishing is not only tiresome but very disagreeable; yet there is a kind of pleasurable excitement about it, after all. One is not half as timid after he begins to skirmish as he was before the guns began to crack around him. After he once begins, after he fires the first shot, his timidity is gone. Such is the case with a truly brave soldier. The man who has no fears before he goes into battle is very apt to experience some thing of the kind

when he comes to realize the real danger. To fear danger is natural—
indeed, it is brutish not to. The truly brave man is not the one who feels
no fear in anticipation of danger, but is he whose noble nature overcomes
that fear and enables him to meet coolly what the boasting braggart would
shrink from, although ever so brave while danger was at a distance.

We had advanced nearly to the Rapidan when our cavalry, a few of
which were in advance, brought back the report that a strong force of the
enemy were at the ford across the river. In fact, a few shots had been
exchanged, and one of the cavalry had been killed and another wounded.

We were again pushed forward, advancing rapidly through the woods.
A fight was now expected, and every man was in his place. The column in
the road moved slowly on with closed ranks, while we were deployed as
skirmishers (as we had been all day) in advance of them. Passing through
the woods, we came suddenly out into an open field along the banks of
the river. We had been gradually quickening our pace until we were
almost on the run, and when we reached the field we started off at a
double quick across it. The gray backs were there on the opposite bank
and gave the skirmishers a sharp volley as they came across the field.

The Rebels were taken by surprise, and our movements were so rapid
that they were unable to make their escape, although a river was between
them and us. They were not expecting infantry, and they supposed the
cavalry to be only a small scouting party. They were at work building a
bridge across the river, and all together, the workmen and guards, they
numbered a little over a hundred men. They had made good calculations
for defense but very poor ones for a retreat. They had a high bank to shelter them from our side of the river, and a few men might have held the
ford against a large force. The river is narrow, not over seven hundred
yards wide. They had the advantage of us in position, as we had nothing
whatever to shelter us. But they did not choose to fight, and to run away
was out of the question. A few tried the latter plan, however, and paid for
it with their lives, as every one that attempted it was shot down. It seemed
hard to shoot men who were running, but they were enemies. After a few
shots had been exchanged, they threw down their arms and came over to
us. We took at that place ninety-six prisoners, among which was one captain, two lieutenants, and a major.

After the skirmish we forded the river and went into camp on the
south bank. We were so fortunate as not to have a single man killed or
wounded out of the regiment. Some of the boys went over in advance and

captured some fellows who were hiding in the buildings near the ford. The river was not deep, although quite difficult to ford, as it was very rapid and the bottom very rough. The ford is at what is called Germanna Mills and is about eight or ten miles from Raccoon Ford, which is about seven miles from Rapidan Station at the foot of Cedar Mountain, near which the battle of Cedar Mountain was fought under Banks, August the 9th/62.

The country along the banks of the Rapidan on the north side is generally very level with but few hills. The timber is principally pine and cedar and the place is almost uninhabited. The buildings known as Germanna Mills are a few old, brown buildings, two of which are grist mills. The stone in these mills has long since ceased to revolve and the old water wheels are standing still. On the south bank there are a few log farm houses, and a narrow strip of land is cultivated along the river bank. Back from this is a forest of pines, which extends for miles almost unbroken. Culpeper is a small city, or what is called a city in Virginia. It is about fifteen or twenty miles north west of Germanna Mills. After having crossed the river, we were getting in the rear of the Rebel army, almost west of Fredericksburg, between it and Culpeper.

The 30th we pushed on in a southerly direction, following an old plank road said to run from Culpeper to Gordonsville, joining one that runs from Fredericksburg. The country along the route was all wild, a wilderness. There are but very few buildings between Germanna Mills and Chancellorsville, a distance of about fourteen miles. We reached Chancellorsville late in the afternoon and encamped on what was shortly after one of the bloodiest battle fields of the war.

The second division had the advance. They met with no opposition, for the enemy seemed to be unaware that an army was massing in his rear. Chancellorsville is about twelve miles west of Fredericksburg and five south, and is set where an old plank road and a turnpike meet. Our movements would bring us almost between Richmond and the Confederate army. The pike road was the one Lee would have to take if he came out of his works to fight us, and here General Hooker prepared to meet and fight him or compel him to evacuate his strong hold on the heights of Fredericksburg.

The Wilderness. This country in the rear of Fredericksburg right well deserves the name of "The Wilderness," for it is a wilderness in every sense of the word—one of deep, interminable forests of pine—not the tall, noble pines of the North, but low, stunted scrubs, very thick, with limbs reaching to the ground. These pines are of a second growth and so thick together that it is almost impossible to force one's way through among them. This pine wilderness is interspersed with little groves of scrub oak not less dense than the pine. This wilderness is almost unbroken. There is here and there a small lot, hardly worthy of the name of farm, with an old log hut or something of the kind, and just enough of the forest cut down to let the light of day down.

Near Chancellorsville, in the midst of the Wilderness, surrounded with a deep, dark, dense forest, is a little stone church known as Wilderness Church. It is a small building, and I have been informed that it was built by the government for the Indians. It was to this church that the brave but unfortunate Gen. Stonewall Jackson was taken after he was wounded at Chancellorsville. Several other Confederate officers were taken there, some of whom died and were buried in the little secluded grave yard. How sad to think that the horrors of war should penetrate even into the midst of a wilderness, and a church known only to the hermits should become the receptacle of ghastly horrors and the pale, death stricken victims of a cruel war—the bitter fruits of an unholy ambition.

Chancellorsville consists, or did consist, of some half a dozen buildings, the major part of which had fallen into ruins. One large brick house still remained; this was what is known as the Chancellor Mansion. This is now also a black and shapeless mass of rubbish. It stood in the centre of a small plain, or, rather, clearing in the forest. North, west, and south of the mansion is the Wilderness; to the east is Fredericksburg. The road to Banks's and U.S. Fords is a dirt one running nearly north east. These fords are about eight miles from Chancellorsville.

We arrived at Chancellorsville in the afternoon of the 30th and bivouacked for the night near the Chancellor House, a short distance to the west of it between the plank and pike roads. The pioneers were at once set at work cutting down the timber around the camp, and steps were taken to fortify the position. Every ax in the corps was in motion, and until long after midnight the ring and clatter of axes and the crash of falling timber could be heard all along the line. Our line faced towards the pike road—the direction which the enemy was supposed to be coming from. The 11th Corps was on the extreme right, reaching far into the Wilderness.

On the 1st of May we were mustered for pay. It was a warm, bright morning, such as the May Day celebrator loves. Every thing as yet was quiet, not a shot had been fired. I never saw a brighter or more peaceful morning; but it was only the calm before the storm. The muster that morning was the last for many a soldier in our regiment, for before another muster day came round, many had gone to answer at that last great roll call, death's muster above.

On the morning of May 1, while Lee's army moved westward from Fredericks-burg, Union troops were initially sent on the offensive in accordance with Hooker's plan. The 3rd Wisconsin, now in Williams's division of Slocum's XII Corps, was sent to secure Banks's Ford, a river crossing point located between Fredericksburg and the farther crossing that most Union units had used. The regiment's assignment was to push back the enemy so that Union reserve artillery could cross over to south of the river.

At this moment, Hooker had a fatal lapse of courage and, over the fervent protests of his subordinate generals, decided that he had to shelve his attack plans and switch over to the defensive. He gave as reasons that he could not maneuver in the Wilderness and didn't know where the Confederates were. Had he kept to his plan, the disasters that overtook him would not have occurred (or possibly a different set of misfortunes would have befallen him). Instead, he chose to consolidate his forces at the edge of the Wilderness in a clearing just east of the Chancellor house at Chancellorsville, where they awaited events.

Williams's division was ordered to fortify a position near the house and just south of the pike. Then Willard's unit and another regiment were sent forward across an open field toward some woods and a stream called Lewis's Run to establish a skirmish line. There they ran into the Confederate advance, which was already in the woods. A sharp fight ensued, after which the Rebels withdrew. The 3rd Wisconsin's lieutenant colonel, John W. Scott, was killed, as were four men of the other Union regiment. This ended the 3rd's fighting on May 1, and the men built a breastwork. Interestingly, the identity of the second regiment is the subject of some disagreement: Willard claims it was the 20th Connecticut; Bryant, the 27th Indiana; and Stephen Sears, in his recent book, Chancellorsville, *the 123rd New York.*

We had hardly finished mustering before we were ordered to fall in. The 1st Division was now in motion, moving down towards Banks's Ford, which was held by the enemy. We (the 3rd Wisconsin) were deployed as skirmishers. A few cannon shots and a little skirmishing was all the amusement we had at that time. We drove the Confederates from the ford, however, and opened communications with the main army. We returned to the Chancellor Mansion but did not stop at our encampment, for we had more work on hand that afternoon. The whole division, except the 20th Connecticut and the 3rd Wisconsin, went into camp again.

Between the plank road and the pike, there was a ravine. The roads and ravine run east and west, or nearly so, at that place. The 20th Connecticut had followed the ravine up along its north bank. We pushed rapidly up the plank road for a mile west of the Chancellor House and then turned southward, coming in on the right of the 20th, which was skirmishing with the enemy. The Rebels were attempting to ascertain our position, and a brigade of them were endeavoring to cross to the north bank of the ravine. At the place where we joined the 20th, there was a large, open field in which there was an old log house and a small orchard. The ravine was in the edge of the woods beyond the field. The land on the south bank was somewhat higher than on the north, and thickly wooded. This gave the Rebels much the advantage, which they did not fail to improve. The movement was being made to flank the 20th just as we came into the field a little distance to their right.

A brisk skirmish now began, the enemy having the advantage of the ground, being covered by a thick forest. The colonel of the 20th had thrown his skirmishers across the ravine into the woods beyond, driving back the Rebel skirmishers; but they were reinforced and recovered the ground, driving our men across the ravine. Their advance was quickly followed by a larger force, and a Rebel line of battle advanced and poured a withering fire into the 20th. We were just getting into position and also received a severe fire, most of the shots, however, going over our heads.

The 20th at first broke but rallied again and returned the fire with spirit. We were not in a position to do much execution. Our lieutenant colonel was killed at the first fire, and some wounded. We had thrown down a rail fence, which we used for a breast work. The firing grew more severe, and at last the 20th gave way and fell back into the timber. We were then ordered back out of range. The Rebels did not follow, but just at night began to throw shells over into the timber. Three pieces of artillery from our side opened, and a very lively cannonade was carried on for a few moments. It did not last long, however, and at sunset all was quiet again. The enemy had been repulsed, as they did not gain a footing on the north bank of the ravine, and the troops were not disturbed in their work on the fortifications, which were being built a short distance in the rear. We were only an advance guard or picket.

During the night we built a breast work of rails, while in the rear, along the whole line, formidable works were being erected. Long before day light we were up and in line, expecting an attack, but none was made. Our skirmishers during the night had advanced to the ravine and hid themselves. Sharp shooters were also posted. A few shots were exchanged as a greeting.

Learning from Stuart's cavalry that the far right of the Union line was unsupported and dangling ("in the air," as he put it), Lee saw an opportunity and had the boldness to seize it. He met with Stonewall Jackson on the night of May 1, in what was to be their last council of war, and determined on a daring and dangerous maneuver. Lee would again divide his forces, leaving some to hold the front opposite Hooker's advanced troops, and send Jackson's 26,000 men on a fourteen-mile march west across the entire length of the Union line on over to its right, there to attack it from the far flank. This movement took place on May 2, in broad daylight and in full sight of the Yankee enemy. There was ample time for the Union forces to intercept Jackson and perhaps inflict a major defeat, but the Confederates' march was permitted to continue unmolested. When Jackson's men reached their goal and then attacked Hooker's right later in the afternoon, it came as a surprise to those who were assaulted, despite the fact that thousands of their comrades (including Willard's 3rd Wisconsin) had seen Jackson's troops on the march. Gen. O. O. Howard, whose XI Corps held the Union far right, admitted in his report to having been apprised of Jackson's movements but excused his inaction by saying he was hampered by the Wilderness and lack of precise information. This failure to intercept Jackson was quite likely the most serious—and inexplicable— Union blunder of the war.

Howard's corps was on the far right of Hooker's army, and the XII Corps, to which the 3rd Wisconsin belonged, occupied the position next to them. While Howard's men were cooking their dinner, Jackson attacked them with everything he had. The XI Corps was crushed and sent reeling back for miles in panic and confusion. The Confederate strategy had been completely successful.

The 3rd Wisconsin heard the incredible commotion and was soon brought into a line of battle near the Chancellor house just south of the turnpike. Its orders were to stop the rout of the XI Corps, as its troops came running back through the

woods to the clearing by the house, and to meet the Confederates who were pursu-
ing them. Meanwhile, night had fallen, and Jackson's forces, which had become
disorganized during the pursuit, ceased their forward movement.

Jackson wanted his men to follow up the advantage without waiting for day-
light and, while reconnoitering at the front, got in advance of his position. He and
his party were mistaken for Yankees by his own men and were fired upon. A num-
ber of them were killed and wounded, including Jackson himself, who was badly
injured. His arm was amputated, and he was unable to further lead his forces. They
were assigned to General Stuart in his absence.

Before Stuart assumed command, Jackson's forces came charging out of the dark
woods, giving the Rebel yell, and made a nighttime attack on the 3rd Wisconsin
and other nearby regiments on the Union right, who were now stationed west of the
Chancellor house. The following is a firsthand report on what it was like to be
attacked by Stonewall Jackson's foot cavalry.

This was Saturday the 2nd of May. The 11th Corps held the extreme
right, the 12th next to it. The other corps were not yet in any position.
The 3rd and 5th were on the ground, ready to form a line wherever
needed. The 5th was near the river, the 3rd near the Chancellor House.
The 6th had not yet crossed and were in front of Fredericksburg, the 1st
was also on the [north] bank of the Rappahannock. The 6th and
1st were to attack in front. All these preparations had been made, and
every thing seemed to be working finely. The forenoon of the 2nd
passed away more quietly than we had expected. About noon, some of the
sharp shooters from the 3rd Corps crossed the ravine and captured quite a
number of Rebels.

About noon a column of Rebel troops could be seen with a glass
moving along the pike westward. For three hours this column could be
seen, and it was well known what it meant. They were allowed to go on
unmolested, save now and then a shell from a single gun from our side. I
cannot see why so large a force was allowed to go so far to the right, and
the 11th Corps not put into position to receive them. It seems strange that
General Howard should lie still and allow an army to pass almost around to
the rear of him and surprise him. This has always looked very strange to
me, and I have never heard or read any explanation in regard to it.

About four o'clock in the afternoon, a portion of the 3rd Corps and
the 1st Division of the 12th were put in motion towards the pike road.
We had the extreme left, and the 3rd Regiment as usual was deployed as

skirmishers. We crossed the open field and over the ravine into the Wilderness. During the day the woods had been burning, having been set fire to by the bursting of shells and by the Rebels, in order to hide their movements. The woods were full of smoke, and the ground was charred and blackened.

Severe skirmishing began on the right and soon extended along the whole line except directly in our vicinity. We did not fire a shot. A little to the right of us, quite a fight took place, and a portion of the first brigade was repulsed. But we were pushing our way rapidly toward the pike; indeed, we had almost reached a position on the enemy's flank. This would have cut the Rebel army in two, and Jackson would have had to turn around and protect his rear.

But while we were pushing our way through their lines, Howard was idle. The Rebel general, the indomitable Jackson, had marched fast and far, and before Howard was aware of it, his rifles were ringing almost in his rear. It was nearly sunset, and we were about to charge on a Rebel battery which we had advanced upon to within less than five hundred yards, unbeknown to them, and in a few moments more would have been through their lines and have gained the point in view.

Just then came a tremendous uproar in the rear, the booming of a score of cannon, the bursting of shells, and the roar of musketry, mingled with the most terrific yells. The Rebels had burst like a thunder bolt upon Howard, crashing through his lines almost before he was aware of their presence. His troops gave way and fled panic stricken towards the river. The whole right wing was swept away and fled in one wild and shameful rout.

We as skirmishers were far in advance of the troops massed in the rear. As soon as the firing began in the rear and the 11th Corps had been routed, the whole force under Sickles was ordered back to prevent it from being surrounded and captured. By some mistake we did not receive the order until all the other regiments on the right and rear had gone, thus leaving us alone in the midst of the Rebel army. It was long after dark, and we were still in the Wilderness waiting for orders. The uproar and thunder of conflict in the rear had died away, but the batteries in front of us kept up a rapid firing over our heads, and the red flashes from the cannons' mouths seemed to light up the forests with a wild purple glare. It was a most dismal place, there in that black forest, dark and gloomy, lit up only by the bursting of the fiery shells and the flashing of the red mouthed cannon. Silently but anxiously we waited there until at last the order came for us slowly to retire. This order should have reached us half an hour before, but by some mistake it did not. It was by the narrowest chance that we managed to make our way out. The Rebels must have seen us as we passed them but probably supposed us to be some of their own men. When we, after wandering for a long time, at last joined our brigade, we found a part of our corps in position and other regiments forming in their places.

There was every indication of the rout and panic which had occurred. Wagons overturned, broken down gun carriages, loose horses and mules galloping here and there, squads of men gathered, regiments marching and counter marching, batteries galloping across the fields, the shrill tones of the bugle, and the loud commands of the officers. Indeed, the whole line of battle had been changed. Instead of facing southward, we were looking westward for the enemy to come down the very plank road which we came on from the Rapidan. Before we had got into position or even out of the Wilderness, this part of the conflict was over, so sudden, so brief and resistless had been the wild onset, and a deep, strange silence followed, unbroken by a single gun.

In a short time a new line of battle was formed, the men moving rapidly into position, noiselessly, shadow like, taking their place without a word. The night was calm and still, the sky serene and star gemmed, and the moon in the fullness of her bright and lustrous beauty smiled softly over the Wilderness, as though within these dark and gloomy woods death was not already reaping one of the richest harvests ever gathered on the red field of battle.

Up to eleven o'clock, that strange, almost oppressive silence continued. This seemed strange, for if the advantage gained by Jackson had been followed up as he generally follows up an advantage, nothing could have checked him; for before the 12th or 3rd Corps could have got into position, he would have burst upon them with his wild, drunken, yelling legions. And with Lee thundering on our left, Longstreet in front, and we in confusion with our right wing swept away, nothing could have saved us from the most fearful carnage and probable rout, which would have ended in almost complete annihilation or capture. But he whose presence seemed almost a guaranty of victory had fallen, and the charm was broken, the spell was gone.

Charge and Repulse of Jackson's Corps. About 11 o'clock the silence was broken. Our skirmishers were out in front, and the main force was quietly laying down in the rear. Many of the men were asleep. The line of battle was formed partially in a half circle, the apex being near and a little west of the Chancellor Mansion, which, as I have said, stands nearly in the centre of a small plain surrounded by the Wilderness. We were in line just in the edge of the woods west of the plain. This was the new position Saturday night.

We had begun to think that the fighting was all over for that day, when suddenly—

> There rose so wild a yell
> As though all the fiends from Heaven that fell
> Had pealed the banner cry of hell,

and the rebel legions came charging down through those dark woods, yelling like very demons; not a round, full, manly cheer, but shrill and sharp, prolonged and continuous, rising and falling, growing faint sometimes and dying away, and then bursting out again louder and more shrill than before. The charge, although a furious one, sudden and unexpected, was a failure, for they failed to make the slightest impression on our line. Their fierce and fiery onset was met by cool determination. Their yells stuck in their throats, and they went back more silently, and as rapidly, as they came. They did not come within a hundred yards of our line, but broke at the first fire.

One who has never witnessed such a sight cannot form a correct idea of an artillery and musketry fire by night. Our artillery was posted on a slight ridge about the centre of the Chancellorsville plain. When the Rebels began to yell, three batteries on this ridge opened on them, throwing their shells over our heads into the woods beyond. Long, lurid tongues of flame leaped from the guns on the ridge, and the shells could be tracked through space by the burning fuse, which gave them the appearance of liquid balls of fire. And when they burst, rings and circles of flame and fiery sparkles illuminate a space of several yards around. Looking back through the woods, it seemed as though that ridge was bursting into one sheet of flame, and a huge, white volume of smoke rolled up into the sky like clouds.

The musketry firing was not much less grand. When the Rebels had advanced to within a short distance of us, we opened on them all along the line simultaneously. Not a word was said, not a shot fired until the Rebel line came sweeping up in full view, firing and yelling as they came. When the word was given, every man sprang to his feet, and one long line of flame blazed along the line, fringing the edge of the woods with fire. The Rebels retired, the firing ceased, and all was still as before. The remainder of the night I spent in front of the line of battle, as a portion of Co. G was sent out as skirmishers. Several killed and wounded were brought within our lines.

While the firing was going on, when the Rebels charged on us, another regiment was in line behind us a few rods distant and either mistook us for the enemy firing at them, or else some of the careless ones foolishly attempted to fire over our heads, and many of their bullets came whistling through our ranks, which put us between two fires, one in front and another in the rear. This was so sudden and unexpected that we thought the Rebels had got behind us. Quite a number of the regiment were wounded and some killed.

The stillness deepened with the night until not a sound broke the deep silence of the Wilderness. Darkness, danger, and loneliness seemed to be concentrating there in that gloomy forest. We all knew that the morning would bring with it a renewal of the engagement, that the morrow would be a day of strife, of bloodshed and death. Many a soldier lay down to sleep his last sleep on earth that night and looked for the last time on the moon and stars that had smiled for him in other and better years. The soldier's heart was with those he loved. His thoughts were of them, and if he slept, he dreamed of them.

But although the men knew their danger, they looked calmly on the dark prospects of the next day. There were no signs of fear or nervousness. The very magnitude of the danger and the greatness of the occasion seemed to exalt the feelings above the reach of fear. There in the shade of that gloomy forest, with the fierce enemies of their country around them, thousands of soldiers brave and true consecrated their hearts to their country and their God; and the stars seemed to look down from above to witness their solemn covenant; and the forests seemed to whisper—amen.

The Confederates resumed the attack on May 3, and the day saw furious fighting. Although they were thrown back by Ruger's Brigade, which was composed of the 3rd Wisconsin and other regiments, the Southerners were more successful elsewhere. After suffering significant losses and running out of ammunition, Ruger's men were relieved by fresh troops, and they passed to the rear amid the ongoing dangers of battle.

The few hours remaining between midnight and dawn soon passed, and the morning came, heralded by streamers of light flashing up in the east. Never dawned there a more calm or lovelier Sabbath morning than that of the 3rd of May, the day of the battle of Chancellorsville, peaceful as Eden's garden ere the fall of man, and the birds of early spring had begun to sing their morning songs. But this calm was soon to be rudely broken, and the thunder of artillery and the clash of arms to take the place of nature's quiet and the songs of birds.

The men were silent and grave, but not nervous or excited. They talked in low tones and moved about slowly and quietly, gun in hand, ready to take their places in the ranks at an instant's notice. We knew that for some of us the light of another morning would not dawn again on earth, that death's mark burned on many a brow.

Scarcely had the light of day begun to penetrate the depths of that gloomy wilderness before the fight began on the left of us. Our pickets or skirmishers were driven in about five o'clock, and in less than half an hour the battle was raging in all its fury. Some troops that were in advance of the line on our left were quickly driven in, and the Rebels, supposing that they had broken our line of battle, began to yell like a legion of fiends. They had not appeared in front of us.

The firing on the left grew sharper, rapidly working up the line, and the yelling grew louder and nearer, until suddenly the Rebel line of battle appeared in front of us and came sweeping down through the woods, making the Wilderness ring with their yells. As soon as they appeared in sight, we opened on them and continued to load and fire for some time. They came very near us, to within less than fifty yards, where they began to waver and finally broke, scattered, and ran back through the woods in wild disorder. The charge was a brave one, however, and when they began to fire, their volleys were fearful ones. In less than ten minutes after the firing began, the woods were filled with smoke. They fared no better along the other portions of the line but were repulsed at every point.

We advanced, firing into the retreating enemy, until we met another line advancing to their support. Then began another struggle, longer and fiercer than the first. We stood there for a long time, loading and firing. Their line wavered several times, at last was broken and shivered, the men scattering back in confusion. We followed again, passing on over the dead and wounded that were thickly scattered over the ground. As before, dense columns of smoke rolled through the forests. The Rebel lines could not be seen, and we only knew that they were there by the flashing of their guns and whistling of bullets.

We advanced again and found another line drawn up to oppose us. Our ammunition was now nearly gone, only a few more rounds remained, some had none. We exchanged a few shots with them, and then the order came to—*Charge*. For a moment the ringing of steel was heard along the line, then, with fixed bayonets, we rushed on through the smoky woods. The enemy did not receive us but broke and fled. We were again masters of the field. But our ranks were sadly thinned and our ammunition was gone.

Just then a line came up behind us and we were relieved. We had been in the engagement over two hours and had driven the enemy for nearly half a mile back into the wilderness. Our loss, though severe, was not near as great as one would have supposed it would have been. We lost one hundred and eight men in killed and wounded, being over a third of our number. The ground all through the woods was thickly strewn with the wounded and dead. We fell back to the edge of the woods, helping our wounded back with us. The roar of conflict still went on in front; we could hear it now that we were out of it. The cannonading was most severe, and the air seemed alive with hissing, screaming, bursting shells. A thick, white cloud of smoke hung over the plain, wrapping gun and gunner in its sulphurous folds, giving them the weird, shadowy appearance of spectres, seen by the flashing of the guns.

In order to get to the rear, we had to follow a ravine running between our batteries and the woods we had just come out of. At last we got around to the rear, but here we found ourselves in danger of being blown out of existence by shells that were dropping on all sides, tearing up the ground here and there, bursting above, behind, in front of and all around us. No one was hurt out of our regiment, but a large number from other regiments were. Half a dozen men would be torn to pieces by one shell. The plain was literally covered by dead horses, dead men, and wounded ones that had crawled or been helped back from the field. It is a miracle, almost, that more men are not hurt on such an occasion. It seems to me now, as I look back over those scenes, as though it would be an impossibility to live through such dangers.

Willard again shows his passion to observe the events swirling around him. Having been in combat for hours, and then moved back to a place of comparative security behind the Chancellor house, he asked for and received special permission to return to the scene of strife. He paints an exciting and vibrant portrait of the chaos at the Chancellor house as the battle peaked and Confederate troops poured into the clearing, and describes the responses of Hooker and Slocum as they surveyed the scene.

Having crossed the plain to the east, or rear, of the Chancellor House, we found another line of battle drawn up behind breast works. This had been thrown up during the night. The troops that had relieved us in the wood were compelled to fall back, the enemy following them closely, yelling most furiously. The regiment halted in rear of the troops behind the breast work, and being anxious to see what was going on in front, I got permission to go back to the Chancellor House. The scene there was one of wild confusion and excitement. The building had been used during the night and morning as a hospital, and a large number of wounded had been taken there. These were being moved away, as the Rebels were shelling in that direction most furiously, several shells having already gone through the house, and it was on fire and the walls would soon tumble in, burying all within a mass of fiery ruins. What a fearful situation for those poor, bleeding, helpless fellows to be in. Men with limbs shot away, legs and arms broken, torn with bullets, there in that burning building with shot and shell crashing among them.

Generals were there, and their orderlies and aides were galloping here and there over the field. General Hooker was there, fearlessly riding in the very thickest of the storm, his eyes flashing and his cheeks glowing with animation. General Slocum was there, sitting on his horse, coolly and quietly watching the progress of the battle, never heeding the missiles of death that rained around him.

The firing in the wood came nearer, and the yells of the Rebel hordes grew louder and more demon like, until at last our men were seen coming back out of the woods, slowly loading and firing as they retreated, until they reached the open field, when they ceased firing and came rapidly back behind the batteries along the ridge. Here they went into line again.

Meanwhile, our artillery had been playing on the Rebels in a most fearful manner. The ridge was black with cannons, which belched a perfect tempest of iron hail among them, mowing them down by hundreds. Yet they came on to within a few yards of the guns, when their lines began to waver and at last broke, falling back across the plain, seeking the woods for shelter. They made two other attempts to charge (and capture) those guns but failed, and retired, leaving that field thickly strewn with their wounded and dead. They, however, succeeded in forcing our batteries to retire by means of their sharp shooters, who, concealing themselves in the woods nearby, picked off every gunner that dared to show himself. Towards night the Rebels attempted to make a flank movement but were repulsed, and with the setting of the sun the battle ended. A few cannon shots boomed along the line, then all was still. Thus ended that memorable Sabbath day, the 3rd of May.

Hooker was wounded shortly after Willard saw him and was unable to lead the army. His subordinates lacked the leadership to go on the offensive. They retreated toward the Rappahannock River from the battlefield and on May 6 withdrew to its north side. The Chancellorsville campaign was over, and the Union had suffered another painful defeat. The 3rd Wisconsin had lost nineteen men killed, seventy-three wounded, and eight captured or missing.

That night the Rebels held the battle field. They had won a victory, but it was one most dearly bought by them. The laurels they won withered on their brows, and if there was rejoicing in the South over that victory, it must have been mingled with many tears and bitter sorrow for the dead—the many dead and maimed that fell on that field—the Plains of Chancellorsville.

We remained in the woods east of Chancellorsville until after dark, when we were sent to the extreme left of the line which rested on the river. Here we remained until the morning of the 6th. In the meantime, the 1st Corps had crossed the river and captured the Heights of Fredericksburg. The 6th Corps had also crossed and occupied the heights. The 1st Corps recrossed and joined us at Chancellorsville. After Hooker's reverse, Lee turned his attention upon Sedgwick and compelled him to retreat across the river.

While this had been going on, Stoneman had made his great raid in the rear of the Rebel army, cutting their communications and destroying their means of obtaining supplies. But Hooker could not remain to take advantage of this as he intended to do, on account of a tremendous storm, which swept away some of the rail road bridges between Falmouth and Aquia Landing. This deprived him of his supplies and compelled him to retreat. The Rappahannock rose rapidly, the pontoons were in danger of being carried away, and our eight days' rations were gone. It had rained considerably, but the afternoon of the 5th there came up one of the most furious storms of the whole season.

Early in the evening, the artillery moved off, and we had orders to be ready to march at a moment's notice. All that night we stood around in groups, shivering in the cold, anxiously waiting to move out since such must be the case. All the other troops went out, and we were left in the works alone. We remained there until long after day light, expecting the Rebels to discover the movement and attempt to capture us; but none made their appearance. Our pickets were called in, and about 7:00 A.M. we started for the river or, rather, the ford, which was about a mile and a half distant. On arriving, we found that a portion of the army had not yet crossed, owing to the delay in taking one of the three bridges, which was necessary in order to lengthen out the other two, as the river was so high that the bridges did not reach the shore. As soon as we arrived at the ford, we had orders to return to the breast works again, so we started back, nearly the whole regiment being deployed as skirmishers on the left and right of the road.

We thought, as we pushed through the woods, to meet the Rebel skirmishers every instant. But none had yet ventured to come near our lines, and we took possession of the deserted works with no opposition. We expected to see them come down on us, as they had had time enough to have discovered the fact that the army was retreating, and had they attacked the troops while they were crossing the river, there would have been danger of a panic among the men and a great slaughter would perhaps have been the result. None were in sight even, and though we remained there an hour, we were not disturbed.

We had been exposed during the whole night to a cold, drenching rain and were chilled through, and our guns, many of them, were in an unserviceable condition. If we had been attacked, we were to fight and detain the enemy as long as we could, and then surrender as prisoners of war. That was not a very pleasant situation to be in, and the hour we remained there in those breast works was a long one to us.

The companies the farthest back began to move out very slowly. Others followed, and at last we in the extreme front withdrew, and the breast works were again deserted. We were not a moment too soon, as the

Rebel skirmishers closed in behind us. Ten minutes later and we should have been cut off from the ford. We reached the river, however, and crossed, and at once began our march back again towards Stafford Court House, where we arrived just after dark, having traveled twenty-two miles that day over one of the worst roads imaginable.

The weather was quite cold, and having no overcoats or blankets, and being wet through to the skin, we suffered very much. It rained all day and all night, and with no shelter whatever, one can readily imagine that the night of the 6th of May was not passed in a very pleasant manner. A strong picket was sent out that night on the Kelley's Ford Road, and I was among the elected. The night was extremely dark, and we lost our way. Such grand tumbling over logs and stumps and scrambling through brush and treetops (much of the timber having been cut down and the bodies used for wood) and such tall praying would have been very amusing for one not of the afflicted who could have been a looker on.

It was nearly midnight before we got out on the road to the place designated. That was a miserable night for us—cold, wet, and hungry. We had not a mouthful to eat and had not had for twenty-four hours. When we left the breast works Saturday evening and went down into the woods, we left our knapsacks, and as the Rebels soon after came in there (having routed the 11th Corps), they fell into the hands of the enemy. Thus we were left without tents or blankets.

Those nine days were the hardest that we ever experienced. That campaign was a terrible one for both sides, the losses were severe, and when all was over, every thing as far as the situation was concerned remained unchanged. The two armies stood as before on the banks of the Rappahannock watching one another. Although we deeply regretted the result of the campaign, yet it was of little or no advantage to the enemy. The Wilderness is a dreadful place, and we were glad to get out of it, though it would have pleased us more to have beaten the Rebels and gone out on the Richmond side.

The wounded suffered most cruelly after the battle, being left on the field uncared for by anyone for several days. During Sunday night the woods were all ablaze with fire, and many a poor wounded soldier, unable to help himself, was burned to death. When those who were sent for that purpose went to gather up the wounded, they found in the woods hundreds of charred and blackened human bodies, men who, wounded and helpless, had been overtaken by the cruel fire!

Stonewall Jackson died on May 10—a serious blow to the Confederates. Not only was he venerated in the South for his victories, but there was something about the flair and extent of his successes that made him a subject of interest in the North as well. Photographs of him in his prewar Federal uniform were reproduced for sale in the North, and his exploits were followed closely there. Many have considered him the war's finest tactical general. It might truly be said that he was an all-American hero, the first to emerge from the war. His death elevated him to a legend, and he remains so after more than a century.

Willard devotes a special section to Jackson's death. He does not gloat over his death or vilify Jackson. Instead, he treats the subject tenderly. For a Union soldier, in the winter of 1863–64, to write this is little short of remarkable and illustrates an odd kind of affection.

After the Battle. The battle was over, the thunder of conflict had died along the banks of the Rappahannock, and the smoke of battle that had gathered over the Wilderness had rolled away. The little church there was one of the Confederate hospitals. Its deep silence was broken by the death wail of men in mortal anguish. There, among the secluded and lowly graves in its grave yard, hundreds of brave men died, and the Wilderness became one vast receptacle for the dead. In that little church, among the stricken ones, was one of high and noble presence whose name had almost ever been the precursor of victory. He was dying, but no sigh of pain or murmurings came from his pale lips. Death was all around him, but he heeded not its presence. It laid its pallid hand on his brow, but he shrank not from its touch. His was a spirit brave and true, and he was appalled not at the approach of death. The night had nearly passed, the moon had gone down, and darkness deep and profound had settled upon the Wilderness. A storm was approaching, the stars were lost in clouds, and the low muttering of distant thunder came rolling up from the west.

The dying soldier's eyes kindled and flashed as he heard the thunder tones, mistaking it for the language of battle. "Good by," he said, "I shall be with you on the battle field no more"; and amid the crashing of the tempest, the bellowing of the thunder, the spirit of the noble soldier took its flight, and the lurid lightning flash gleaming through the Wilderness lit up death's dark passage to that better land.

After receiving our tents and supplies, we fixed up a new camp on the crest of a low hill surrounded on all sides by a forest of low pines. It was a delightful camping ground. Spring had touched every thing around with its magic wand, and freshness and beauty smiled on every side. The forests were clothed in the richest green, and the earth was dotted with flowers of every hue.

The respite from action lasted only a month. Lee's spectacular run of victories had come at a great cost. At Chancellorsville, he lost about 20 percent of his men; Union casualties, though higher in number, accounted for less than 15 percent of Hooker's army. More important, Lee knew that he would not be able to replace his losses, whereas his foe could count on more than adequate reinforcements. Moreover, the war in other theaters was not going well for the South, and the Union blockade of Southern ports was becoming more and more effective. A war of attrition would clearly work to the South's disadvantage, so time was not on his side.

Nevertheless, Lee and his men were at the height of their confidence—in fact, were perhaps overconfident—and he wanted to follow up his string of successes with a blow so powerful that it might bring the war to an end. He again opted for boldness, a strategy that had served him so well in the past, and determined to invade the North. The same reasons that had prompted him to invade Maryland in 1862 applied in 1863, though there was even more urgency. It therefore seemed to him that he had little to lose and much to gain. If he battered the Yankee army in its own country or captured a major Northern city, the North might well sue for peace. If he could not accomplish either of these, he would still wreak havoc in the enemy's country, resupply himself there, and also remove the center of war from long-suffering Virginia. The possibility of being badly beaten himself most likely never occurred to him. And so, on June 3, his troops left their works at Fredericksburg and started on a road that led to Gettysburg and immortality. The Union army followed.

We remained at Stafford until the 6th of June, when we began the longest and hardest campaign of the war. Late in the afternoon of the 6th we had orders to be ready to march immediately and to leave every thing behind which was not absolutely necessary. Just at night we started on this expedition. It rained nearly all that night, and it was very dark. Only two regiments from the 12th Corps [were] moving, which were the 2nd Massachusetts and the 3rd Wisconsin. There was one battery of 6-pounders with us and two or three regiments of cavalry. We took the Kelley's Ford Road as far as Harwood. At Harwood Church we were joined by one regiment from the 11th Corps. From Harwood we pushed northward to the rail road, which we struck at Bealton Station, where we remained until dark the night of the 8th. We then went up the Rappahannock River, keeping about five or six miles from it, until we were opposite Beverly Ford, where we went into camp about midnight.

Reports about Confederate movements had been coming in to Hooker, but he needed more reliable information, the kind available only by sending his own men on reconnaissance. He dispatched his cavalry to cross the Rappahannock and feel out the enemy. J. E. B. Stuart's Confederate cavalry had the reputation of being unbeatable, and certainly the Union cavalry to that point had known nothing but defeat at its hands. Believing, perhaps wrongly, that his cavalry was outnumbered by the vaunted Confederates, Hooker sent 3,000 infantry along to its support. The 3rd Wisconsin was not originally slated to be a part of this contingent, but at the urging of the 2nd Massachusetts, which was participating and wanted dependable men at its side, it was included at the last minute.

The Union force crossed the river on June 9 and took a Confederate brigade posted near the crossing completely by surprise. The infantry units rushed up a hill, through a small stand of woods, and took position at the far edge of the woods. There before them stretched an open field that seemed ideal for a cavalry engagement. The Union cavalry formed near the edge of the woods, and Stuart's men, now awake to the immediate presence of the enemy, were gathering at the far side of the clearing.

The battle that developed, known as Brandy Station because of its proximity to that place, became the largest, most classic cavalry battle of the entire war. The scene seemed almost straight from a novel, complete with spectacular charges, sabers swinging overhead, mounted men shooting with pistols, and excited horses. The contenders fought head to head for hours. The infantry played an important part, both in keeping Confederate skirmishers from picking off Federal cavalrymen with impunity and in meeting enemy charges with a wall of flame from their rifles. Then, as Rebel infantry troops were brought up, the Union cavalry retreated, leaving the field in Confederate possession.

Though Stuart could thus claim victory, an assessment of the battle reveals otherwise. Confederate general H. B. McClellan thought that Brandy Station "made" the Federal cavalry, and it certainly had the three important effects of giving it confidence, proving that it could be a match for Stuart, and diminishing the prestige and aura of invincibility surrounding the Confederate cavalry.

Willard was in a position to observe this important battle and gives us a stirring account.

One very small fire was allowed to be built by each company to make coffee by, and then all fires were put out. We knew nothing of the object of the expedition, though we suspected that we were going out to support the cavalry, a large amount of which had joined us. We were awakened before day light the next morning and allowed to cook coffee as before, then moved out rapidly for the river about three miles distant. We were soon at the ford. The cavalry had already crossed, and a sharp fight was going on on the other side, and the firing of revolvers and carbines could be distinctly heard. We pushed on silently and rapidly, knowing that there was sharp work on hand for us. We had started out in the rear of the column, but on arriving at the ford, the other regiments halted and we were sent ahead. Without halting a moment, we began fording the river and, when across, pushed on almost at a double quick over an open field to the woods beyond. It was early in the morning, and a heavy fog hung over the river, the fields, and woods, hiding every thing at a distance from view.

The cavalry had dashed across the river and surprised the Rebel pickets. Another regiment or two came up. The 8th New York was driven back but the 8th Illinois in turn repulsed the Rebels. The Rebel bugles had sounded their "boots and saddles," and their whole force, some sixteen thousand, were quickly in line. Our whole force was now brought up and gallantly charged, driving the enemy before them through and out of the woods.

We followed rapidly, nearly all being deployed as skirmishers. The piece of timber we were in was triangular shaped, the base resting on the river and the point extending westward. It was about half a mile wide at the river and came to a point about one mile back. The country is very open all around that little piece of timber and resembles a Western prairie. About three quarters of a mile west of the point of timber is a wooded hill, long and low but rough and rocky. About one mile south of the point of woods is the rail road, and about two and a half miles south west is Brandy Station, a rail road station between the Rappahannock and Culpeper.

The Rebel cavalry drew up in line across this open country or, rather, around the piece of timber we were in. One regiment of our cavalry charged and broke their line, going straight through it, and turning around, cut their way back again. The Rebels charged repeatedly but were repulsed every time most handsomely. The Rebel cavalry outnumbered ours at least three to one, but there were other portions of our troopers that the braves of the South heard from before the battle was over. Our three regiments of infantry numbered in all about nine hundred men. The 2nd Massachusetts and 3rd Wisconsin numbered about two hundred and fifty each, and the 38th Massachusetts five hundred, many of which were not in the engagement.

It was a fine sight to see the cavalry in long lines as they swept across the open field, meeting in full career, mingling in a deadly hand to hand conflict, the bugles ringing over the din of strife, the clashing of swords flashing brightly as they rose and fell, the waving of banners, the cracking of revolvers and carbines, the rearing of steeds, the Rebel yells and Federal cheers, the wild swoop of charging squadrons. Indeed, a cavalry fight is one of the most *stirring* scenes.

But the fighting was not confined alone to the cavalry. Soon after the fight began the Rebels were reinforced by several hundred mounted riflemen, and before we were aware of it, they had gained a position in the edge of the timber, having driven in our skirmishers before they could be reinforced.

We were at the time on the opposite side of the woods, having been sent there on a double quick to repulse an attack in that direction. A wild, demonic yell arose from the other side of the timber, and the firing in that direction became very rapid, almost swelling up into the terrible roar of a general engagement between lines of infantry. We at once hastened through the woods in that direction. Meanwhile, the Rebel artillery kept up a rapid cannonade, throwing shot and shell into the woods from a dozen guns. Several shells burst very near the regiment, some even swept through the ranks; but strange to say, without hurting a single man.

The yelling and firing continued, and when we came to that side of the woods, we found our cavalry being pressed back, not being able to cope with the Rebel riflemen that had gained a footing in the timber. The cavalry at that place, which happened to be only one company, found it impossible to rout them from among the fallen trees, stumps, and brush. Our cavalry stood their ground well, sitting on their horses and never turning their backs on the enemy, although fair marks for the Rebel riflemen. Several of them dropped from their steeds dead while we were passing them.

As soon as we arrived on the ground, we were deployed as skirmishers and advanced into the fallen timber ahead of the cavalry. Several of the men were hit before we could get into position. The Rebels soon found that they had some thing besides cavalry to contend with, that they were fighting with those who could use the rifle as well as they. The fight now, in this portion of the field, became a scientific game, the result depending on the skill as well as courage of the combatants.

When once we were deployed, every man chose his own manner of fighting, sheltering himself behind a tree, stump, log, or any thing else that kept him partially out of sight. He gets shot at every time he moves or shows himself in the least, and also shoots at every enemy that he gets a fair glimpse of. Good marksmen will do fearful execution when skirmishing, often more than the firing of a whole battalion when firing in line of battle. The skirmisher, if he is good, has a good gun, and is cool and steady handed, will make sure of his mark almost every time. The firing often begins at long range, but good skirmishers will soon work their way up into close quarters.

Some very severe little fights often occur between skirmishers. This affair at Beverly Ford was one. The sharp ringing of rifles chimed in along the lines for some time. We worked up very near the Rebels, and in such a way as to make some of them change positions. And having once dislodged them, we soon forced them out of the woods altogether.

There is a right way and a wrong way to conduct a skirmish. Men may be ever so brave, but if not properly handled they will often be beaten. I have been in quite a number of skirmishes, but I have never seen a line deployed as I think it should be. Skirmishers are always deployed in a straight line, and in this way advance on the enemy. I think the line should be formed so as to be slightly curved, the wings a little ahead or in advance of the centre. By forming a line in this manner, an enfilading fire can be had on the enemy. This would not matter if the ground was all clear, but where there are rocks and trees etc., a curved line would enable the skirmishers on the wings, the right and left, to dislodge the centre of the enemy's line.

Once, they supposed that they had broken our line. Seeing a few who were wounded going back, and thinking that the whole line was falling back, they sent up one of their wildcat like yells and *some* of them sprang forward in pursuit. This brought them from their covers, a hundred rifles rang out along our line, and *some* of those yelling fiends found "cover" in the shade of the Valley of the Shadow of Death. The brush and fallen timber [were] so thick that it was impossible to see through to the open field beyond, and this enabled the rest to make their escape by crawling off through it. Finding that their firing had ceased, we began to advance rapidly down to the open field, where we found they had gone back.

A few moments after, we saw the Rebel cavalry suddenly thrown into a confusion, and turning from us, they galloped off across the plain in the wildest disorder. Men, mounted and dismounted, and steeds without riders all wildly scattered off. It was a strange sight to us, and we stood there in the woods wondering what it could mean. Soon, however, a large body of our horsemen came dashing upon the plain which the Rebels were so suddenly leaving. Just then we heard the sullen booming of cannon far away towards Brandy Station, and we knew that our brave troopers had gone around in their rear, and as we saw the flying, broken squadrons dashing into the woods, we also recognized their pursuers as another division of our cavalry which had crossed at Rappahannock Station. We immediately advanced across the plain, finding quite a number of dead and wounded Rebels on the way.

A severe fight occurred at Brandy Station, Kilpatrick finally succeeding in routing the enemy and driving them far beyond the Station. All that afternoon we lay near the Station, and after picking up all of our dead and wounded, and providing for the wounded Rebels also, and having accomplished our object—the breaking up of their cavalry camp—we returned without being molested to the east bank of the Rappahannock. The Rebels used their artillery to good advantage, but we were not aided in the least by ours, as it never crossed the river. Our loss was severe. Not less than three or four hundred of our cavalry were killed and wounded.[3]

The loss among the infantry was light. In our regiment it was one killed dead on the field and fourteen wounded. This loss was just what it cost us to drive the Rebels out of the woods. Only two or three of the wounded have yet returned to the regiment. It was impossible to ascertain what the loss to the enemy was, but it could not have been less than our own.

The battle of Beverly Ford was a brilliant affair in which our cavalry boys won immortal honors and will, [in] years to come, be spoken of with pride by many of those brave troopers. The Rebels fear them, and the infantry speaks of them with pride.

> May the wreath they have won never wither
> Or the star of their glory grow dim.

The sun was very low when we recrossed the Rappahannock, the infantry, or a portion of it first, followed slowly by the cavalry. On the crest of a slight eminence, I paused and, looking back, could see a portion of the battle field which still smoked and burned where the bursting of the fiery shells had set the woods on fire, and where the enemy had burned a few wagons which they were not able to take with them in their flight. There were the woods, the plain beyond, and in the distance the wooded hills to which the Rebels fled, and the red sun low in the west cast a crimson glow over all.

That night we returned to Bealton Station, where we remained until the 13th. Then we started for Fairfax Court House, our corps having moved in that direction. While we were at Bealton, the 1st and 5th Corps passed us on their way up the river. Lee's vast army was now on the move, a portion of it having gone west of the Blue Ridge into the Shenandoah Valley. A long, hard campaign was before us, with deprivation, suffering, and danger, and we knew it well. Long marches were to be made and hard battles fought. Yet the men were cheerful and pressed on without a murmur.

The morning of the 13th found us up and ready to move, and we were soon in motion. The day was a very warm one, the roads were very dusty, and the country parched and dry. But we pushed on and at night camped near Bristoe Station, having traveled fifteen miles. We resumed the march the next morning, passing around a little to the north of Brentsville, a little town through which we passed on Pope's retreat the day that Banks's Corps got cut off from the main army then at Centreville. Brentsville is a small town or hamlet some distance (eight miles perhaps) south and west from the stone bridge at Bull Run. The town does not contain over one hundred inhabitants, and as in all other towns, most of the whites have gone and most of the buildings are used by the Negroes. The buildings are mostly log ones, very old and rotten.

There was one Union man living in that little town at the time of Pope's retreat. I happened to be walking along alone by the side walk while the troops were passing through. I saw an old, gray haired man standing at one of the gates with a pail of water. Being thirsty, I stopped and took a drink from the cup which the old man handed me with the remark, "I am a man of peace, but I am your friend, for I love my country and I love its defenders. I am a Southern man, a native of Virginia, but I am for the Union and pray God to stay the progress of the Southern army and give you the victory. My interests as far as property is concerned is all here, but my heart is with the North—with your cause. I am very old, can hardly see, but I came out here to see you go by and look once more on the old flag. I did hope to live and die in a land where that old flag was loved as I love it. Good by." Tears were in the old man's eyes when I left him, leaning against the gate, sadly watching the soldiers as they went by.

From Brentsville we went around the Rebel army at Manassas. We struck the rail road near Manassas Junction, where we halted to rest, and then pushed on across the dry, dusty Plains of Manassas to Bull Run. The day was extremely hot, with not a breath of air stirring. The sun poured down its untempered heat, burning and scorching, heating the sand until it burned the feet through the shoes. There was no water to be had. and we suffered greatly with the thirst. Many of the men dropped down by the wayside overcome with the heat; some were killed by sun stroke. Those that could kept on across the plain.

After crossing the plain, we came into the Bull Run country, which here is very rough, the banks high, rocky, and covered with timber. But there are no signs of there ever having been any formidable works there; in fact, there is not any where along the Run. Bull Run is not what I had, before I ever was there, supposed it to have been. The country is covered with huge rocks in most places and at the time of the first battle was thickly timbered. The Run itself is no larger than a large spring creek, a mere streamlet. There are none of those terrible bluffs and rocky peaks, deep dark ravines (save at Union Mills), and frowning ramparts and breast works which we have heard of. It was a strong position, but not stronger than can be found any where in Virginia.

Passing down the rail road, we came to what is known as Union Mills. Here we halted; the men would go no further but, being completely exhausted, lay down along the banks of the stream to rest. We remained there until late in the afternoon, when we resumed the march and pushed on to Fairfax Station, where we bivouacked for the night. The country around the Station and all the way from Union Mills is thickly wooded, the timber being that of a second growth forest or, rather, thicket of low pine trees. But very few inhabitants live in that part of the country. The soil is very poor and the water bad, the farms or plantations are uncultivated, and the buildings old and many of them deserted.

The next morning we joined the brigade at Fairfax Court House. Our corps had moved up from Stafford to there. Fairfax is one of those old dilapidated towns one so often meets with in Virginia. The buildings are log and frame ones, small, old, and gray with age, many of them overgrown with moss. Fairfax is a very ancient town, named after Lord Fairfax, who had an extensive grant of land east of the Blue Ridge. There is a little old church at Fairfax built many years ago. It has nearly gone to ruin now, and its walls are tumbling down. An old grave yard is near by, but it has been sadly neglected, and one can hardly discover the traces of a grave. The fence is gone, and the graves have been trodden down by the cattle of the common. A few old, gray tomb stones still remain, bearing up the records of the dead.

Fairfax is the county seat and has a court house, an ancient looking structure resembling some old prison. There was, before the war, a few small stores and one or two taverns. The town consists of less than two hundred buildings altogether. I do not think there has been a new building built in Fairfax for the last fifty years. Take it all in all, the whole country from Alexandria to the Rappahannock wears the appearance of a blighted land, cursed and dying with old age.

Some might say that all this has been caused by war. Not so. War did not give to a few those broad plantations while so many were without homes. War did not make a few thousand planters owners of the whole state. War has not prevented the wider circulation of papers or the building of school houses, and it was no war that has made the common people so poor and indolent, and ignorant too. No, all this was the same before the war. The whole country is owned by a few wealthy planters who lived sumptuously from the products of their slaves and cared not what became of the poor whites while they fared well.

Throughout the whole South you will find but few small farms, few neat and well cultivated fields or small white cottages so common in the North, no farms tilled by white labor, but broad, half cultivated fields of tobacco or hemp, labor all done by the hand of the unwilling slave, who toils because he must. Instead of the happy farmer, cheerfully working at his plough, you will see the poor slave whose heart is not with his work, and his driver standing over him with the whip.

Such a country with such planters cannot prosper, for with every furrow that is turned, the land cries out against him, and the wrongs of the slave are recorded against him, and his shadow falls like a withering blight on the land. It matters not how prolific the soil may be or how healthful the climate or serene the skies, such a country cannot thrive. The withering curse of slavery that rests on the unhappy south like a deadly blight, absorbing its energies, degrading its people, and darkening its prospects, casts its shadow like an ill omen all over the land.

The 15th of June we joined our brigade at Fairfax Court House. The other regiments were glad to see us. Great numbers from the brave old 27th Indiana, 13th New Jersey, and 107th New York came to learn how we had fared while away.

The whole corps was now moving, and early in the morning of the 16th we left Fairfax, turning northward in the direction of Dranesville. We were in the advance that day. The country between Fairfax and Dranesville is wild and wooded, with but very few inhabitants. Sometimes you will not find a house for miles. We camped for the night near Dranesville, a small village, where, or in the vicinity of which, was fought one of the first battles of the war. Dranesville is not a very bad looking village and is located in a fine, sightly locality. From it may be seen nearly the whole of that beautiful country known as the Leesburg Valley.

At Dranesville the whole appearance of the country changes. The forests of dwarf oaks and pines gives place to a fine, open country dotted with green fields, orchards, and meadows, with slight wave like rolling hills or undulations covered often with timber. There is no fine or better looking country to be found anywhere than Leesburg Valley.

The 17th was a most dreadful warm day, and the march to Leesburg was a very hard one. A soldier, loaded down with all his luggage, finds it no light task to march all day in the midst of a cloud of dust, sweltering beneath a Virginia sun in summer. It seems that one of the Confederate generals was on his way to Leesburg in order to get possession of the river at Conrad's and Edwards's Ferries and compel us to cross the Potomac farther down near Washington. It was thought that some of the Confederate forces had already reached Leesburg. Notwithstanding the extreme heat and dusty roads, the column was pushed rapidly on. Hundreds sank down, over powered by the heat or choked down by the stifling, smothering dust.

We still had the advance. About four o'clock in the afternoon we reached Goose Creek, a small stream three miles from Leesburg. Finding no enemy there as was expected, we crossed and after a brief rest pushed on for the town. While we were resting at Goose Creek, a most violent storm came up. This was hailed with joy, for anything was better than the burning heat. We had been praying for rain, and when the black clouds began to roll up in the west, shading in the sun, and the low, deep muttering thunder came up from the distance, it sounded to us better than the sweetest music. The clouds spread rapidly over the sky, and their shadows rested like a blessing on the parched earth. The air soon became cool, and the crisped and withered leaves seemed to lift themselves up, looking to the clouds with gratitude.

The large drops soon began to fall, and it seemed as though the thirsty earth drank them most eagerly, and the leaves and drooping flowers expanded and their usual freshness and beauty returned. A thunder storm in Virginia is no small affair. The fury of the storm, the vividness of the flashes, and tremendous crash and roar of the thunder surpasses any thing of the kind in the North. These storms come up suddenly and often in less than half an hour change the whole aspect of the skies from cloudless serenity to one of darkness.

But we got more than we had bargained for. We had been wishing for coolness, and it not only came in the shape of rain drops but also in ice drops, and not small ones at that, and they did not come slow either. Hail stones fell as large as large marbles, and the wind drove them into our faces, sometimes eating through the skin; but we pushed on against the storm through the town to Fort Hill. The remainder of the corps halted before they got to the town.

No Rebels had as yet made their appearance near the town, save a small roving band of cavalry which passed through a day or two before our arrival. They assured the people that the Rebel army would soon be there and the Yankees would never again trouble them. The people had already prepared a dinner for Longstreet and staff; but lo, the "Yanks," the pesky Yankees, came and frightened their dear Rebel friends away.

That night, the 17th, we camped near Fort Hill, one mile west of Leesburg. The fort is built on one of the commanding hills near the town, and from its summit, an extensive view of the surrounding country can be had. There are several other forts in the vicinity of Leesburg. Fort Johnson is the best constructed and commands a passage of the river at Conrad's Ferry. These fortifications were built by the Confederates about the time of the fight at Ball's Bluff to prevent a flank movement on Manassas. The position was a strong one but was abandoned without a struggle. They could not have remained at this place or Manassas after Banks had begun to move up the Shenandoah Valley, as either position could have been flanked by an army from that direction by passing eastward through the Blue Ridge, by the way of any of the several mountain passes from Manassas

Gap to Snicker's Gap. Had the Confederate army remained in their fortifications around Bull Run and Manassas until Banks could have reached Massanutten Gap, he could have forced them to fight east of the Rappahannock or have cut off their retreat by way of the Gordonsville and Alexandria rail road. But the Confederate general was not to be caught in that way, and before Banks had reached Winchester, the Rebels had evacuated Manassas and Leesburg, retreating across the Rappahannock.

Leesburg is a fine old town or, rather, city located in the midst of one of the best looking counties in the state. It once contained, in those better days before the war, about seven thousand inhabitants, but now many, very many of the finest dwellings are deserted. The town is nicely laid out, and most of the buildings are red brick. They are large, fine looking ones, built after the good old fashioned style of a half century ago—not high and lofty, but broad and square, affording ample room without climbing to the fifth story to find it. Many very wealthy families lived in Leesburg prior to the war, indeed it was a city of the wealthy—the FFVs (first families of Virginia) were the principal residents of the town. The Loudons, the Lees, the Uptons, and Middleburgs lived in the most aristocratic style, with their slaves around them and hundreds of poor whites to bow down at their bidding.

It is not often that you find the real aristocrat living in a city or town, but out in the country on their broad and extensive farms or plantations. There, in their fine, old fashioned mansions, in the midst of their slaves, with waiters at their elbow, these proud gentlemen live in all the ease and luxury of the English nobleman. These FFVs pride themselves on being connected with some of the titled ones of Mother England.

The traveler will always receive a cordial welcome if he stops for the night at the house of a Virginia planter. These planters are usually very generous, full of good humor, kind and genial in their manners, ready to talk with you on any subject, generally well informed in regard to the history of our country, and especially of the Old Dominion, in which every Virginian takes great pride. They will sit and talk for hours about the Smiths, the Fairfaxes, the Lees, the Culpepers, the Staffords, and a hundred other English noblemen who came to this country long before the Revolution, and will tell you many marvelous stories and legends about Virginia's revolutionary heroes.

These planters have large estates, many of which have been owned by the same family ever since the country was first settled, having been handed down from sire to son, and no price hardly could induce them to part with it. Many of them will live in the same house built by their great grandfather's grandfather, and although they have grown rotten with old age and over grown with moss, still their present owners have such a desire to live, a religious one I might say, to live and die in the same old house their forefather lived and died in, that they would rather live in the old house, decaying as it is, than to build a new one.

The rooms are large and square, lighted by high bow windows with deep casements and generally shaded by long curtains reaching from the ceiling to the floor. They are well furnished, the furniture being of that heavy, massive kind so much in use one hundred years ago. The huge armchair with its high back and great, stout legs, and the fireplace with its broad mantel piece, polished irons, and nicely swept hearth, the cozy rooms with useless ornaments and no light, the free, easy, and altogether cheerful, self confident, and generous manners of the occupants, make one feel at home in the house of a real old fashioned Virginia planter.

These same planters have entered into a strange, mad scheme to work out their own ruin. They have invited war and brought upon poor old Virginia the terrible curse of being the great battle ground. Much of this open, generous hospitality has passed away with its advent. It has swept over the state in a perfect tempest of death and destruction, and its fearful course may be traced by the charred and smouldering ruins of homes destroyed and villages given to the flames, and the Genie of ruin sits enthroned in the midst of this wilderness of desolation.

The view from Fort Hill is a fine one, for from the crest of the hill one can look over many miles of one of the finest appearing countries I have ever seen. Leesburg is about four miles south of the Potomac and the fort the same. Looking northward, one can trace the course of the Potomac as it rolls smoothly on towards the Chesapeake. The country rolls up here and there into swelling, wave like undulations, presenting a steep bank to the river, beyond which swell up the higher and rougher heights on the Maryland shore. Far away, over the river, on a clear day the little village of Poolsville can be seen, and still farther northward in Maryland looms up the Sugar Loaf, its rocky crest crowned with clouds. This mountain stands alone like some proud sentinel overlooking the fair country around it. The Sugar Loaf has an elevation of nearly three thousand feet above the level of the Monocacy River, which flows near its base, one of the most beautiful little rivers to be found in the South. The country around the Sugar Loaf is rich and, seen from the crest of the mountain, presents an appearance of varied beauty hardly surpassed any where. In summer, large fields of grain, green meadows, and blooming orchards are seen, with here and there belts and groves of timber still in its primitive beauty, while white farm houses, single or grouped in clusters, dot the whole landscape. Frederick City, a fine old town, is situated in the midst of this lovely valley three miles from the Monocacy and eight miles north of the mountain. The Sugar Loaf has been used by both the Federals and Confederates as a signal station, and while we were encamped near Frederick in the early part of the war, the red, white, and blue signal lights used to burn and swing from its crest by night, flashing intelligence of the enemy's movements here in the Leesburg Valley.

About twelve miles up the Potomac from Leesburg is what is called Point of Rocks. A range of mountains here cross the river but seem to have been rudely split apart to allow the grand old Potomac to pass through on its way to the sea. The Baltimore and Ohio Rail Road passes here along the north bank of the river at the base of the mountain. Looking directly upward from the rail road, one sees hanging over him at the height of more than two hundred feet, a huge mass of rocks, looking as though about to fall on him, and making him feel how small, how insignificant he is when in the midst of nature's grandeur.

This mass of rocks can be seen from Fort Hill, shadowing over the little old village beneath it, as can the blue crest of Maryland Heights at Harpers Ferry and Loudon Heights on the Virginia side. Westward from the fort, far away in the distance, dimly seen through the blue, smoky clouds that always hang around its crest, is the Blue Ridge, stretching to the southward like a bank of clouds. A little farther south and much nearer are the Thoroughfare Mountains, and directly south are the Bull Run Mountains. East of these is the Manassas Plains and the Bull Run country. Aside from these heights and mountains, the land south of the Potomac is very level from the Blue Ridge to Alexandria, and from the summit of any one of them one can look over the country for miles.

This fine country around Leesburg is not what it should have been, and the lack of thrift, industry, and agricultural skill is sadly apparent. The old, worn out farms and plantations, dilapidated dwellings, and small and ill contrived out buildings all seem to give the whole country an air of decay. It seems old long before its time, ready to die with old age. It is no uncommon thing to see the farm house or dwelling surrounded with a dense forest of scrub pines, and all the fields in the vicinity overgrown in the same way, while some distance from the house, perhaps a mile or two, are the cultivated fields. It is often the case that on one side of the road will be found pine thickets of this kind, without a single bush of any other kind of timber, while on the other may be seen forests of other timber with no or but very few pine trees in it.

The land has been worn out, completely exhausted by the continual growth of tobacco or hemp on it without proper care. The soil after a few years becomes worthless, and the planter leaves it and plants a new field. Left to itself, nature at once begins its work of restoring the soil to its former fertility. Nature is the universal restorer and ever seeks to keep every thing in its proper relation. In a few years these deserted and worn out fields are over grown with pine thickets, and so very thick are they that the sun's rays are shut out entirely. Beneath the dark shadows of these pines, the soil gradually resumes its former fruitfulness. In these thickets, quails, hares, and foxes are found in great abundance. The planters never disturb these old farms, hence the reason why Southerners wish to own vast tracts of land, so that when one plantation is worn out, they can begin a new one. All that is required to redeem these waste lands is a little agricultural skill and industry, and I believe if these lands as they are now were owned by Eastern or Western farmers, Virginia would have none or but few of these dark jungles which cover one fifth of the whole state.

While we were at Leesburg, one of those affairs occurred which, though sad and seemingly cruel and useless, are nevertheless right, namely the shooting of three deserters. They had had their trial and had been found guilty and were to die—to be shot by the side of their grave, kneeling on their coffins. It was very sad, yet it was just; for all deserters should die. Not that the crime is so cruel and wanton, but because the army and the country demanded it.

It was a bright afternoon on which the execution took place, and the whole of the 1st Division was paraded to witness it. The division was formed in a square, except one side, which was left open. The lines were formed, and at 2:00 P.M., the general and his staff and escort, all mounted, galloped around to their places. Then came the prisoners and the guard, following the music, ahead of which was borne three coffins. The band played a march, and the slow beating of the muffled drums sounded sad that day, for it was the death march to the grave. The men walked firmly and lightly around to the open side of the square, where three graves were dug. The coffins were placed by the graves, and the victims, after the charges and findings of the court martial were read to them and a prayer offered by the chaplain, knelt on them. A moment they knelt there alone and a death like silence reigned, broken at last by the rattle of eighteen muskets, and the unfortunate men rolled from their coffins dead. The regiments then in turn marched around their graves and returned to their quarters.

We remained at Leesburg until the morning of the 26th, when we crossed the river at Edwards' Ferry and once more stood on the soil of Maryland. Lee was already in Maryland and Pennsylvania. The Confederate general had boldly pushed westward through the Blue Ridge and crossed the river with a powerful army, determined to invade the Northern states, defeat the Potomac army, capture our vast stores, take Baltimore and Washington, and, as they boasted, dictate peace on their own terms from our capital.

It was a dark, rainy morning, that of the 26th, and a heavy mist hung over the river, the fields, and woods. In going to the river, we went over the renowned battle ground known as Ball's Bluff. A small elevation on the bank of the river goes by this name. Some graves were still to be seen, and bones were thickly strewn over the ground. It was here on this battle field where the brave and deeply mourned Colonel Baker fell, with hundreds of others, victims to the treachery or incompetency of one man.[4] The sad story of that battle will be remembered, the fallen ones will not rest in their graves, and the dead tongues will not be still. It was a foul thing to send those brave men over there in old, leaky scow boats to attack such a place with no supports and no way of escape and, when overpowered by vastly superior numbers, with nothing remaining but to rush to the river bank and plunge into the foaming stream to perish or be shot down by a heartless enemy. The battle of Ball's Bluff will always be spoken of with indignation, and the white bones on the banks of the Potomac will ever flash back their bitter condemnation. The Army of the Potomac has suffered many defeats, but there was never one like this, one where so many lives were lost so uselessly.

The night of the 26th, we bivouacked near the mouth of the Monocacy. The weather was dark and disagreeable. The movements of the army were a profound mystery, for the soldier knows nothing of what is going on outside of his own brigade or division. The next morning we crossed the Monocacy and followed up the river towards Harpers Ferry. We camped that night in Middleton Valley, about eight miles from Harpers Ferry.

About this time the army was turned over to General Meade. We heard of it with deep regret, for although Hooker had failed at Chancellorsville, we still had confidence in his ability. The next day we crossed the Catoctin Hills and camped near Frederick City. The following day we marched through the city on our way to Pennsylvania. The people were glad to see us and came out in crowds all along the street, many mingling in the ranks to shake hands with us. Our regiment, if it never won honor on the field, surely won the esteem of the good people of Frederick City, Maryland, when we were provost guards of that city during the winter of 1862. This was the second time we have passed through that place on our way to give battle to Lee. Our ranks had been sadly thinned out since we passed through the city the autumn before. We had fought the battles of Antietam, Chancellorsville, and Beverly Ford, and full one half of our number had been left behind, many in graves on the banks of the Potomac, the Rappahannock, or in the Wilderness. Our flag was torn, having been pierced with scores of bullets.

That day we crossed the state line into Pennsylvania and went into camp late at night near Mechanicsville; resumed our march early the next morning. While we were resting by the road side, news came to the general that the Rebel cavalry and our own were fighting near the little town just ahead. We were at once ordered to "fall in" and marched rapidly forward.

Skirmish at Littleton [Littlestown]. We were at Littlestown in less than half an hour and found the people in a most dreadful fright. The Rebel cavalry had been there and had begun to plunder the town, when our boys burst in on them like a thunder bolt. A fight took place in the streets. On the approach of the Rebels, the people had closed their doors and hid themselves. Our cavalry dashed into the town with wild yells, and the Rebels answered with shouts of defiance. Horsemen met horsemen, sabres clashed with sabres, and revolvers flashed for a moment. But they were not equal to our brave troopers when fighting thus for their own homes, as it were, and under the eyes of their own people. The Rebels were worsted and driven out of town, where another encounter occurred.

We came in just then on the double quick, our artillery galloping on ahead, making a most terrible uproar in that usually quiet, little town. The women and children were wild with fright, and men were running up and down the street wildly. We were on the ground in a few moments, but none (save the dead and wounded) of either party were in sight. We passed through the town and camped for the night one mile west. Littlestown is a fine, little town in southern Pennsylvania. It must have been a strange thing for the people of that quiet town, where all had been peaceful, to have that quiet so rudely broken by the wild galloping of steeds, the clashing of swords, and yells of two thousand combatants. The people of the North are unaccustomed to such scenes.

Littlestown is about ten miles from Gettysburg, and Willard and his comrades were still there on July 1 when the battle of Gettysburg began. He gives a brief, general summary of how the battle started, likely based on reports he heard in camp either during or after the event.

A part of the army had taken one road and a part another. The 1st and 11th Corps were already near Gettysburg, the 1st commanded by General Reynolds, the 11th by Howard. Our cavalry had been there, but the Rebels had driven them back through the town the 1st of July. During the afternoon of the 1st, the 1st Corps attacked the Rebels on the east side of the town and, after a hard fight, drove them to the west side. The 11th Corps then joined in, but the enemy, having been strongly reinforced, returned to the fight, and after one of the [most] hotly contested struggles of the whole war, the brave 1st Corps had to yield and fall back slowly through the town.

When the 1st Corps attacked the enemy, no other corps save the 11th were within supporting distance, while nearly the whole Rebel army was in the vicinity. The fight was a fierce one, and at last the Rebels gave way before the determined onset of the 1st, but rallied again, and we were forced back; but we in turn rallied, and again the Rebel legions were forced to give way. Then came the 11th and they with the 1st gained the heights beyond. Fresh battalions opposed them and the conflict raged with terrific fury; the roar of musketry could be heard for miles. But our little army there were soon exhausted and their ammunition gone. The Rebels fired two large barns filled with grain and, under cover of the smoke and flames, made a flank movement on the left and right. Our cavalry posted on the wings were forced to give way, and our band was forced to yield the heights so gallantly won. Such was the first day's fight of the battle of Gettysburg. We were defeated with heavy loss. Here General Reynolds was killed. He fell at the commencement of the battle.

There was a picture of war—the burning buildings, the flames leaping high in the air and dense clouds of smoke rolling over the fields, the cavalry breaking on the right and left, the retreating Federals and pursuing Confederates, yelling as only Rebels can yell, the flashing and booming of cannons, the bright flashes of many thousand muskets in the meadow and on the hill side, the smoke settling down over the fields, at times hiding the combatants from view, the city behind and the dark heights before.

As the 3rd Wisconsin marched the few miles to Gettysburg, the men could increasingly see the shells bursting and smoke lofting over the field of battle, and then could discern soldiers in the distance. Refugees streamed away from the field of conflict. No one knew the state of affairs at the front, and all were anxious for news. Willard gives an account of the Union army's march into Gettysburg.

We left Littlestown early on the morning of the 1st of July and marched towards Gettysburg. When about half way we were massed afield to await orders. While we were there we could hear the sound of the cannonading at Gettysburg as it rolled down to us from those heights like combined thunder. We knew a great fight was going on and expected soon to be ordered to the scene of conflict. We could see the shells as they burst in the air, shattering their myriad sparkles of fire and fragments of iron on every side. At last we could see the vast volume of smoke rising up above the heights and rolling away along the sky, and we could see, too, columns of troops moving in long, dark lines along the crest of the hill. Had they fallen back or were they going to the front were questions anxiously asked by every one, but none could answer.

At last the order came to "pack up," which was obeyed quickly and silently, and in less than five minutes we were in motion, one regiment after another passing out of the field into the road, the head of the column turned towards the scene of conflict. On the way we met many citizens, men, women, and children, hurrying to the rear. The faces of some were pale with fear, others were red with excitement. One old man had lost his hat, a woman her bonnet, and children were hurrying along the road alone. Some were terribly frightened, others smiled and seemed to take the whole thing as a good joke.

"What is the matter?" inquired one of our men of a young man on horseback, "Are they fighting much up there?" "They have been," he replied, "but they have killed all our men and burned the town." "Oh, I guess not," returned the soldier, coolly taking a chew of the weed, "suppose you take a musket and go with us and see." The fellow shook his head and turned to the rear again. We saw an old man sitting by the road side with two little children by his side. Tears were in the old man's eyes, and he clung fondly to his two grandchildren as though he would protect them with his own arms, old as he was.

But we had little time for observation, for we were moving rapidly to the front and expected to go straight to the fight. "Have they driven our men back?" asked a soldier who paused for a moment to take a drink of water offered by a young lady. "I believe they have," was the reply, "but they won't drive *you* back," she added with a smile. "We don't mean to let them, lady," said the soldier, lifting his cap and turning to go on his way to the front.

In camp the soldiers are always noisy and "full of fun," and on the march, songs and laughter are always heard, save when going to the battle field. At such times soldiers that have seen service are always grave and silent. The true soldier does not go to the battle field boastingly. No songs are heard then, no loud talk and buffoonery. The men close up to their places and silently and soberly move on. If anything is said, it is in a low tone. Some faces may be pale and voices may tremble a little; for what man, knowing the danger of battle, will not feel a sensation of dread creeping over him. It is often said that soldiers lose all sensation of fear, but not so; he may be in a hundred battles, but he will dread the last one as much as the first. One who has been in military hospitals and witnessed the terrible suffering of the wounded will never forget it and will always dread to run the risk of being put in their situation. He is not a coward but has a nobleness of nature which, though he knows his danger, overcomes his fear and gives him the mastery. To have no fear, to know no danger is unnatural and is not bravery. The truly brave man is one who knows his danger but can look that danger in the face and overcome his fear.

The old soldier will perhaps exhibit less excitement than a new one, but he has his secret dread. He may go [to] the field of death coolly and with seeming carelessness, but he knows what he has to meet and will not let his fear overcome him. The soldier who goes to the battle field in a boasting mood, with songs and jokes, is apt to have his song stick in his throat and possibly may use his legs more than his tongue. I had rather see men go to the front silently and soberly than to see them going with songs and laughter.

The balance of the Army of the Potomac, now commanded by Gen. George Meade, was brought up and into place during the late afternoon and night of July 1. The 3rd Wisconsin came in from the east via Wolf Hill, where it skirmished with members of the Stonewall Brigade, which constituted the far left portion of Lee's army. This area was, however, beyond the Union defenses, and Willard's men were ordered westward to join the rest of the army.

The Union forces were deployed to the south of Gettysburg in a position shaped like a fishhook. The hook portion started at the eastern slope of Culp's Hill (an excellent defensive position just southeast of Gettysburg), curved around the hill's north end, and then west over to Cemetery Hill, south of the town. The hook then bent and ran south in a fairly straight line over Cemetery Ridge down to Little Round Top.

The XII Corps, assigned to defend the Culp's Hill sector, was commanded by Maj. Gen. Henry Slocum. Brig. Gen. Thomas Ruger was now the division commander, and Col. Silas Colgrove led the brigade to which the 3rd Wisconsin belonged. Gen. George Greene's brigade was given the task of holding Culp's Hill itself, while Colgrove's brigade was placed at the far right, on the southeast slope of the hill. In effect, Colgrove's brigade held the same position on the northern end of the Union line that Col. Strong Vincent's brigade, which included the 20th Maine, held at the southern.

South and southeast of Culp's Hill was a large, marshy meadow, about a hundred yards wide, called a swale, and at its northern edge at the foot of the hill was Spangler's Spring, from which men on both sides took water during the battle. To the south of the swale lay a low ridge running from Rock Creek on the east over west to the Baltimore Pike. At the eastern end of the ridge was a low granite hill covered with boulders and a grove of trees known as McAllister's Woods. These woods ran right up to Rock Creek, and to their south was more marshland. Two of the regiments in Colgrove's brigade were stationed on the lower southeast slope of Culp's Hill, while the 3rd Wisconsin and two others were placed across the swale on the small hill in McAllister's Woods. Confederate units were stationed in a meadow and woods across Rock Creek, facing west.

On the evening of July 1, the XII Corps set about building breastworks with the vigor of men whose lives depended on it. All day on July 2 the corps expected an attack, yet none came, and except for a little skirmishing and artillery fire, the entire front was quiet. At about 4:00 P.M. the Confederates struck Dan Sickles's III Corps, which was in an exposed position toward the south end of the Union lines. The action was terrific in what would come to be called the Wheatfield, the Peach Orchard, and Devil's Den. The Rebels also launched attacks on Cemetery

Ridge, where the 1st Minnesota gave its "last full measure of devotion," and against the V Corps at the southernmost Union position, Little Round Top, which resulted in some of the toughest fighting of the war and led to eternal renown for the 20th Maine and its colonel, Joshua L. Chamberlain. Casualties were staggering, and the wounded came streaming back in sight of Colgrove's men. There still was no action in their sector, but they were ready.

It was nearly dark when the call came. Colgrove's men were to immediately vacate their breastworks and move to the southwest across Baltimore Pike, leaving another brigade to defend their sector. This would bring them in the rear near the center of the stem of the Union fishhook, where they would be in position to plug holes in the Union line wherever needed. They came under Rebel artillery fire on the march to their new location. But they arrived too late, as the Confederate assaults that day were virtually over. The fighting tapered off, night deepened, and Colgrove's troops were finally ordered to return to their breastworks without having taken part in the main action.

They were in for an unpleasant surprise, however. While they were gone, the enemy had attacked their position, which had been left with an inadequate number of defenders. A staunch defense by Greene's brigade had prevented the Confederates from overrunning Culp's Hill itself, but the works that Colgrove's brigade had built were now in the hands of the Rebels. The works erected by the 3rd Wisconsin on the low hill southeast of the swale in McAllister's Woods had not been occupied by the enemy, so most of Colgrove's units were stationed there. Now Spangler's Spring and the swale separated them from Culp's Hill.

That afternoon we took our position on the right of the 1st Corps, forming our line along the crest of a wooded ridge, facing westward to the right of Gettysburg. As soon as we were in position, we at once commenced building breast works along the crest of the hill. The 3rd Brigade of the 1st Division, however, was not placed in position until the next day. We were sent farther to the right the afternoon of the 1st in order to ascertain whether the enemy were in that direction or not.

We left the main road and struck off through the country to the right, following byroads or crossing over fields and meadows. The country in that vicinity is a very fine one. Great and well tilled farms and magnificent orchards, large dwellings, were all around us. It seemed strange that hostile armies were in that peaceful land.

Skirmishers were kept constantly in front of us, [as] we passed through fields and woods. Just before sunset we found the enemy's skirmishers, as we supposed, but it was only their advance cavalry. A few shots were exchanged without any one's being hurt on our side. We held them in check until our cavalry were in position to guard the flanks of our position and then withdrew but remained in the vicinity all that night, as the movements of the enemy were unknown.

All was quiet that night along our lines, and the soldiers lay down on the grass and slept. The moon never shone brighter and the sky never looked bluer or the stars more lovely than they did that summer's night. It was a novel sight to look over the field where the 3rd brigade was lying. Hundreds of men were sleeping there on the ground, their knapsacks for pillows and their guns by their side, ready to spring to their places at a moment's notice, the moon smiling softly down, seeming like a kiss on the soldier's brow, and the dew in his hair like angels' tears.

The next morning we moved along the line to the left, our skirmishers well in front. The object seemed to be to find the enemy's position or see if any forces had advanced in that direction. We were nearly on a line with the main force but far to the right of them. While working slowly towards the right flank of the main line, we happened to come in contact with a regiment or two of riflemen, which, like ourselves, seemed to be out on a voyage of discovery. A sharp, little skirmish followed, lasting half an hour or more, when the Rebels retreated. The loss in the 27th Indiana was quite severe. This occurred principally in a large orchard, in one of the finest of pearing places I saw on the whole route.

Before noon we were in our place on the extreme right of the whole line. We at once commenced building breast works on the crest of a little hill, separated by a marsh from the main ridge. Trees were cut down and logs rolled into line, rails were brought from a distance and piled up, brush thrown over them, which was covered with earth, and more brush thrown on so as to hide our works from the enemy.

It was not near night when it was finished. It does not take soldiers long to build a formidable breast work—when there is any prospect of its being useful to them, they will work with a will. Well, our work was all done, but no enemy had yet appeared in our front. The ax of the pioneers had leveled down the trees along the foot of the ridge, and we sat down among the rocks to wait the developments of events in other quarters. Many of us went beyond our works to a creek running near to bathe, our skirmish line being just beyond. Some light and irregular firing had been going on some distance to our left. But the afternoon up to three o'clock was very quiet. The day was cool and pleasant, and a thousand birds sang among the trees.

The 2nd day's battle. Late in the day (three in the afternoon, or perhaps a little after), we were startled by the heavy booming of cannon far around to the left of that horseshoe like line that had been formed. The firing was almost in the opposite direction from that in which we were looking for the enemy, and at the time we supposed the Rebels had gone around to our rear, as they had done at Chancellorsville. Gun followed gun, roar after roar, so rapidly that when our batteries opened in return, the cannonading became one continuous roar that rolled over those heights like a hundred thunder bolts combined. No language can describe it or give an idea of the terrible uproar. Many of the Rebel shells, not bursting where it was intended they should, came over to where we were, often tearing up the ground in our vicinity. These shells that do not burst go far beyond the spot where they are intended to burst and make a strange sound as they go end over end. They are called by the soldiers "Wandering Devils." They seldom do any harm, however. The terrible cannonade on the left continued, and we began to grow restless.

"The 3rd Corps is on the left," said Colonel Ruger, and we were glad to hear it, for we knew that if any troops in the army could hold that point, it was the old 3rd Corps and General Sickles. After an hour and a half of this terrible uproar, it began suddenly to die away, and soon only a few batteries were in play and there were brief intervals between the discharges. But there came up to us the "still small voice" of musketry, still and small it seemed compared with the cannonading, yet we knew that there was more death in that voice than in the thunder tones of the artillery. The cannon often sweeps down whole platoons and companies at a time, it is true, but in almost every battle more men fall before muskets than the cannon.

As the cannonading grew less and less, the roar of musketry grew louder, until it swelled up in one vast volume of sound. We had the order to "fall in," and all were sitting in breathless silence behind our breast works. When the cannonading was at its height, the wagons all were hastily driven to the rear, and ambulances, wagons, loose horsemen, and straggling footmen might be seen going along the pike in more than double quick time. The road for some moments was thickly crowded. It was very amusing to see them go. Some laughed and other cursed them for their fear. There is nothing more maddening to the soldier (at least a great many) than to see a lot of teamsters in a panic, and see them dash along pell mell at a wild gallop.

Once we had orders to retire from the hill and go to reinforce those on the left. We had gone but a short distance before the order was countermanded and we returned; but just before sunset, we received the same order again and hastened across the field to the left. Shells were falling thick and fast all around us, and the fight was still going on. We were at a loss to know whether our lines had been broken or not. We thought perhaps that the left had been crushed and we had got to retreat. The fact was, the left had been twice forced back; but when we arrived, the brave old Pennsylvania Reserves, or a part of it, had been sent in and had forced the Rebels back.

We halted for a few moments, waiting to see, I suppose, if the Confederates would again renew the attack. They did not, for they had been most terribly repulsed. While we were in line, the broken and shattered regiments of a part of the 3rd Corps passed around the rear. Many of the regiments would not number fifty men, and often regimental flags would not be fifty feet apart— the length of a regiment!

The old 3rd Corps fought nobly, and the 5th sustained themselves well. The Reserves fought as they always have, like heroes. All was quiet along the line save the hum of many voices coming from the battle field, mingling with the groans of the wounded. Our line was beyond the place where the fighting had been, for the Reserves, not content with having repulsed the Rebel hordes which had been massed on our left, drove them back far beyond the original line of battle. This was the second day's battle.

It was dark before we started to return to our position, and we little thought that the enemy had already advanced on our breast works on the right, though we heard heavy cannonading in that direction—the red flashes of cannon lighting up the sky with a lurid glare. It seemed to us to be too far away. But on reaching the crest of the hill, we saw that the flashes were not so far distant after all. The smoke had settled down so thickly that the flashes of the artillery could only be seen glaring red as blood through it. The thick clouds settled down over the hills, fields, and woods like a pall, illuminated at times with the crimson fire of the artillery as it flashed and burned against the sky. There is no more sublime a scene as an artillery fire by night; it is most magnificently grand.

We hastened back to our old position, but lo! The Rebels were already there, except a few rods on the extreme left of the ridge occupied by our corps and the little hill on the very extreme right where we had thrown up our breast works. This hill was separated from the main ridge by a marsh some twenty rods wide.

Greene's brigade of about fourteen hundred men had been left and held their ground. All the other space from the right of his brigade to the last regiment on the extreme left was occupied by the enemy, they having come in while we were away. The 2nd Massachusetts, the next regiment on our left, attempted to take possession of their works across the marsh but found them well cared for by their Rebel friends. Our whole brigade, the 27th Indiana, 2nd Massachusetts, 13th New Jersey, 107th New York, and 3rd Wisconsin, were at last posted on the hill north of the marsh, and the breast works were silently and cautiously lengthened out, built along the side of the hill towards the hill across the marsh occupied by the Rebels.

We could hear the Rebels talk across the swale, but we were as silent as the grave; not a word, not a whisper above our breath. Before midnight our works were complete, and we lay down on the grass to sleep or dream, perhaps of home and loved ones far away in our own loved Northland. Many a sleepless eye, however, watched the stars as they came up in the midnight sky that night, wondering if we would ever see them again on earth, and many an eye grew moist as his thoughts wandered away to those he loved and thought perhaps they might soon be weeping for him as among the lost. The night was calm and still and starlit, not a breath of air stirring among the leaves, while the night birds kept up their songs—the whippoorwills gaily singing in the forests and the owls dismally hooting from some distant crag or blasted tree.

We knew we would have hard fighting to do in the morning, that death would come to many of us there on that hill. Death had, we felt, already set his mark on many a brow. Solemn indeed are the thoughts that come to the soldier at such times, for it seems to bring him almost to the very gateway of eternity. Nature seems to smile a sad smile, and the stars above gleam with a subdued lustre, as if in sympathy. A heavy weight seems to press upon his bosom, his heart beats with a stronger throb, and drops of sweat stand upon his brow. Life, though it may have been ever so dark, wears at such a time a dearer and brighter glow.

Several times during the night, heavy firing broke out along the line on the hill beyond the marsh. Several times the Rebels attempted to force back Greene's Brigade, and twice did they charge up to their works up a steep, rocky hill side. But they failed, and in the morning those heroes stood where they did at night, firm and undaunted.

In the morning on July 3, the Confederates launched a major assault on Culp's Hill from the northeast. Meanwhile, the 3rd Wisconsin and its brother regiments exchanged fire with the enemy stationed in their old works at the southern slope of that hill. General Ruger knew that possession of the breastworks on the hill's south side would permit Colgrove to assist those engaged in holding the hill, and he ordered Colgrove to send two regiments across the meadow to the woods where the works were to feel out the enemy and dislodge them if they were not there in too strong a force. Whether the order was garbled by the general's aide who delivered it or was misunderstood by Colgrove is unknown but it arrived when cheering from the Union positions on the hill seemed to indicate that the Confederates were being driven back (which was incorrect at that time). An out-and-out attack was ordered on the Rebel entrenchments, rather than just a probing action. Generally accepted historical accounts relate that the 2nd Massachusetts charged across the swale toward Spangler's Spring, and shortly thereafter the 27th Indiana headed slightly to the east across the broader part of the swale. The 3rd Wisconsin was held in reserve, nor were the 13th New Jersey or the 107th New York in the charge. The Rebel positions were strongly held and well protected, and the Union regiments that participated suffered devastating losses. They were forced to retreat, pursued by the enemy into the meadow. This gave the 3rd Wisconsin an opportunity to fire on the Confederates, which it took advantage of greatly and effectively.

Union troops now moved forward throughout the sector. Connecticut and New York men charged Confederate works on Culp's Hill itself, while their comrades on the far right exploited an opportunity to push the now vulnerable enemy. According to Bryant, the 3rd Wisconsin was ordered in and, with the Union troops already in the fray, swept the Confederates off the hill, out of the breastworks, and back across Rock Creek. Ruger then ordered the Wisconsin men to take possession of the works, which they did.

This is the only spot in Willard's story that appears to contradict what has been reported elsewhere. He reports that the 13th New Jersey and the 107th New York attacked through the east meadow, where the 27th Indiana is generally given sole credit, and that the 27th was sent in to save the 2nd Massachusetts. His assumption about the Indiana men may have been encouraged by the fact that they certainly charged after the Massachusetts troops were already engaged. It is also possible that the New York and New Jersey men may have commenced a movement, as seen by Willard, but did not follow through.

This ended the action around Culp's Hill, and silence reigned in that sector. The Confederate assaults on the hill had been a failure. They had lost two to three times as many men as their Yankee counterparts without gaining new ground, nor had they drawn any Union troops away from other sections of the battlefield.

With the first dawning of morning we were awakened by the simultaneous discharge of at least twenty cannon, the shells going into the woods across the swale and screaming in a most frightful manner. These were followed by hundreds of other shots from our batteries, the shells crashing among the trees, splintering them and scattering the limbs over the ground.

But we knew that the Rebels could not be driven out in that way, for there behind the breast work we had built and among the rocks and trees, they could find shelter and remain in comparative safety. The better way would have been, I think, to have charged the works from the meadow before light in the morning and not have waited to fire a shot but rushed on them with the bayonet. The cannonading only served to wake them up, to be in readiness to receive us when we came.

The cannonading ceased after a few moments, and the charge was ordered to be made all along the line, which was done at half past four. The 3rd Brigade of the 1st Division was crowded on the little hill north of the one the Rebels held. The remainder of the corps, save Greene's brigade, lay in the meadow east of the ridge, hid from the enemy by a long, low swell or ridge. The bugle sounded, and the whole line rushed up over the swell across the marsh and, with a yell, disappeared in the woods. At the same instant, three regiments from our brigade, the 2nd Massachusetts, 13th New Jersey, and 107th New York, started from the hill also. One, the 2nd Massachusetts, went straight across the swale, the other two around to the left, coming in from the east.

The firing was most terrific from the Rebel side, and a perfect tempest of bullets swept through the ranks of the brave old 2nd [Massachusetts], cutting them down fearfully. But on, right on they swept, heedless of the hissing bullets and those that fell, on across into the woods beyond. The woods and underbrush were so thick that we could not see either our own men or the Rebels, but we could see the bright flashes of their guns gleaming among the rocks and trees, like a thousand lightning flashes dancing, and a vast cloud of smoke rose slowly up along the ridge. It seemed as though no one could have lived a moment in that forest. The 13th and 107th were forced back, but the 2nd Massachusetts held their ground until the Rebels, having followed the other regiments to the edge of the wood, turned upon the 2nd, attacked them on the flanks, and were fast gaining a position between them and us—such was the word brought to Colonel Colgrove, who was commanding the brigade.

The 27th Indiana, one of the best regiments in the service, was then ordered to cut their way through to the 2nd with their bayonets. "Men of the 27th Indiana," shouted brave old Colgrove, "you are to save the 2nd Massachusetts, and unless you do, I never want to see one of you on this hill or anywhere else again." "Forward," shouted Lieutenant Colonel Fesselier,[5] and the brave old 27th, with fixed bayonets and a yell such as only the 27th can give, rushed across the swale, already thickly strewn with wounded and dead, into the woods. The Rebels scattered before this resistless charge, and a way opened for the 2nd Massachusetts to retreat, which they did slowly and cooly under the most withering fire. The 27th also returned, fighting fiercely as they fell back to the swale.

The loss in the 2nd Massachusetts was fearful—eleven officers were killed and wounded, and out of less than three hundred men, 136 fell either killed or wounded. Thirty-six men fell dead on the field and not less than twenty have died of their wounds since. The loss in the 27th was also very severe. Never was there a better regiment, or one that has engaged in a more desperate hand to hand struggle, than the old 2nd Massachusetts. Every man of the Color Guard was shot down, but as soon as one man was shot down another took his place—their banner could not be taken.

While the 27th Indiana was slowly retreating down the rocky side of the hill, their flag got entangled in the branches of the trees, and as the Rebels were close upon them, they came very near losing it. But seeing the state of affairs, the whole regiment fiercely turned upon their yelling pursuers, and a brief but bloody struggle ensued. For full five minutes the contest raged around that banner, when the Rebels yielded and the flag was saved. The instant the Indianians began to retreat again, the Rebels rushed upon them. Their color bearer was shot down, but the adjutant caught it up and bore it out in safety.

We were so very fortunate as not to be sent into that terrible struggle, being held in reserve. The troops farther to the left gained a footing on the ridge, and the fight was kept up fiercely all along the line. The firing at times was terrific, then it would die away, then break out again with yells and shouts as reinforcements arrived. The whole ridge would seem to be illuminated by a thousand lightning flashes gleaming and dancing among the trees.

In the meantime, after the repulse of the 2nd Massachusetts, a part of our regiment was deployed among the rocks at the foot of the hill and kept up a galling fire on the Rebels across the swale. Thus the fight was kept up for seven hours. At half past eleven, another charge was ordered, and we (the 3rd Wisconsin) were ordered to cross the swale. But it was known that the Rebels were being hard pressed, and this would be an attack on their flank. Co. G and B were sent ahead as skirmishers. We were followed by the remainder of the regiment, while several other regiments came in from the east. We received a brisk fire while crossing the swale, but without hardly checking ourselves, we rushed into the woods, up the side of the hill, and were in the breast works before the Rebels were hardly aware of our approach. Nearly forty of them surrendered, while others ran away, yielding us the hill without hardly firing a shot. The Rebels were about to abandon the hill before we came, as our fire from the hill across the marsh was getting too hot for them, and our men were slowly but surely gaining ground farther to the left. A few shots were exchanged, however, between us and the retreating Rebels, but by the time our other troops had come up, all had disappeared.

The ground was covered with abandoned arms, many of them loaded and capped. A large number of Rebel wounded were also left behind, while nearly a hundred dead ones were found on the side of the hill. Farther to the left, where the most of the fighting was done, the hill was literally covered with the dead and wounded of both sides. As soon as the Rebels had gone, we, or part of us, went to work caring for the wounded, giving them water and doing every thing for them we could; the Rebel wounded as well as our own men were cared for.

I went up along towards the left for a quarter of a mile or more, and I found the farther I went in that direction, the more wounded and dead I found, until I came to Greene's brigade, which had held a portion of the breast works and the Rebels could not move them. On the crest of that ridge there is an open field of perhaps two acres. On that little space there could not have been less than five hundred dead and wounded. One could not look in any direction, let him turn which ever way he would, without seeing scores of dead and wounded men, shot in every way a bullet could hit them, lying just as they had fallen. Some of them had been killed instantly, others had struggled fiercely with death, tearing the earth with their hands, dying at last with expressions of the most horrible agony lingering on their distorted features. Some had died as if without a struggle, others had been thrown into the most terrible convulsions, their bodies crumpled and twisted in every shape, their limbs extended or thrown out from the body, their mouths open and their eyes glaring with the ghastly light of death. One who has never been on a battle field and seen for himself the grim and ghastly faces of the dead, their distorted limbs and convulsed bodies, can form but a poor idea of its horrors. It is a mercy to him, if he is to fall, to die instantly, for the suffering of the badly wounded is beyond description. It is hard to die on the field of battle, yet there is no nobler grave than that found on the field of strife for one who dies in a noble cause.

There was not a tree on that ridge that had not been scarred by bullets, and many of them had been struck by scores of them. One tree had been struck by thirty-eight bullets. It would have seemed that no one could have lived there on that hill. Those old woods will bear the marks of that battle for hundreds of years to come.

At twelve o'clock, all was quiet along our line, save now and then a stray shot from some hidden Rebel sharp shooter, who paid us his compliments in a manner not altogether agreeable. Indeed, so very attentive was he that several of the 13th New Jersey who were behind a stone wall behind us were hit by him. We looked for this fellow a long time, and at last one of our sharp shooters discovered him and brought him down with the first shot.

Then every thing was quiet along our whole line, from right to left—not a shot was fired, not a cannon heard. We knew that the enemy was massing somewhere, intending to make another dash on some point on the line. That is the Rebel's way of fighting—to mass a vast command, hurl it upon some one point, and if possible crush it before reinforcements can arrive. It requires troops of wonderful coolness to stand these fierce and overpowering onsets. The Rebel soldier, maddened by liquor mixed with gunpowder, will rush up to the cannon's mouth and, as some of the Western soldiers said of Longstreet's men at the battle of Chickamauga, "They will come yelling like devils with their gray caps drawn down over their eyes, and stagger right by the cannons like a lot of drunken men." He was right. But if they meet with determined resistance and coolness, after a few shots they will turn and stagger the other way. They rush fiercely to a fight, and if the troops opposed waver, they are sure of a victory, or at least of routing them. A few well directed volleys, however, will check them.

The cannonade that preceded Pickett's Charge was generally considered by the soldiers to be without peer. Probably more than two hundred guns were in play. The 3rd Wisconsin and those on the Culp's Hill front heard the screaming shells, saw many explode, and felt the earth tremble. They were close enough to the intended Cemetery Ridge destination of the Confederate missiles for those that overshot their mark to screech, explode, and break around them, bringing down tree limbs and wreaking havoc.

About one in the afternoon a most tremendous cannonade burst out near the centre of our line. The first volley shook the whole ridge. Then came another and another, until the hills seemed to rock to their very foundations. The enemy had massed nearly his whole force behind a ridge or wood crowned hill extending in a parallel line along our front near the centre. He brought not less than a hundred and fifty guns to bear on our batteries, and so sudden was onset that for a few moments our men were thrown into confusion—the shells dropping among them in a perfect shower. Our batteries were soon in operation to toss shells in return. Nearly all of our vast reserve artillery was brought up, and in less than half an hour, we had as many guns in play as the Rebels. This cannonade is said to have been the loudest and fiercest ever heard. We were at least a mile from our batteries, and even there the hill trembled perceptibly. We could see the flashes of the artillery. It seemed as though the whole ridge was one vast billow of flame, and the whole sky to the southward became dark with clouds of smoke that rolled up, shading the sun, which glared through it like a red ball of fire.

Willard provides a breathtaking description of Pickett's Charge, full of exceptional detail, but it presents a question. Bryant states that the 3rd Wisconsin was not in a position to witness Pickett's Charge. Julian Hinckley, author of another regimental history of the 3rd Wisconsin, says that he "took occasion" to seek a better view of what was going on, but from his spot he could only hear but not see the famous charge. Willard states that he had not read any accounts of the battle of Gettysburg before writing his own. If we accept these above statements as factual, we must conclude that Willard obtained his information in one of two ways: either as an eyewitness or from others who had participated. We can be certain that the story of the battle was the principal topic of conversation around the campfires of the Army of the Potomac for some time after the event, so we may have an account that

Willard gleaned directly or indirectly from actual combatants during the weeks and months between the battle and his writing the following passage.

On the other hand, we know that Willard (and apparently other men, such as Hinckley) made a practice of leaving his regiment to find vantage points from which he could personally view the unfolding of great events. Willard specifically mentions doing so a number times, such as his return to the Chancellor house during the battle of Chancellorsville, and we know that he was away from his unit's position for a time, walking over Culp's Hill. He certainly relates his account as if he actually saw the charge. Weighing all this evidence, I believe that he likely was an eyewitness to Pickett's Charge. You must come to your own conclusion. Either way, this account is an incredibly early one, and it makes compelling reading.

While this was going on, the Rebels were being massed behind the hill and a grand charge was to be made. The Rebel soldiers were being drugged and maddened by stimulants until they were no longer men but very fiends. In the meantime, Meade had gathered his forces and brought up his reserves. The artillery still thundered from opposing hills, and the air was filled with hissing, screaming shells. Many guns were disabled and gun carriages torn to pieces; the infantry coolly awaited the onset they knew was to be made.

An hour and a half passed, and no Rebel infantry had appeared. Suddenly a long line of them rushed over the hill and down into the fields below, followed by two other columns. Our artillery was brought to bear, and shot and shell were poured into them; but although they were thrown into some confusion, they still continued to press on. A hundred and fifty cannon blazed and burned on the crest of the hills, sweeping them down by hundreds. But they came on, their ranks being closed up as fast as they [were] broken, fresh men taking the places of the fallen. These men were crazed and madly rushed on, many of them to their graves.

The field was crossed by them in a few moments, and our guns could no longer play on them from the heights. No, all depended on the bravery of the infantry. The Rebels were already ascending the slope—had reached to within a hundred yards of our line—when our boys with great coolness rose, and one long girdle of flame burned along the hill side and ten thousand rifles sent their leaden messengers of death hissing through the Rebel ranks. Another and another volley followed. The Rebels [return] the fire for a moment—[rush] on again—another volley—they stagger, their line wavers, surges to the left, reels into position again—then breaks, becomes ragged. The wings scatter over the field, and at last the whole line becomes confused, those in the rear press up, and all becomes one stirring, moving mass of men. Finally those in front press back to the rear—those in the rear press to the front—until at last all become panic stricken and rush wildly back across the field to the woods beyond.

But instantly another mass of troops rush forward, the others are rallied, and again those crazed warriors rush towards our batteries. Again the artillery open from the opposing hills and the infantry wait coolly to receive the charge. They come on as before but were again repulsed. A third time fresh troops were thrown forward, only to meet the same leaden and iron hail when within a few yards of our line, to turn and scatter back in broken and confused masses to the rear.

The hills and valleys became enveloped in smoke, through which the red flashes of the artillery burned and gleamed angrily from the heights, and the flashes of musketry fringed the hillside with a sparkling belt of fire. The last charge was made just at sunset, and the sun glared luridly through the smoke upon their broken and shattered columns. The Rebel batteries withdrew, and as the sun went down, the last gun boomed from the heights of Gettysburg.

The soldiers wiped the sweat from their brows and with thankful hearts sat down to rest beneath the smoky canopy of battle. The stars came out in the summer sky, smiling sweetly on that field of the dead. The contest had been a fearful one, and—

> Thousands sunk to the ground overpowered,
> The weary to sleep and the wounded to die.

Thus ended the battle of Gettysburg, which will always be counted as one of the most hotly contested and most important battles of the war. I have never seen a full account of those battles.

The Confederate dead were buried in a mass grave at the foot of Culp's Hill. While this gruesome task was being done and the Union soldiers were celebrating the 4th of July, the battered Lee left Pennsylvania and attempted to retreat back across the Potomac in safety. Union troops were immediately dispatched in pursuit.

A terrific thunder storm came up just after dark, which probably prevented Meade from following up his advantage. The rain storm was a good thing for the wounded, as it cooled the air and bathed their wounds. All night we lay behind our breast works, the storm in the meantime raged most violently. The thunder and lightning seemed to be trying to equal the uproar of the battle. The bright flashes burned and gleamed along the sky, lighting up those dark heights around which the tempest of strife had swept during the day. Through that terrible storm the Confederate legions pulled back, covered by the darkness, and when the morning came, all had gone from our front.

Early in the morning of the 4th we reconnoitered our front but found no enemy. The woods were thickly strewn with the wounded and dead, while vast quantities of arms were scattered around every where. After we returned from our reconnoitering expedition, we began the humane work of burying the Rebel dead. A deep, wide trench was dug in the meadow at the foot of the hill; there we gave them a friendly and decent burial. All the wounded were removed to the hospitals and cared for. The 4th of July was a happy day for us, though we spent it burying the dead on the ghastly battle field.

Our troops entered the city over and around which the battle had been raging amid the joyful acclamations of the people, who hailed us as their deliverers. The Rebels were completely disorganized. That night they began their hasty retreat towards the Potomac. Our cavalry, as soon as it was known that the enemy were retreating, were sent in pursuit. The results to the Rebels was most disastrous. Some portion of our army followed the retreating Rebels. The cavalry was already at work, the brave and daring Kilpatrick and his followers and Gregg and Buford were doing fearful work in the enemy's rear and on his flanks, falling upon them like thunder bolts from an angry sky. The storm had passed over Gettysburg, and the low muttering of the distant guns told how it was whirling away towards the Potomac.

The results of the campaign are known to all, and I will not attempt in this little book to speak of them. The invasion of the North by the Rebel army, vast as it was, proved a failure; their legions were broken, their hopes crushed, and their prospects darkened. Beaten and disheartened, they fled from Pennsylvania back to their own blighted land, and among the mountains of Virginia collected their scattered bands, reorganized their shattered army, and again the rival armies stood on the banks of the Rappahannock.

The march from Gettysburg back to Harpers Ferry or, rather, Williamsport was a hard one. We took the same road back that we came on and camped for the night near Littleton, where our cavalry met the Rebels the 30th of June. The next day we reached Frederick City, having marched nearly thirty miles. It rained continually and the roads were very bad. From F. C. we pushed westward through Middleton Valley and over South Mountain by the way of Crampton's Pass. We arrived at the top of the pass about dark, where we remained all night. It was through this pass where the battle of South Mountain was fought where Burnside drove the Rebels at the same time they were driven through Boonesboro Gap by Reno. These mountains are portions of the Blue Ridge. There are three ranges of mountains that run nearly parallel. One range, known in Maryland as the Catoctin Hills, strikes the Potomac at the Point of Rocks, one at Harpers Ferry, and the other between those two points, at or near Knoxville. The mountains on the Maryland side divide the country into several of the most lovely valleys in the world. Middleton Valley, Pleasant Valley, and the country east of the Catoctin Hills cannot be beaten anywhere, and south of the Potomac, the valley of the Shenandoah and Leesburg Valley are also formed by these mountains. The country in the Shenandoah is very fertile, the water abundant and of the very best quality, often coming from springs high up in the mountains. Some of these springs are the finest in the world, being twenty or thirty feet in circumference and often ten feet deep, while others will be found gushing up from a seam in a huge rock, cold as ice and clear as crystal. The principal productions in that valley are wheat and corn, of which vast quantities are, or *were*, yearly grown.

The valley is quite thickly settled compared to other portions of Virginia—it is the garden of that state. Many of the very best troops in the Confederate service come from there. Jackson's old brigade, which by its firmness at the first battle of Bull Run won for itself the title of the "Stonewall Brigade," came from that section of the country. The people are mostly very wealthy, or were, at least, before war, with its desolating breath, swept over their homes. The conscription absorbed the men, the Negroes ran away, the women moved southward, and today a large portion of that rich and fertile valley is barren.

From Crompton's Pass, we pushed on to near Boonesboro and halted for dinner in the same field where we encamped the first night after we left Hagerstown, when we first came into Dixie. There was the same field—the same old tree standing like a sentinel in the centre. I shall never

forget that first night after the first day's march—how weary we were—
and how it rained that night—and how we had to lay in the water or stand
up all night. The next morning it was not a little amusing to see the men
wringing the water from their clothes. We little thought at that time that
we would ever have to come there to fight Rebels, but such are the varied
changes and vicissitudes of war. At times the clouds hover over our own
borders and darken our own land, then are suddenly swept back and the
sound of strife is heard only in the distance.

That night we camped near the river. I was on picket, and being short
of rations, went with my friend Beebee to a house, where we for the first
time in many months sat down to a table. The man of the house was loyal,
or at least claimed to be, and told us how the Rebels had treated the people in that vicinity. He assured us that the Rebel army could not cross the
Potomac, and how the people had all been praying for the rain and the
Yankees. "And now," said he, "thank God the rain and the Yankees have
come."

The next day we passed westward over a part of the Antietam battle
field. We passed through Keedysville, the place where I was taken after I
was wounded at Antietam. We passed the little church, which was at that
time used as a hospital. I shall never forget those dreadful days I passed at
that little church—I shudder when I think of them.

The 10th of July found us in front of the enemy again. Skirmishing
began after the old style, and the familiar sound of the popping of rifles
echoed all around us. After a severe skirmish the Rebels were forced back,
and during the night, we and one other regiment advanced under the
cover of the darkness nearly a mile and a half. The advance was a cautious
one, and the men moved along like shadows, silent as death—not a word
was spoken. When we reached the designated spot, all save a few who were
sent out as pickets lay down to sleep, which most of us did in as sound a
manner as though we had been at home. It is a little strange, but nevertheless a fact, that soldiers, no matter how great the danger, as long as they are
allowed to sleep, will drop down any where and sleep as though there was
no such thing as getting shot, perhaps within the next ten minutes.

Well, that night passed, and the next morning we were up bright and
early, expecting to see the enemy before us or have some of them dash on
us, as we were some distance in advance of the main force. At first there
were none in sight, and they could not have been seen even if they had
been within five hundred yards of us. A heavy fog rested over the fields
and woods, making every thing, even at a short distance, wear a ghostly

weird appearance, and a nervous person would be apt to transform every stump or bush into a human being or something worse. A fence across a field, just beyond the hill behind which we were, seemed to us very much like a line of battle; such was the effect of the imagination.

When the fog lifted, we discovered the Rebel skirmishers or pickets about one thousand yards from us, posted along the edge of a woods beyond a wide, open meadow. When they saw us they were a little confused, not expecting to see us there. They began at once to tear down the fence and pile up the rails in the shape of a V, as picket stations. We did the same, but as there were more of them than of us, they had their Vs up before we did and began to pop away at us, sending some of their bullets singing too near us to be comfortable; but we kept at work building rails until our work was done. One Rebel, in the meantime, had crept up among the weeds until he was within fair range of us. I had seen him and watched his motions. He thought he was safe, I suppose, among the weeds; but a Yankee got his eye on him and sent him where he had been trying to send us—to Kingdom come.

Light skirmishing was kept up all day, but no engagement took place. Our whole line advanced as far as we were, and it was thought by all that an advance on the enemy was to be made, but such was not the case. That day passed and the next, yet all was quiet save a little skirmishing. And what seemed still more strange was the order to throw up breast works all along the line. Thus the golden opportunity passed when the Confederate army might have been destroyed. The Potomac was so swollen with the late rains that it for some days could not be bridged, even if Lee had a bridge, which he had not until one was made of such material as he could find and sent to him from Richmond. His position was most critical—driven to the banks of a deep and rapid river with no way of crossing until the floods had subsided, with the Union army stretching half way around in front and the foaming river in the rear.

The Confederate rear guard under Gen. Henry Heth was assigned to keep the Yankees at bay while Lee waited for the swollen Potomac River to subside so that he could build a pontoon bridge and cross into Virginia. On July 14, the day Lee intended to cross, Heth was attacked by elements of the U.S. Cavalry at Falling Waters, Maryland. The Rebels retreated at the end of a sharp engagement in which Confederate general James J. Pettigrew was killed. They did succeed, however, in preventing the Union forces from interfering with the crossing, which took place unmolested.

The night of the 13th came on dark and stormy. Just at night our pickets on the right were thrown forward, and a sharp, little skirmish was the result. That night, covered by darkness and storm, the Rebel army crept away from our front and crossed the river, and when morning dawned, they stood once more on the blighted soil of the Old Dominion—all save their rear guard.

We were up long before light on the morning of the 14th and in line, ready to move at a moment's notice. We expected a great battle was now to be fought and looked down from our breast works over the field lying darkly between us and the enemy's works on the hill beyond, thinking they were soon to be covered with the slain. All stood silently waiting the order to advance, which came at last, and the whole line moved slowly forward, looking in the gray twilight like a wall of shadows.

The whole of the 3rd Wisconsin was thrown forward as skirmishers. We advanced from our works down into a ravine and through a belt of timber, out into the open field, across which, in the edge of the woods on a hill, was the enemy's lines of breast works, which we could see crowning the crest of the ridge. As soon as we came into the open field, we expected to be fired on by the Rebel pickets, but a little to our amazement, we were not. We kept on across the field, expecting at every instant to hear the bullets whirring past us or perhaps be shot down. The field was crossed, and we began to ascend the hill. Now, thought we, if the enemy is here, they will rise and give us a volley very soon, and we expected to see a thousand Rebels suddenly spring up behind the breast works. We quickened our steps almost to a run, and in a moment we were on the works, but no Rebel was there. One long, loud cheer came up from those below, but surely there was no occasion for rejoicing, for the enemy had escaped, and I had fondly hoped that such would not be the case.

We pushed on rapidly through the woods. Their camp fires were still burning, but there were no evidences of haste or disorder. The cavalry now swept past us, we following them as supports. The main column halted, but a few regiments kept on with the cavalry. When near Falling Waters, we heard suddenly the booming of cannon and the rapid discharge of small arms. Our cavalry had overtaken or, rather, had come upon, the enemy's rear guard. They found them posted on a hill with strong earth works, but after a severe fight they stacked their arms and signified their willingness to surrender. The 6th Michigan was sent to take them and slowly moved up to the foot of the hill. It had begun to ascend it when the treacherous villains again took their loaded guns and resumed the fight, pouring a most deadly volley into the unsuspecting men who were only coming to take them prisoners. Fully one third of those they had so basely deceived fell either killed or wounded. But maddened by this base and cowardly act, the brave Michigan boys spurred their steeds up the hill and over their works into their midst. The Rebels threw down their arms and fled. Our cavalry were among them, cutting [them] down as they ran, their long bright sabres rising and falling like lightning flashes and their horses trampling them down in the mud. Full two thousand Rebels were scattered over the field, and what was left of the 6th, stung to madness at their treachery, was rushing among them like so many messengers of death. The Rebels fled wildly toward the river but found some of our cavalry there. About fifteen hundred were taken prisoners, and a large number killed and wounded.

We followed our cavalry closely, and when we got to the scene of the conflict, many were yet quivering in the agonies of death. Our men were stretched out on the hill side, where they had been shot down by the treacherous Rebels, but behind the earth works and scattered over the fields beyond and in the woods near the river, could be seen the work of the avengers. The Rebels in this instance exhibited an unusual amount of meanness. They were neither brave nor honorable and justly deserved the punishment they received at the hands of our cavalry boys. This was the battle of Falling Waters. The Rebels lost not less than two thousand, many of whom were among the killed and wounded. But few of them would have been hurt had they not fired on our cavalry after having once surrendered.

These were dark and gloomy days while the Rebel army was in Pennsylvania, and deep indeed was the interest with which the people watched the conflict raging so fiercely around the Heights of Gettysburg. They might well have inquired "does the star spangled banner still wave," and the fierce cannonade by night and the red flashes burning on the midnight sky would have assured them that "the flag was still there." When the storm had passed, they saw with grateful hearts the Rebel army broken and its shattered fragments hastening backward.

Thus terminated the campaign in Pennsylvania and Maryland. Our southern borders were again free, the capital safe, the Rebel army broken and disheartened. The people looked up and saw the dark clouds that had gathered so thickly above them, overshadowing our land, rolling away, and their hearts, thrilling with joy, beat with a new life.

The loss on both sides during the campaign was great, but ours was not as heavy as that of the Rebels. Ours would not exceed twenty-five thousand, theirs not less than forty. We were cheered by a victory unequaled by any of the war; they were disheartened by defeat. We then became the invaders, and their homes were at our mercy. Never did any soldiers fight better or exhibit more daring than the Rebel soldiers during those three days. But their daring was equaled by the firm, steady coolness of the Northern soldiers, who met every onset firmly and repelled every charge.

When the history of this war is written, it will be said that the Rebellion received its hardest blow at Gettysburg. Had the Rebel army been victorious there, Lee and Davis could have done their will, the people would have been overrun, their cities sacked and their homes burned. Washington would have fallen into their hands, Maryland been lost to us, and the Union, I fear, would have been broken. But He who rules the destinies of nations willed it otherwise, and the Southern legions were swept back beyond the Potomac.

Having finished our work up by Williamsport, we returned to the main force near Falling Waters, where we remained all night. The country in that vicinity is a fine one, and the Rebels, when they went back into Virginia after their brief visit, must have felt that there was a vast difference between a country where war has not desolated the land and one where desolation sits crowned on every hill and ruin smolders in every valley. The great fields of grain, the green meadows, and blooming orchards of the North form a strange and painful contrast with the barren hills and desolated fields of poor old Virginia. How sadly, how lowly she has fallen, the proud state; how poorly it becomes her thus to sit at the feet of her Master. But the day will some time come when, freed from the curse of slavery, she will again take her position as first among the great states of America.

The morning of the 15th found us on our way towards Harpers Ferry. We camped that night about half way up the side of the mountain known as Maryland Heights. We were in the advance, and the main bulk of the army was encamped far below us. Camp fires were soon burning far up along the mountain side and gleaming in the valley below, and as darkness came on, it was a fine sight to look down from the mountain over the myriad fires that dotted its side and sparkled in the valley. One might suppose he was looking down on a great city, only the fires burned more brightly, seeming like some vast illumination. Soldiers become so accustomed to scenes like these that they look on them with indifference. The charm of novelty wears away, and he cares more for a little rest that he does for the most brilliant scenery.

The march was resumed the next morning, and by ten o'clock we stood on the summit of the mountain. I had been there often before, but so changed was the appearance of the Heights that I should hardly have known the place. The timber had all been cut down and a large strong fortress built on the summit, while other forts crowned all the smaller hills, and rifle pits and earth works linked them together like a chain. The general features of the country, however, remained—the same grand lofty heights were there; and Harpers Ferry, the ruined and deserted town at the mountain's foot, looked nearly the same, the charred ruins of the old armory and arsenal and the piers of the burned bridge remained unchanged.

We camped on the same ground where we passed our first month in Maryland. It seemed not a little strange to come back there after two years had passed. There were many who did not return with us who had often answered to "roll call" on that same ground, but who had gone to answer to the last great roll call in the courts of death.

We remained in our camp until the morning of the 19th, when we crossed the river, and once more the Army of the Potomac began its campaign southward. The 3rd Corps had crossed [on] the 18th and was marching rapidly up along the Blue Ridge. The march to Warrenton Junction was a hard one. The Rebels were headed off at several of the mountain passes, but at last they succeeded in getting east of the Blue Ridge by the way of Thornton's Gap. They made an attempt to get through at Manassas Gap, but the old Excelsior Brigade of the 3rd Corps drove them back and held the pass. Much credit is due to that brigade and its brave commander, General Spinola, for their gallant conduct in that affair.

After many days of toilsome marching, we arrived at Kelley's Ford on the Rappahannock. On the way, we passed through the Bull Run Mountains via Thoroughfare Gap. These mountains are a short range of perhaps fifteen miles in length. Thoroughfare Gap is a deep, natural cut through the mountain, and the Warrenton and Strasburg Rail Road runs through this cut. It may well be called Thoroughfare Gap as both armies have made a thoroughfare of it since the war began. I was a little surprised to see a farm built in a little notch in the side of the gap where there was hardly room enough for a house to stand, and nothing around it but rocks, scarcely a green shrub growing. After passing the main mountain, there are several other, smaller elevations. Among these there are several families living who, like their neighbor in the mountain pass, seem to cultivate rocks, as nothing else can be seen around their homes save perhaps a lean pig so poor that even Blenker's stragglers would not have taken it for plunder.

There is a little stream among these hills formed by the many springs in the vicinity. Someone has put up a mill on that stream, a "right smart one it is, too," as a Virginian would say. When in running order, it would, as the miller told me, grind nearly "twenty bushels of wheat a day." But the stone in the old mill was standing still and the old water wheel was broken down. The miller was a New Englander but had lived in the South so long that he had forgotten he was an American.

A few miles east of the mountain is the little village of Hay Market, or at least the place where that little village once was. Now three buildings and long rows of black chimneys are all that is left of it. All the others had been burned down by the Rebels after the first battle of Bull Run, and the tall chimneys stood like grim sentinels among the ruins. The question came up in my mind as I stood among the ruins, where are the people who once lived here?

From Hay Market we went to Fair Play, and across White Plains, and at last on the 26th arrived at Warrenton Junction. After a brief rest, we pushed on down the rail road to Bealton Station, and from there to the banks of the Rappahannock. The army went into camp there, holding all the fords from the U.S. Ford to Waterloo. We (1st Division of the 12th Corps) were stationed at Kelley's Ford about eight miles below Rappahannock Station.

For the 3rd Wisconsin, the Gettysburg campaign now came to its conclusion. The regiment had lost two killed and eight wounded, and the men felt lucky to have come through its trials and battles with so small a loss. The men of the Army of the Potomac had resented the stinging criticisms leveled against them over the past two years for their failure to win the war quickly, and they felt that their performance at Gettysburg should put to rest any doubts about their fighting abilities.

The campaign was now over, and both armies resumed their old positions on opposite sides of the Rappahannock. The campaign had been a hard one, one of almost continual toil and hardships. From the 6th of June, the day on which we left Stafford Court House, until the 29th of July, we were constantly on the move and in that time marched nearly four hundred miles and fought seven battles besides several skirmishes, and that, too, during the heat of summer. And yet we often hear and read in the paper how the Potomac army does nothing. That army, it is true, has often been misled by incompetent generals, and as yet has failed to accomplish its object, namely, the taking of Richmond; but in the meantime, it has fought some of the severest battles of the war. In such battles as Antietam, Fredericksburg, Chancellorsville, and Gettysburg, its losses are not counted by hundreds, but by thousands. Yet it is said the Potomac army does nothing.

The next day after reaching Kelley's, we crossed the river, and during the day a fierce combat took place between a portion of our cavalry and that of the Rebel General Stuart. The combat was a fierce one, fought with about equal numbers, and for about two hours raged with desperate fury. It was fought a few miles northeast of Culpeper Court House in an open country, well adapted for cavalry contests. But little artillery was used on either side, and the fight was carried on in true cavalry style, both sides using the sabre and revolver freely. Several charges were made by both sides with great gallantry but were met with steady, firm coolness or with counter charges. At last, however, the enemy was forced to yield and were driven back to within a mile of Culpeper, where a large force of infantry were posted. Our cavalry were forced to retire, which they did slowly, for the Rebels, although brave enough, were not anxious to again cross sabres with ours and kept at a very respectable distance.

That night we recrossed the river and went into camp with the rest of our division. We remained in that camp until the 16th, when we started for New York City. Our camp on the Rappahannock was a pleasant one, situated on the north bank of the river on a small, green prairie or meadow. This prairie was perhaps half a mile in width, running along the river bank nearly two miles. The meadow was level and covered with a rich vegetation of long, green grass. A high ridge or range of wooded hills bordered the plain on the east, rising like a huge wall several hundred feet above the level of the plain. On the very crest of this ridge was a spring that welled up among the rocks, cold as ice. The whole division was encamped on this plain, and it was a fine sight after clambering to the summit of the heights to look back down on the encampment below. Hundreds of white tents dotted the green meadow, while regimental, brigade, division, and corps flags waved and fluttered in every breeze. Many of those regimental flags were torn and perforated with bullets and were old, stained, and battle worn like those over whom they waved. But the soldiers were all the more proud of them for that and looked with pride on their old banners, which had been with them on many a crimson battle field.

Drills were again the order of the day, and every forenoon and afternoon the regiments were out going through the various and complicated movements of brigade and battalion drill. Some brigades drilled in brigade or battalion drill in the forenoon and in company drill after dinner, others in the opposite order. During these drills a fine and stirring sight was afforded from the heights. Thousands of men all dressed alike, with their sky blue pants, black coats and capes, were all moving—some wheeling to the left, others to the right, some forming squares, some regiments "closing in mass," then deploying at a double quick into line of battle, others sweeping across the plain on a charge with leveled bayonets, all rushing along in line, their ranks closed and solid. Other regiments would be drilling in the manual of arms, loading and firing, while way over near the river would be perhaps a regiment drilling in the skirmish drill. The banners would all be out, the field officers mounted, every belt brightened, "brasses" polished and arms glittering and flashing in the sunlight. Such were the drills of those days, and under such discipline, no troops can help being effective in time of battle. It not only accustoms the men to move with ease in large bodies, but gives them healthful exercise. There is nothing so apt to destroy the health and weaken the soldiers more than inactivity. If the general wishes his men to be healthy and able to endure the hardships of actual service, he must not fail to give them plenty of exercise. Yet too much drilling is not best, for the men soon learn to consider it a task, and it fails to answer the object as exercise. Then other means should be resorted to.

Drills may be made interesting if the general or colonel will try to make it so and knows how, but not while the commanding officer treats the men as mere machines and drills them as such. He must put life into every movement, not by being spiteful, but by his own manner. He must not elevate himself so much above them in his own estimation and speak to them as though he was some deity speaking from the clouds. Such a way may do with some people, but Americans cannot be made good soldiers of in that way, and unless they are deeply interested in what they are contending for, I do not believe they would fight well. They certainly will not fight as well as they would if treated more like men. Severity on the part of officers is not discipline. Men will obey orders and will not shrink from danger, but their hearts are not with a severe officer, and they will only do what they are compelled to. But when the commanding officer has won the confidence and love of his men, he can put more dependence on them; the men will be more interested in whatever they are called upon to do, and will do it.

The country in the vicinity of Kelley's Ford wears the same desolate appearance as other parts of the state; a fine country naturally but allowed to die, so to speak, with old age. Most of the land has been cultivated without proper care, until it has become worthless and abandoned. Then low scrub pines grow up, affording shelter for hares, foxes, and even beasts of prey which prowl through these dense jungles, roving where once the wealthy planter rode about among his slaves. This is one of the many evil effects of slavery. There are but few people living in that vicinity. In other times there was an inn and a small store near the ford, around which had sprung up a few other buildings. An old mill stood on the river bank, but the miller had gone, the wheel was broken down, and the sound of the millstone was heard in *that city* no more.

The place was inhabited by Negroes, there being only two white families living there. I went to one of the wells during the day after water. It was dry. "No water thar," said the man of the house, a gray haired old man, "the water has done gone out on't ever since the war began, and there will never be any more in it until the Yankees are all done gone and the Southern Confederacy is acknowledged." "Indeed," said I, "then I am afraid you will never draw water out of that well again." "Yes, I shall, and that too within one year." "I don't wish to quarrel with you, but I think if false prophets were served nowadays as they were in olden times, you would stand a fair chance of getting a severe stoning." The old man laughed and said he "hoped the war would soon close, either in favor of one side or the other," for he wanted peace, his heart ached, his neighbors were all gone, his wife dead, and his son, his only child, had died in the army and he was alone. Tears came in the poor old man's eyes as he spoke, and he turned sadly away, muttering a prayer for peace. There are many such victims of this war.

The Confederates had a strong draft law, and their armies had many conscripts. It wasn't until March 1863, however, that Congress passed a draft law for the United States; up to that point, all Union soldiers had enlisted. There was widespread opposition to conscription, and when the first names were drawn on July 11, riots broke out in New York City. Mobs roamed the streets, fighting with police and committing outrages against blacks—whom the rioters blamed for the war. At least seventy-four people died, and the draft was suspended there.

The government scheduled to resume the draft on August 19 and moved some battle-hardened veterans from the front to New York to prevent, or at least deal with, any further violence. They had no cause to fear that the soldiers might sympathize with the mob, as the men who had so often risked their lives in battle perceived the rioters as slackers and traitors. The 3rd Wisconsin was one of the regiments that went north to the metropolis.

We remained in our camp on the Rappahannock until the 16th of August, when we started on a new and unexpected expedition. The great riot in New York City in opposition to the draft made it seem necessary to send troops there, and for several days before we received the order, it was rumored around among the men that we were going there, and so it proved. Early in the morning of the 16th we were up, and by sunrise wound our way to Rappahannock Station. There we took the cars with several other regiments for Alexandria, where we arrived late in the afternoon and went into camp. It was several days before we embarked, but at last the boats arrived, and we were on board. The steam ship or transport *Merrimac* was a fine boat, capable of carrying three whole regiments such as ours. When all were aboard, the ship swung out into the stream, where we remained all night, rocking upon the bosom of the old Potomac.

Early in the morning the anchor was hauled up and we were soon under way, dashing swiftly down the river. The morning was a fair one, but a dense fog hung over the river, almost hiding the many boats upon it from sight, but their dark hulls and towering masts could be dimly seen through it as they seemed to glide by us. The sun came up a few moments after, shining warmly upon the fog and clouds, which soon caused them to ascend, and caught by the morning breeze, they rolled away over the city in huge, white banks. We passed Aquia Creek about noon. A great change had taken place there; the government buildings had all been burned down, and a few blackened logs were all that was left of the large, fine wharf which had been built. Every thing had disappeared save the dark heights and a heap of timbers. Several other heaps of ruins may be seen along the river bank, and I noticed three little villages that had been destroyed, nothing but the chimneys remaining.

It is about fifty miles from Aquia Creek to Point Lookout, where the Potomac joins the Chesapeake Bay. Our ride was a very pleasant one. Passing smoothly and swiftly down broad, old Potomac, we were soon out on the broader waters of the bay, and the fine, old ship danced gaily over the waves. Night soon came on, and the low lands along the coasts were lost to view. The full, round moon came up early in the evening, smiling gloriously over the dark waters of the bay, tipping the waves with a silvery crest. The night was warm and the scene a fine one. The bright moon and glittering stars, the deep blue sky, and the dark waters of the bay formed a new combination of nature's loveliness, at least new to me, and for hours I sat by the railing along the side of the ship looking out over the bay, watching the waves as they rose and fell or washed along the sides of the vessel.

Virginia has fine facilities for commercial operations afforded by the many large, and for many miles navigable, rivers which find an outlet into the bay. The York, the James, the Rappahannock, the Potomac, and the many smaller river tributaries provide water thoroughfares to a great part of the state. Chesapeake Bay affords one of the best harbors in the world. But all these blessings have remained unimproved, and the old and insignificant town of Jamestown and unimproved streams remain where a great and flourishing city might have been and a thousand mills and factories might have been built, turning out wealth and affording employment to thousands of men and women; the hum of industry and the songs of the contented and happy laborer would have been heard, where now idleness, ignorance, and silence reign alone.

The night passed quickly away, and when morning dawned we found ourselves out on the ocean. As we looked out over the wide waste of waters which seemed to meet the sky on every side, that strange, indescribable feeling of wonder and awe which every one feels when he first finds himself on the deep, far out of sight of land, came over us, and we looked out upon the wild waters so deep, so blue in silence, lost amid the magnificent grandeur of the scene.

The sun came up, glaring through the mist, paving a broad track across the waves with fire. The ride from Alexandria to New York City was a very pleasant one. We were about fifty-two hours in making the voyage. It was a fine, bright morning that the old ship dropped her anchor in New York harbor, under the guns of the Battery. We were all very anxious to get ashore, but it was nearly noon before that much wished for event occurred. At last we disembarked and formed into line along the landing.

We were soon moving through the city. Crowds of people thronged the way, and cheer after cheer rang along the street. Arriving at City Hall Park, the column halted, and after some delay, we were marched to our quarters in the American Camp, which for the time was to be our home. The change from a dull and lifeless camp on the Rappahannock to barracks in the heart of a great city was a novel one to us. On the Rappahannock all was quiet and still; here, all was noise and confusion. The rumbling of street cars, the roar of coaches, the ceaseless tramp of many hurrying feet, the endless flow of human beings, and the life and activity formed a strange contrast with camp life. Our visit in the city was a very pleasant one, as we had good opportunities of seeing it and visiting all the prominent places of amusement.

While we were in the city, the draft, which had been delayed by the riot, came off with little or no disturbance. The spirit of violence was awed by the formidable array of military power and the undaunted firmness of the government. The rioters were assured that the soldiers brought to the city were tried and true ones, and if brought in collision with them would not scruple to do their work; for they knew how bitterly the soldiers hated them. No disturbance occurred, however, and on the 6th of September we left the American Camp and embarked on board the transport *Mississippi*, bound for Virginia again.

One thing, however, deserves notice before we leave the city, and that is our fare while there. It was the poorest we ever had any where. Mr. Walker, the contractor, was a soulless scamp mean enough to steal the soldiers' rations, which he did every day. It seemed hard to us to be treated so meanly when we knew it was done only to rob us. There are many base and soulless beings calling themselves men, who have no interest in their country's welfare and whose only object is to coin money out of their country's blood. Such men have long since dug a grave for their manhood and have buried it deep down beneath the filth of their own selfishness. They would rob the widows of their last dime and steal the last mouthful of bread from a fatherless child. They would sell the heart's blood of the nation, ay, sell their own nationality and give up their only hope of

Heaven for gold. Such a man was *Walker*. And there are many more of them, men in the government employ getting high salaries who make it their business to rob the government, and not that alone, but men who rob the soldiers of much of their scanty fare, making him go hungry often while *they* grow rich and do nothing—but *steal*.

The soldiers toil on in the ranks with no hope of reward, while the officer rests quietly and safely in the rear, and while the soldier is facing the enemy, he *robs* him of his own. Yet in times to come those very men will be lauded, flattered, while the private who has done the work and fought the battle will be looked on with cool indifference and often with contempt. To be an *officer* elevates a man to the sky, to be a private sinks him to the level of a dog. The former receives high salaries, the latter a mere pittance; the one has but little to do, the other is broken down by extreme hardships and toil; one is in comparatively little danger, the other stands in the front rank of battle; one, if wounded, is immediately taken care of and has every attention paid him, while the private is often left on the field to die or, if taken to the hospital, is deprived of every comfort and often dies of neglect; the one does the work, the officer receives the pay. Such is the difference between an officer and the private. Well, it is so in all wars, such is a soldier's life; but still, it is hard to be robbed of all rights, and worse to be ruled by some villain who has no object save that of filling his own pocket.

We remained in the harbor until morning, when the transport *Mississippi* got under way, and we were soon again dancing over the blue waves of the ocean. It was a warm, bright morning, and the waves seemed to fairly glitter in the sun light. As we glided slowly out of the harbor, we had a fine view of the shipping. The harbor was crowded with boats of every kind, from the little pleasure boat to huge ships that often crossed the seas. The great city loomed up along the shores, and it was a fine sight to us who had been spending years in the lonely camps on the old Potomac and the Rappahannock. Our visit, brief as it was, served to recruit up the health of the men. The many interesting changes, the novelty, and the sea breezes were better than all the physics in the medical department. One would hardly have recognized in the hale, healthy men on board the *Mississippi* that bright autumn morning the wan faced, dim eyed soldier that left the Rappahannock not a month before.

Many of the men were sea sick when we got out on the open sea, where the waves rocked the ship like a cradle, lifting her high up and then plunging her deep down among the foam; but the weather was very fair, and only a moderate breeze ruffled the bosom of the deep.

We arrived at the mouth of the Chesapeake the next morning and laid off Fortress Monroe a short time, waiting for a pilot. The low, white beach was all that could be seen of the shore save the dark blue high lands in the distance, near which is the fortress.

We anchored at the mouth of the Potomac that night, and the next day went up the river to Alexandria. Alexandria is now used as a great military depot, as nearly all of the supplies for the Potomac army are shipped to that place and from there to the front. The old town looked dull enough when compared to the city of New York. Alexandria might have been a large, flourishing city, situated as it is on the banks of a large river, capable of bearing on its broad bosom the largest ships, and with a country around it which might have been with proper cultivation, a fine one. There is no good reason why Alexandria is not a large city unless we conclude that the people were not of the right kind. Why should it not be equal to hundreds of other cities which, with less advantages and a much younger age, have grown to be several times larger, filled with wealth, business, and prosperity, while Alexandria with all its many advantages, remains only a town almost dead with old age.

Washington City, had not the capital of the nation been established there, would today have only been a small town, and now it is a poor apology for a city, as it is one of the most miserable looking places to be found anywhere north of the Potomac.

We landed in the afternoon of the 8th and went into camp, where we remained until the afternoon of the 10th, when we began our weary, toilsome march back to our proper place at the front. The distance from Alexandria to Kelley's Ford is about sixty-five miles. We marched that distance in less than three days. The weather was excessively warm, and the roads were very dusty. The march was a very hard one, and when we arrived at the ford the men were nearly exhausted. We went into camp on our old camping ground. The other regiments seemed glad to see us and came out in line and gave us three cheers as we passed them. We moved camp the next day to the high lands but did not have a very long rest, as we received orders to march the next morning. We knew we were to cross the river and looked for a stirring time. The Rebels were north of the Rapidan, and we expected at least to meet and fight them on the banks of that river.

By day light the column was in motion, moving across the meadow towards the river. Our cavalry had driven the Rebel cavalry beyond Culpeper. We camped for the night near the little village of Stephensville. That day our cavalry again attacked the Rebels and drove them over the river. One of the most daring charges ever made by our cavalry or any other was made by General Kilpatrick's division. There is a little mountain or, rather, a high hill near Stephensville known as Pony Mountain. On the crest of this the Rebels had planted a battery, and their cavalry, having been beaten in the valley below, fled to the summit of this hill, where most of them, at least most of one brigade which went up there, dismounted and formed a line along the crest. One of our brigades, composed mostly of Michigan men, was ordered to charge up the hill, which they did in fine style, heedless of shot or shell, and in a few moments had reached the summit, galloping into the very midst of the dismounted Rebels, who fled in every direction.

The hill side was not very rough yet it was a daring act to ride up there, and nothing but a brave heart and a good steed would have carried a man to the crest of that mountain. But our cavalry have learned to fear nothing. Better troopers than those of Kilpatrick's division can be found no where.

The next day we moved forward towards the river. We were not aware that the Rebels were all across the Rapidan and, as we were in the advance, thought we might perhaps have a skirmish near the river. Within a short distance of the Rapidan, we heard firing in front. We supposed it was our cavalry advance, and as we were ordered to load our rifles, we thought we were to meet the enemy soon. The firing in front was irregular, like that of skirmishers. The men closed up to their places and moved forward silently and steadily, not with that appearance of excitement, noisy bravado which is generally to be seen among new and inexperienced troops, but quietly with closed ranks and firm steps. However, there was no fighting to do that day; the enemy were all across the river, and the firing was only between the pickets.

A cold rain storm came on that afternoon, and those dark pine woods were very dreary. The storm winds swept through the pine boughs over head with a strange, mournful sound while the rain pattered against the trees and on the ground. We (our regiment) were to go on picket to relieve our cavalry, which had been doing duty along the river. We were now near Raccoon Ford, which our cavalry were guarding. The country in that vicinity is on the north bank similar to that around Germanna Mills, but on the south bank rises into heights like those at Fredericksburg. The river is very narrow, and the Rebels had a line of earth works near the river bank, which completely covered all approaches to the ford from our side of the river. A little further back loomed up the dark heights crowned with bristling guns. These heights were all well fortified, and I have heard men say that they considered the position stronger than that at Fredericksburg.

A short distance up the river, the heights arose almost to the dignity of a mountain. We could see from the edge of the woods the enemy's batteries frowning down upon us. No fires were allowed, as the smoke would show them where to fire. Five companies of the regiment were sent out on picket; the other five remained in the woods about half a mile from the river. During the afternoon several shots were fired into the woods where we were, but no damage was done to any one.

There was one post that could not be relieved until after dark, as it was on the bank of the river at the ford and was within half musket range of the Rebel rifle pits. Our main picket line was some distance back out of range, but it was thought best to send one company to the ford after dark, where they would be obliged to remain until the next night, as no one could approach the ford by day light. Co. G was chosen as the company to go. The night came on, dark and dismal enough for any purpose, if rain and darkness was all that was required. The darkness was broken at times by red lightning flashes that gleamed for an instant along the sky, and the low, deep toned thunder rolled away in the distance. We left the woods shortly after dark and moved down to the picket line. Slowly and cautiously we moved from there across the fields towards the river. The lightning flashes at times lit up the scene with a momentary glare, showing the way to go. There are several buildings near the ford, and in these we were to post ourselves and remain secreted until darkness the next night allowed us to be relieved. We found the company of dismounted cavalry there, which we were to relieve, and from their officer received our instructions.

The company was divided into squads, one half to remain as reserve. Six men and a sergeant were sent to the building nearest the ford, and six more to another house a little farther up. I was among the first six. Two of us were to be posted, one on either side of the road on the river bank. Our orders were to resist if attacked in the daytime as long as possible, and as there was no way of escape, to surrender. No assistance could be sent us, as the enemy's works covered the whole field back of us. The day before we went there or, rather, the morning we did go there, just before day light, a party of Rebels rushed across the river and captured nearly a whole company of cavalry, killing some and wounding several. A very lively firing was kept [up] the whole day, and several cannon shots had been sent through the buildings.

We took our positions silently, and the two sentinels were posted. I was on the "2nd relief" and had an opportunity of reconnoitering the place. I examined the yard, surrounding grounds, the fences and out buildings, and then went to reconnoiter the inside of the house. It was as dark in there as any place could be, and my first adventure was to tumble over one of the men who had laid down and was already asleep in the hall. I found this hall to be a narrow passage leading from the front to the back door. While feeling my way across this, I bumped my head against a door leading into another room, and I thought I would go in there. But after stumbling over two or three trunks and upsetting several chairs and a stand with a globe lamp and numberless other little things on it, I concluded to adjourn my exploring until day light. I came out into the passageway and groped towards the front door, but on the way, I hit my foot against a knapsack, and in stepping around that, I slipped and went rolling down stairs into the basement. This ended my voyage of discovery.

At ten o'clock I went on post at the ford, and a dreary two hours I spent there. An old mill stood on the river bank, and its huge water wheel was still in motion, groaning and creaking in a most dismal manner. A mill dam was built across the river, and the water seemed to tumble over it with a strange roaring sound, the river dashed furiously along and among the rocks, and the rain pattered sharply against the sides of the buildings. The dashing of the river, the roaring of the dam, the pattering rain, and the dismal creaking and groaning of the old water wheel, the extreme darkness, and the peculiar situation were enough to make the hours lonely and long.

The night passed quietly. I went on again just before day light. As soon as it was light enough to see across the river, I returned to the house where we remained cooped up. During the day the Rebels amused themselves by shooting into the house, and many balls went through it. We had orders not to fire and paid but little attention to them. They became very bold and took no pains to hide from us, but walked along their earth works shooting their guns now and then. They were not a hundred yards from us and we could have shot them if we had wished to, but we have always considered it a mean thing to fire on pickets, even if we had no orders against it.

The house we were in was well furnished and belonged to a Mr. Stringfellow, who we found to be a captain in the Confederate army. He had left every thing in his house. There were several feather beds and a large, fine library. We spent the day very pleasantly, reading and lounging in his great arm chairs, started a fire in the chimney down in the basement, and made ourselves very comfortable. At night we were relieved and joined our regiment again.

In the following account Willard witnesses the execution of a soldier suffering from what is now recognized as post-traumatic stress syndrome—called "shell shock" in World War I and "battle fatigue" during World War II. Before the advent of psychiatry in the late nineteenth century, psychological traumas caused by war were rarely taken seriously, and this soldier was treated as just another deserter.

At Brandy Station one of the 3rd Maryland was shot for desertion in [the] presence of the whole division. It is known that the man was a fool. A shell burst over his head at the battle of Chancellorsville and had such an effect on his brain that he became deranged. He had run away from his regiment, had been caught, tried, and sentenced to be shot, and on a bright autumn morning he was led out to die, sitting on his coffin by the side of his own grave. He was unconscious of what was going on, and while the guns of the executioners were pointed at his breast, a horrible, idiotic laugh burst from his lips, and the next instant he rolled from his coffin dead.

At the little village of Stephensville, we found the grave of one of the 3rd Maryland who had been hung by the Rebels to the limb of an apple tree and left there. After dark some Negroes cut him down and buried him at the foot of the tree. He had been taken prisoner at Beverly Ford when Pope retreated from the Rapidan. Some of those captured with him saw him executed, and it was those who now found his grave.

It was thought an advance would surely be made, and a great battle was daily expected. We remained near the ford several days, and in the meantime, the great battle of Chickamauga was fought. It was rumored that Rosecrans had been severely beaten, his artillery nearly all lost and his army cut to pieces. The rumor then began to spread that the 12th Corps was to be sent to him, which proved true, and the 24th of September we left our camp on the Rapidan.

Longstreet had been dispatched west to support Confederate forces in the West, and this had resulted in success at Chickamauga. To counter this move, the Union XII Corps was sent west to Tennessee. It ceased being an Eastern unit and served the rest of the war with the Union's Western forces. This gave the men of the 3rd Wisconsin and their corps comrades the distinction of having served at Antietam, Chancellorsville, and Gettysburg, and then participating with Sherman on his Atlanta campaign and the march to the sea.

The prospect of going to the South West was a cheering one. We wished for a change and longed to leave Virginia and enter upon a new field of action. It was hard to leave those old battle fields where the 12th Corps had seen many a dreary day and passed through many scenes of danger and had fought several hard battles. Its ranks have been sadly thinned, and many hundreds of its best men are sleeping in lonely graves on the Potomac and the Rappahannock.

BOOK FIVE

All Brothers Together

Oh! I wish air castle building
Had not pleased my fancy so;
Then perhaps life's real gilding
Had not worn so faint a glow.

What thoughts, hopes we fondly cherish
Prove elusive, false, and vain;
Soil that one neglects to nourish
Afterwards may teem again.

After their defeat at Chickamauga, the Union forces retreated and took refuge in Chattanooga. They dug in and, with the Tennessee River at their backs, prepared for a stay. The victorious Confederates occupied the mountains that surround the city—Lookout Mountain, Missionary Ridge, and Raccoon Mountain—and waited for the Yankees to evacuate.

This delay by the enemy came as a godsend to President Lincoln, who had no intention of withdrawing from Chattanooga. It gave him time to send two corps from Virginia to Tennessee to salvage the situation. Willard and his comrades in the XII Corps first received word of the Union loss at Chickamauga from the Rebels, then heard rumors that they might be dispatched to the Western sector to reverse the fortunes of war there. This was confirmed, and they packed up and left the Eastern front, traveling west.

>─┤─◆〉─○─〈◆─├─<

On the 24th of September the 12th Corps left the Rapidan to reinforce the Army of the Cumberland. It was a bright afternoon in early autumn and a September sun shone from the sky with a mild, subdued lustre o'er field and wood, bathing the blue hills of the "Old Dominion" in a shower of golden light, drifting down through the dark woodlands and glimmering on the rippled bosom of the Rapidan. The Army of the Potomac had been encamped along the north bank of the river for several days. On the opposite bank lay the Rebel army of Virginia behind their entrenchments, strongly posted on the heights. Their batteries could be seen, and a long line of earth works marked their line of defense. They held a strong position, well fortified, but the Union army quietly and confidently waited for the order to advance.

In the meantime, the disastrous battle of Chickamauga had been fought and lost by the Army of the Cumberland. This was one of the most disastrous battles of the war. It was fought on the 19th and 20th of September 1863. Rosecrans had crossed the Tennessee at Bridgeport, Battle Creek, and Shellmound, south west of Chattanooga, and moved up and invested the town, compelling the Rebels to evacuate. Bragg, who commanded the Rebel army of Tennessee, backed into northern Georgia south of the little river Chickamauga. Rosecrans pushed on over Mission Ridge toward Dalton. A portion of his army crossed the Raccoon Mountain. Bragg, heavily reinforced by Buckner's corps and Longstreet's veterans from Virginia, attacked the Army of the Cumberland and, after two days of the most desperate fighting, forced it back to Chattanooga.

The Rebel army occupied and fortified Mission Ridge and Lookout Mountain, which form a semicircle extending around the northern, eastern, and southern sides of the city about three miles distant. Mission Ridge is a circular hill about four miles in length, its northern extremity resting on the river, and has a height of three hundred feet. Lookout Mountain at the Southern extremity is a high, bold bluff twenty-three hundred feet above the level of the Tennessee and stands on the bank of that river like some huge, grand old monument. In the valley in which Chattanooga is situated lay the Army of the Cumberland, surrounded by this wall of earth and rocks, bristling with Rebel cannon and Rebel bayonets. It was for their relief that the 12th and 11th Corps were detached from the Army of the Potomac.

On the night of September 22nd, about ten o'clock, the Rebels seemed to be very jubilant over some thing. Cheer after cheer went up from their encampment, bands of music were out, songs and shouts and the most extravagant expressions of rejoicing were kept up nearly all night. They had heard the news that Rosecrans had been defeated long before we heard a word and were rejoicing over it. Our pickets and those of the Rebels were on "speaking terms," and the next morning one of our boys in blue shouted across the river, "Good morning, Johnny." "Good morning, blue back, have you heard the news?" "No. What the deuce were you fellows about last night?" "Oh, only having a wake." "Well, I should think you did, and some thing else. I should think by the pow wowing that your whole army was on a drunk or an Indian war dance. We shan't allow any more such pow wows, for don't you know that it is against the law for folks to break the peace and disturb quiet people like us?" The Rebel then proceeded to inform us that Rosecrans and his whole army had been captured. This was an exaggeration of course. The Rebels always got the news from the West and South West long before we could on account of their greater facilities of communication.

Much of the blame for the disaster of Chickamauga may, I think, be laid to our enemies in New York City. The treason and rioting in that city took from the army a large number of soldiers, not less than fifteen thousand. This, of course, convinced the Rebel authorities that an advance by the Potomac army was not intended at that time, and they could safely detach a corps to reinforce Bragg, which was done; the unfortunate consequences followed. The Copperhead democracy of the North have always worked for their masters—at the South. It is hardly known at the North how much mischief such creatures do to our cause by their violent and treasonable opposition to the war and the administration, their miserable and cowardly clamoring for peace.

I have heard Rebels say that they were expecting assistance from friends in the North. Rebel papers are filled with imported treason, borrowed from disloyal journals north of Mason's and Dixon's Line. The shameful whining for peace, the bitter language and disloyal sentiments that drift through the social atmosphere of Northern society, all poison like the deadly miasma that floats up from the filthy pool. They weaken our cause, strengthen that of our enemies, and retard the dawning of that peace for which they so wildly clamor.

When the order came to "pack up and be ready to march," it was supposed that an advance was intended. All expected to cross the river and that a great battle was about to be fought. The fearful experience of Burnside's crossing at Fredericksburg, the rocky and rapid river we should have to cross, the strength of the enemy, their strong position, the dark heights crowned with batteries—would we cross the river was the thought first in every mind. And it was not the most agreeable thought. Had the advance been made, the Rapidan would have run red with blood, and dead bodies would have drifted down among the rocks.

In a short time every thing was ready, and the line was formed facing the river. We were a little surprised, and very agreeably, too, when we moved off by the right flank and marched back toward the Rappahannock. We arrived at Brandy Station about ten o'clock, and as the night was cold, huge fires were soon burning, illuminating the plain around the Station. We remained at the Station until the morning of the 26th. In the meantime the paymaster called to see us. The visits of that worthy individual are always agreeable to soldiers. He brings his money box and a few thousand dollars for a few thousand of Uncle Samuel's boys. The green backs were accordingly issued out, and the men pocketed the insult with much less grumbling than is heard on some other occasions.

At midnight on the 27th we got on the cars and began our journey toward the West, passing through Washington up as far as the Relay House, where we took the cars again and started westward on the Baltimore and Ohio Rail Road, crossing the Potomac at Harpers Ferry. At nine o'clock P.M. we reached Martinsburg, Virginia. It was at this little Union town that Banks's broken and shattered fragment of an army was treated so kindly by the people when we passed through there on our retreat from Winchester. By midnight we were among the mountains of Western Virginia.

It was a clear, bright moonlit night, and the grand old mountains and the lofty peaks loomed up darkly against the blue sky. A ride by night through the mountains, with a full moon and a clear sky, is by no means an unpleasant affair. The scenery—ever changing—is sublime. The full, round moon and myriads of glittering stars, seeming to dance around the lofty summits of the mountains, the huge rocks and deep, dark passes, all whirl before one's eyes. Western Virginia is a rough, mountainous country but has a brave, loyal people. There are but few slaves in that portion of the Old Dominion; the people are industrious and true to freedom. When the war broke out, these hearty mountaineers took their stand by the Union and the old flag, and notwithstanding the home strife that raged around their very doors, they have been undaunted, and we find them in this bitter struggle standing firmly by the country, the Constitution, and the laws. It would be well if every section of the North could boast of such loyalty and devotion as has been exhibited by these mountaineers. Eastern Tennessee can also boast of being more loyal than some states north of Mason's and Dixon's Line.

On the morning of the 27th, we arrived at Bellaire, Ohio. We passed through Columbus, the capital of the state, and arrived at Dayton in the evening. Here the ladies came out with songs, smiles, and eatables. One could hardly suppose that such a miserable Copperhead and traitor as Vallandingham[1] could ever have lived among such a generous and patriotic people. All through the Buckeye State, the people were wide awake over their state election. Where ever we stopped along the route, the people, men, women, and children, were cheering for their Johnny Brough and cursing Poor Vall. The voting of course resulted, as every loyal man wished it might, in the election of the Union candidate, and the patriotic old state mounted the lofty summit of a hundred thousand majority on the side of freedom. What a rebuke must that have been to the Vallandingham peace sneaks of Ohio!

A little incident occurred at Dayton which will illustrate the sentiments of the soldiers in regard to that class of Rebels—a meaner kind than the Southern—at the North. Just before reaching Dayton some of the 7th Ohio, knowing that Dayton was cursed with a rather large stock of Rebel sympathizers, concocted a plan to give them the benefit of soldiers' regards. They collected on the platforms of the cars, and when the train stopped, proposed three cheers for Vallandingham to a crowd of men standing near. The soldiers began to cheer, the men at the depot joined in; but the soldiers suddenly changed their mode of demonstrating and sprung among the open mouthed gentry before the second cheer had left their throats. They were knocked down, and the three cheers were not given. The soldiers hate the name of Copperhead and have reason, for while they are fighting the enemy in front and standing like a living wall between their homes and the enemy, these snakes in the grass are stabbing them in the back and doing more to prolong the war than the Rebels in arms.

We left Dayton just after dark and took breakfast at Indianapolis, Indiana. The next morning, October 1st—crossed the Ohio. The next morning—took breakfast at the soldiers' home, Louisville, Kentucky. Passed through Nashville, Tennessee, about midnight and arrived at Murfreesboro at day light. Murfreesboro is a fine, old town thirty miles south of Nashville. At twelve o'clock that night we arrived at Stephenson, Alabama, an old town among the mountains, where for the first time in seven days we had the pleasure of stretching ourselves out on the ground and enjoying a soldier's sleep under the blue sky and in the open air.

While passing through Kentucky and Tennessee we saw a great number of very poor people living in log huts, without windows, furnished only with a few old chairs and benches and a bed in one corner of the room. These have a huge, stone chimney, around the hearth of which the family hovers as if anxious to catch every breath of warmth from the smoldering embers, while the chilly winds of autumn come in rude gusts through the open space between the logs, and the half clothed, shivering inmates gather around the cheerless hearthstone to bake their "hoe cake," often the only article of food. But Tennessee has not suffered so much from the effects of the war as Virginia has, especially that part of the Old Dominion between Washington and Richmond and in the Shenandoah Valley.

Losing patience because the Yankees had not evacuated Chattanooga, General Bragg ordered Joe Wheeler's cavalry to disrupt Union supply lines serving the garrison there. The 3rd Wisconsin was sent chasing him, and after a few other brief assignments, the regiment was ordered to Wartrace, there to build a stockade and guard a bridge. This was not hazardous duty, and the men had a chance to rest and recuperate from the year's arduous service. Willard used this time to observe and write.

On the 3rd of October the Rebel General Wheeler, with four thousand cavalry, crossed the Tennessee, attacked McMinnville, and captured the 4th Tennessee [USA]. This was the beginning of one of his most unfortunates raids. General McCook followed him closely and overtook a portion of his command near Anderson's Crossroads and routed them. On the same day a portion of Wheeler's command appeared before Murfreesboro and burned the rail road bridges over Stone River and Stewart's Creek. They were finally overtaken at or near Sugar Creek, five hundred of them captured and the remainder scattered.

The 3rd Wisconsin and several other regiments, after several days of marching up and down, went into camp at Elk River Bridge on the Chattanooga and Nashville Rail Road. Here we had for neighbors a Negro regiment. Their camp was clean and neat; they were nearly all of them large, athletic fellows and looked as if with good officers and proper training they might make the very best of soldiers. They were always orderly and obedient, much more so than some of their near neighbors.

The inhabitants in the vicinity of the station were supported by our government, and rations were dealt out to them by our commissaries. The country is not very good, the people quite destitute.

The 12th and 11th Corps were now under the command of General Hooker, or old Fighting Joe. The 1st Division of the 12th Corps was guarding the rail road from Murfreesboro to Anderson. The 2nd Division was encamped near the western side of Lookout Mountain in a valley on the banks of the little stream Wauhatchie. On the night of the 29th this camp was attacked, but after a brisk fight the Rebels withdrew. In the meantime, Sherman's army had reinforced General Thomas, who was then in command of the Army of the Cumberland.

About two weeks after we went into camp at Elk River, orders came to prepare to march. By day light the next morning we were on our way again towards Chattanooga. It was a cold, wet morning, and we found the mud of Tennessee equal to that of Virginia. At night we camped at the foot of the Cumberland Mountains. The next day we crossed the mountains and encamped near Anderson.

For some reason best known at head quarters, the 1st Division was ordered back, and after two days we went into camp at Wartrace, where we remained for several weeks. Wartrace is in Bedford County and is only a rail road station and a few buildings of a very old and dingy appearance. It is called Wartrace from the fact that it was through that section that General Jackson marched with his army to fight the Indians. His army encamped for several days on a hill side near the village, and names and dates may still be seen cut in trunks of trees.

Middle Tennessee is altogether a fine country with a healthful climate. Bedford County has been one of the most wealthy counties in Middle Tennessee. It has a rich and fertile soil, with numerous small rivers and streams winding among the hills and through the valleys, and a climate as delightful as one could wish. Long after the snow had fallen in the Northern states, in Tennessee the grass was still green on the hillsides, and that most delightful kind of weather which we call Indian Summer prevailed until mid-winter, and flowers were blooming in the gardens. It is a fine farming country, and with a little more skill in agriculture and a little more industry and enterprise on the part of the people, it might be made one of the richest counties in the Union. But in Middle Tennessee, as in all other slave holding communities, industry on the part of the whites is ignored, enterprise lags, and the tone of society is lowered. The miserable buildings and half cultivated farms, the habits of indolence on the part of the whites, and the carelessness of the slaves leave their marks upon society. Most of the people around Wartrace were very poor but loyal, and many of them lived on the charity of Uncle Sam.

War has not effected Middle Tennessee as much as it has other portions of the South. The fences remain and but few building have been burned; the farms have been cultivated according to Southern style in most localities as long as the slaves would remain and work, but of course many of them ran away. Most of the young men were away, either in one army or the other, or had fled to escape conscription. There are but few schools in Tennessee. I do not know that I ever saw a school house. There have been some private schools, but only the most wealthy could attend more than long enough to learn to read and write, and not more than one half of the people ever learned that much at school. Most of them learn at home and a large number never learn.

Nearly all use tobacco. It is no uncommon thing to see young ladies chewing tobacco and smoking pipes made out of corncobs. Dipping snuff is another practice very common among the upper classes. This dipping is to me the most disgusting habit of all. It is confined to the ladies generally, and it is a fashionable habit among the aristocratic. For the benefit of those who may chance to read this who have never been in the South and do not know what is meant by "dipping," I will explain the "modus operandi." The dip cup and dip stick or brush are indispensable articles of furniture in almost every wealthy family in Tennessee. The dip cup is usually a small earthen cup or mug. In this is mixed two or three spoon fulls of snuff and water. The dip stick is usually made from a round bit of hickory, chewed at one end so as to make a kind of brush of it. This they dip into the cup and then put it in their mouths, chewing and rolling it around as men do cigars. They go about the house with their dip sticks in their mouths. Whenever a lady calls on another, almost the first thing will be to pass the dip cup and sticks to the visitor. The snuff is used on the teeth to make them white. Some ladies smoke, dip, and chew.

Every people have their peculiar habits, and these people have theirs. Some of their habits would not be considered elegant here at the North, but custom makes laws. They have good qualities as well as bad ones. Southern people are generally open hearted and generous, though indolent and ignorant, and have much less deceitfulness than their Yankee neighbors of New England. True Southerners are very social, even with strangers, and take a person to be what he professes to be. Being honest themselves, they suppose every one else to be the same. This applies not to the most wealthy or the poorest, but to those who occupy the "middle walks of life." The most wealthy are proud and overbearing in their manners, yet they are generous and free with those they consider their equals.

I have heard many stories about Southerners being spiteful and uncivil to Union soldiers, and how they have poisoned them and the like, but during a three years' experience in the South, I have seen but little incivility, and never knew of a soldier being poisoned by them. I have been treated with kindness and respect by Secessionists. There have been acts of violence committed by women, but as far as I have ever been able to learn, they have been of rare occurrence.

The 3rd Wisconsin was the only regiment at Wartrace; the other regiments of the 1st Division were scattered along the rail road guarding bridges. Two companies, A and G, were stationed at Garrison Creek, one mile from the village. We went into winter quarters there, where we remained until Christmas nearly. It was a very pleasant place to encamp, being in a fine country and among good people. Many of the inhabitants were loyal, and those who were not were social and hospitable. Their sympathies were with the South, which they did not deny; but they were not spiteful or uncivil.

The terms of enlistment of most of the boys of 1861 were coming to a conclusion, and the government launched a campaign to get these veterans to reenlist. A large majority of the 3rd Wisconsin was ultimately persuaded to do so, but the pressure on these men must have been terrific. In fact, Willard seems resentful of the "agitation" used to procure the reenlistments. A veteran of years of service, wounded at Antietam, and survivor of many battles, Van Willard felt that he had done enough and chose to go home. The men who reenlisted were sent home on

Christmas Day for an extended leave, while the others, including Willard, stayed behind in Tennessee. Those on leave returned in early February.

When it was nearly Christmas, the subject of reenlisting began to be agitated in our regiment. The battle of Chattanooga had been fought, and the Rebels, hurled from Lookout Mountain and Mission Ridge, had fallen back towards Dalton. It was supposed by many that the war would soon be over, the men were anxious to visit home, and the bounty of four hundred dollars was some thing of a temptation. By Christmas, over two thirds of the regiment had reenlisted for another term of three years. About seventy-five of the regiment present for duty at that time refused to reenlist and were left behind when the regiment started for home, which it did Christmas morning, most of them in high spirits, cheering and singing, "We are homeward bound, homeward bound." The remnant of the regiment was consolidated in one company and went into quarters at Wartrace, where we remained until the return of the regiment at the expiration of their furloughs. Nothing of importance occurred to break the dull monotony. Every thing went on smoothly.

We attended church in a little meetinghouse about two miles from the village, where an elderly gentleman, formerly a native of Massachusetts, preached an occasional sermon on the Sabbath. The congregations were not large ones, made up of women and children and a few old men. I was told that before the war the church was always well filled, but that the people had nearly all gone away, the young men into either one army or the other or had run away to escape conscription; some of the people had gone north and some south. There were but few, at all events, that remained, and they could tell nothing of the fate of those who had gone. Some they knew had fallen in battle, but they knew not who or how or when or where. The few who came to hear their old, white haired minister preach the word of God came with a sad and cheerless look, as though they had lost every hope and had nothing to live for, only to mourn.

What a sad condition for a people to be in—their country depopulated, every other house deserted, with here and there the blackened ruins of some building burned by one side or the other, and they mourning the loss of kindred or friends, or living in suspense in regard to their fate, not knowing whether they were alive or dead!

The North has suffered by the war, but the people here hardly know what war means; they can't comprehend the amount of suffering that falls to the lot of the Southern people. Well, perhaps they deserve it all. The fearful wrongs that they have inflicted on a portion of their fellow men are being terribly avenged, the blood and tears that they have wrung from the poor slave have all been counted by Him who watches the sparrows fall and numbers the hairs of every head, and now it is being repaid, for as they have meted out to others so shall [it] be meted out to them.

Slavery is an institution that hardens the heart and corrupts the morals of any people; it lowers man from his true dignity. Its evil spirit pervades society like a magic charm, the lofty sentiments of American liberty and democracy are stultified, morals degenerate and nobler sentiments of the heart and religion die out, and industry and enterprise languish.

There is a punishment for national sins as well as for individual crimes. The sin of slavery has rested on our nation for years, North as well as South. The wrongs of millions of people have been noted, their blood has cried out against us, and our punishment come at last. Our depopulated country, our homes draped in mourning, are the tokens of our just chastisement—a mourning people and a humbled nation.

Freedom and slavery cannot exist in the same government, for a house divided against itself cannot stand. Either one section or the other must triumph. Slavery will either pass away or freedom will sink at the feet of the slave power. Slavery must die—the curse of God is upon it; the light of experience and intelligence burns upon it, and it must wither. The school house and academy will take the place of the whipping post and the slave mart. The desolated fields will be cultivated anew, and the spirit of freedom will be born anew along the Southern borders, and the Union, cemented anew by the blood of heroes and patriots and purified by fire, will emerge from the struggle stronger than ever before.

Though the remnant of the 3rd Wisconsin saw little action toward the end of 1863, the same was not true for the balance of the Western armies of the Union. In November, Grant and Sherman broke out of Chattanooga, took Missionary Ridge and Lookout Mountain, and sent the Rebel forces fleeing. Many of the Federal troops had never seen the Confederates run like they did at Missionary Ridge and gladly pursued them southward. These victories made Sherman's famous Georgia campaign of the following spring possible.

Lincoln County in southern Tennessee had been a hotbed of secession and was strongly in support of the Confederate cause. It was also infested with roving bands of guerrillas who had been murdering Union soldiers. Gen. George Thomas levied a fine on the area, the proceeds of which would be used for the relief of the families of the slain men, and in February 1864, the reunited 3rd Wisconsin was ordered

there to enforce the fine and keep the guerrillas at bay. Willard's men had some
interesting scrapes with the guerrillas, as he details in his narrative.

The entry of Union troops into the county seat of Fayetteville was initially
greeted with resentment, but this began to change when the Yankees provided food
to the hungry, without regard to political sentiments, and protection from the parti-
sans who had been terrorizing civilians on both sides. The people also began to see
that the U.S. soldiers were there for the duration and were really quite decent fellows
after all. The conversion of the town of Fayetteville from hostility to a kind of
friendship is as fascinating as it is unexpected.

The regiment returned on the night of the 9th of February and passed
on to Tullahoma, seventeen miles south of Wartrace and seventy miles
south of Nashville on the Nashville and Chattanooga Rail Road, where
we joined them on the 11th. Tullahoma is one of the places where Bragg
made a stand, building strong fortifications, cutting down the timber all
around the place for over two miles, and after all abandoned the place
without a battle. It is not a city, not even a village, and is located in a fine,
level country.

The next morning we started for Fayetteville, thirty miles west of Tullahoma, where we arrived about noon on the 13th. Fayetteville is, or
rather once was, a fine, little city of about two thousand inhabitants, is
built mostly of red brick—had several stores and other public houses, one
printing office, and an academy. It is one of the finest towns in Tennessee.
The people were nearly all Rebels, and it had been one of the favorite
haunts for bushwhackers. Lincoln County is quite rough and hilly, which
made it a resort for the kind of beasts which infested it. Several soldiers
had been captured in the vicinity of the town and murdered by them.
Lincoln County was known to be one of the most rabid Rebel counties in
the state. Several gangs of bushwhackers and murderers prowled among
the hills, burning cotton and persecuting what few Union people there
were.

A tax of thirty thousand dollars had been levied on the county for the
murder of three Union soldiers whom they had captured. Their bodies
were left thrown across the fence by the road side. Three others had been
murdered before and thrown into Elk River. It was thought best to establish a military post at Fayetteville to facilitate the collecting of the tax and
the breaking up of those bushwhacking bands.

Many of the buildings were deserted by all save rats and mice—not more than half of the people were at home—probably had gone visiting among their friends "way down south in Dixie." We took possession of the town and went into quarters in some of the empty buildings. An order was issued to us and the people, stating the object of our visit to the city. The collection of the tax was to go on, refugees were to be protected, and the destitute families of men in either army were to be supplied with food, and for that purpose, contributions were levied on the wealthy secessionists in the neighborhood. We were soon in comfortable quarters, and preparations were made for building a fort in the public square.

It was thought advisable to have a few mounted men scout about the country and hunt bushwhackers. Thirty men were detailed for that purpose, and I happened to be one of the number. We soon supplied ourselves with horses and began our exciting but rather dangerous work. We were in the saddle most of the time, night and day, riding through the country or guarding wagon trains through to Tullahoma and Shelbyville. We were often out three or four days at a time, scouring the country and chasing guerrillas. Small parties would leave camp at night and not return until the next night. We captured a large number of guerrillas and broke up several camps. It was not always a pleasant task to scout among the hills alone, not knowing at what moment you might be attacked or what ambush you might not run into.

We had several skirmishes with them. We attacked a band at Tucker's Creek and captured the whole party after a little fighting and a good share of running. They do not generally stand to fight, but get out of the way as soon as possible; their object is not to fight but to rob and plunder. They are generally deserters from the Rebel army with now and then one from our own. They prowl about the country doing what little mischief they can without any danger to themselves.

The most important skirmishes with the bushwhacking gentry were at Fishing Ford and Markham's Farm. The former occurred on the 17th of March. A small party of our scouts were scouting near Fishing Ford and, while passing through a piece of timber land between two hills, were attacked by a band of guerrillas who were waiting in ambush for them and captured all but one, who made his escape and brought the report of the affair to camp. Orders were immediately given to "saddle up," and about twenty of us were soon ready for the road. We met the men that had been captured coming into town. The captors, having stripped their prisoners of every thing valuable, had let them go. One of the men had heard the commander of the party say that they were to go to the Sulphur Springs. We got on their track, and by enquiring of the Negroes, were able to follow them for several miles beyond the Springs. It was night before we left Fayetteville, and after the moon had gone down, it was quite dark, and about midnight we lost track of them.

It was thought best not to go any further that night, and having taken possession of a house and barn, pickets were stationed so as to allow no one out or in, and the others lay down in the hay and were soon in the land of "nod." All passed off quietly, and by day light we were again in the saddle. We found they had not passed along that road and concluded they had turned off before reaching that place, and had gone up over a hill, leaving the road altogether. Their horses made quite a plain trail, as the ground was soft and there being fourteen of them.

Two men dismounted and followed on foot a few rods ahead of the party. We had not gone a mile when, on coming to the top of a hill, the advance discovered the whole party about a half mile ahead, safely, as they supposed, in among the hills, little thinking that the Yankees were on their track. The place they were in was a good one to encamp in, as they could be seen only from the top of the hill we were on. The country all around was rough and hilly. Nine men and the captain dismounted with the intention to surprise the camp. The others, as soon as we (those who were to attack them) had attacked their camp, were to ride among them and cut off their retreat.

The attacking party moved off rapidly, and after a rapid walk of half an hour, we gained the hill at the foot of which the party was encamped. We could see them sitting on the ground and standing by their horses, smoking their pipes, all unconscious of danger. We crept down the hill among the trees until we were within a hundred yards of them. They seemed to be in a warm dispute about the horses and arms they had captured from us the night before. Every thing worked well so far, but our captain very foolishly hailed them and asked them whether they would "fight or surrender." They did neither, but sprung off among the trees, and before we could hardly fire a shot, they were out of sight. We followed them and had a running fight for half a mile or more. There was a wide, deep ditch which could be crossed only at one place. The guerrillas knew where this crossing was, and those who took their horses were soon beyond our reach.

They had left nearly all of their horses and several carbines and revolvers, two muskets, and one long rifle. They seemed to have but little care for anything, only to get away, which most of them did. One was captured, several wounded, and one killed; but the expedition was more of a failure than a success on account of poor management.

The other incident occurred fifteen miles from Fayetteville at Markham's Farm. We were guarding a government agent through to Huntsville who had thirty thousand dollars with him. We reached Markham's just at night. Lieutenant Haskins was in command and concluded to put up for the night. Markham's farm is in northern Alabama, owned by a wealthy planter, a social, warm hearted old gentleman who knew how to treat every one. He owned a large plantation and had owned a large number of Negroes, most of which had gone a-visiting, never intending to return. Markham received us kindly and extended every hospitality. He did not pretend to be a Union man and boldly admitted that he was a Rebel, and hoped they would come out triumphant. But, said he, "I reckon you Yankees are honorable men, and I allow that it is right to treat even our enemies with respect." A good supper was gotten up for us and the horses well cared for.

The country around Markham's is very open, having once all been cultivated for cotton, but most of the plantations had been deserted, having become unproductive by the numerous crops of cotton that had been grown on them without any change. The soil had, as the old gentleman expressed it, been allowed to "run out." It is no uncommon thing to see plantations of hundreds of acres deserted altogether on account of its becoming so sterile that nothing could be grown on it. All through northern Alabama such barren fields may be found, giving the country the appearance of a vast common or heath. Such was the appearance around Markham's.

Pickets were posted, and the others "turned in" for the night, taking possession of one of the Negro huts, which afforded accommodations for us all. The night was dark and rainy, and the wind sweeping across the deserted fields and the rain pattering a mournful measure on the shingles made the night a dismal one, such as we have always associated with nightly crimes—murders, assassinations, and the like.

Every thing passed on smoothly until eleven o'clock, when we were awakened by one of the sentinels, who had discovered someone creeping into the yard and had ordered him to halt. The man dodged back into the corner of the fence, and a moment after a volley was fired; some of the bullets whistled over us, and some struck the building we were in. No one was hurt, however, and the next moment we were out and had posted ourselves to the best advantage. Shots were exchanged rapidly for a few moments, when the attacking party, whoever they were, withdrew. The darkness prevented either party from seeing the other, and the flashes from the guns were the guides for firing. None of us were hurt, and it is known only by themselves what their loss was, but from the fact that blood was found on the ground and on the fence, it was thought that some of them had been hit. In a short time all was quiet again, and the most of us lay down to sleep.

The scouts have a dangerous task, often riding alone through strange country surrounded by unseen enemies, liable to be captured at any moment; it would be an easy matter to ambush them. We had but little of that during all of our rides through the country, yet we often followed large parties of guerrillas for miles through wild, rough country, which afforded abundant opportunities for ambushing us—dark woods, deep ravines, rocky hills, and narrow passes, where a hundred men might have defied a thousand.

The people began to think better of the "Yankees." We remained at Fayetteville several weeks. The winter had passed quite pleasantly, and two of the spring months had gone by. In the meantime three hundred recruits joined the regiment who had enlisted while it was home on furlough during the winter. During March and April the weather was warm and pleasant. In April the trees leafed out and the grass was several inches high. It would seem quite strange to the Northerner if he were to suddenly change his locality from the North to the South. While his state was yet held in the cold embrace of snow and frost, he would find in Tennessee green meadows and the flowers blooming in the gardens and by the wayside. Yet I prefer the cold winters of the North to the warm, wet seasons at the South. I like snow better than mud. There is no such thing as sleigh riding there. They never know the pleasure of a wild, rollicking, noisy sleigh ride such as we have in the North.

April brought the start of the military season for 1864. Grant had been promoted during the preceding winter and gone east to take effective command of the Army of the Potomac. He left Sherman in charge of the Union forces in the West, which proved to be an excellent choice. Sherman developed a plan to head south from Tennessee into Georgia and take Atlanta, the only large city in the West still in Confederate hands. This great movement was to be crowned with success in September and was followed by the famous march through Georgia to the sea. Sherman's movements had a devastating impact on the South and helped bring the war to a conclusion just three and a half months after he reached Savannah.

The Union forces had been reorganized, and the 3rd Wisconsin was placed in the new XX Corps, with Joe Hooker in command.

On the 27th of April the regiment left Fayetteville. Sherman was about to begin his march toward Atlanta. All winter preparations had been being made for this grand movement. A portion of the Army of the Mississippi, the 15th Corps and the 17th, the 11th, and the 12th, consolidated as the 20th commanded by Joseph Hooker, and the 23rd Corps by General Scofield.

May, beautiful May, came in all the royal beauty of woods and flowers, of earth and sky. Troops had been gathered from all quarters, settling down on the banks of the broad old Tennessee like a cloud of blue. Beyond Ringgold, strongly posted, lay the Rebel army, their lines extending across the rail road at Tunnel Hill. Their position was one of immense strength and well chosen, strongly fortified and entrenched.

The hostile armies, vast and strong, like two huge giants of song or fable, stood confronting one another, prepared to struggle for the mastery. They listened anxiously, dreading the boom of the first gun that should awaken the echoes among the mountains and be the signal of the approaching tempest. It was well known that fearful strife would soon occur and that the quiet that reigned among those hills and valleys would be broken by the thunder of artillery and the shock of battle.

For the soldier, there is something unpleasant, almost fearful in such a situation. However brave or patriotic he may be, a kind of nameless dread will creep over him, unpleasant, horrible dreams *will* haunt him, strange thoughts will disturb him. There is something so unnatural in war, something so revolting in the idea that men should engage in killing one another, that no one of a thoughtful mind can contemplate the preparations for a battle without feelings of regret that there should be an occasion for such things.

The two armies had lain all winter so near one another that the light of their camp fires seemed to mingle as it glowed and flashed up against the dark sky of night. The Rebel line of earth works, rifle pits, and forts extended along the crest and slopes of what is known as Rocky Faced Ridge, from a point nearly a mile north east of the Chattanooga and Atlanta Rail Road to Tunnel Hill, and thence on along the ridge in a southwesterly direction as far as a dark, narrow pass through the ridge known as Buzzard's Roost, which they had fortified. Rocky Faced Ridge is so called from the fact that it is covered by huge fragments of immense rock which seemed to have been broken and scattered over its surface.

Their position was one of great strength, and the soldiers, as they looked up along the dark heights where their old enemies were waiting, could not but feel a sensation of awe thrilling over them as they contemplated the prospect, thinking that the time would soon come when they would be called upon to charge up those rugged steeps and perhaps meet their death among the rocks on the mountain side. They knew if they were ordered up there that the slopes would be reddened with blood and the gray rocks drip with gore.

A tragic murder shows the danger to all civilians posed by guerrillas on both sides. Willard and some others were sent to investigate and provided with horses. This gave Willard another short stint as a cavalry trooper.

One little incident is worthy of notice. An elderly gentleman who had in former times been one of the judges of the circuit court and a resident of Fayetteville was murdered by some Union soldiers who had belonged to what was known as Brixy's Band. They were loyal Tennesseeans. Brixy had been one of General Rosecrans's scouts, and some of his men had acted in that capacity. They were a rough, blood thirsty set of desperados, many of them deserters from the Rebel army. Their motto was "death" and they never spared an enemy (or friend either, I should think, judging from their conduct). The judge was a fine man, a good musician and singer, and was noted for his good humor and great faculty of telling stories. He was a great favorite with the men and spent many evenings in our quarters. He was a secessionist and had the moral courage to admit the fact.

When our regiment left Fayetteville, Captain Brixy with his company were in the town and were to go with us and be the rear guard. Our wagon train was quite a large one, having collected the tax (mostly in corn), and there were a good many Union refugees going along. It was a bright spring morning that we left our old quarters, and the regiment moved down the street with music and banners flying. The mounted troop scoured the hills on each side of the road, as it was thought some guerrillas might be caught prowling around or might venture into town after we left. None were found, though we rode around in every direction.

Some of Brixy's men had stolen two of old Mr. Chillcoth's (the judge's) horses and two little Negro boys. The old gentleman followed us to get his horses back, or at least one of them. Brixy told him that he "could not have his horses, and that if he came near him again or attempted to see the colonel about them, that he would kill him." The old man managed, however, to see our colonel while the troops were resting for dinner and of course got his horses again. But he never reached home with them, as some of Brixy's gang followed him. They overtook him and, after taking him off the road into the woods down into a ravine, shot him seven times and killed both his horses. The old man was found the same afternoon, covered with blood—dead!

We heard of it the next day, and the scouts, some of us, were sent back to Fayetteville to investigate the matter. We started out that night. A terrible thunder shower came up, and it was thought best to halt for the night. We put our horses in one part of a barn and ourselves in another and waited until morning. We were within nine miles of the town and the next morning rode in, to the great alarm of the people, who at first supposed we were Brixy's devils who had threatened to return and burn the town.

But they were glad to see us when they found out who we were, for we had always treated the people well, and they had done the same by us. We were received with great kindness by all. Hundreds of the people came out to see us, and our little party seemed about to be captured, if not by force, by kindness. We were all invited to breakfast by the people. There were only sixteen of us, and had the guerrillas felt disposed to attack us, they might have killed or captured us all, but they seemed to have no disposition to molest us.

A small party of them made their appearance on one of the hills near the town. A few of us quickly got our horses and dashed out after them; but they scampered off, and having a long start ahead of us, we soon gave up the chase. Another party made their appearance just before night and quietly looked down on us, but probably thought it best to remain at a respectful distance and finally rode away slowly, looking back sometimes to see, I suppose, if we were following them. We thought perhaps they might attack us during the night, as we knew that there were not less than a hundred in the vicinity. But the people assured us that we would not be disturbed while in the town, and we were not. The night passed away quietly, and the next morning we left town again and returned to Tullahoma.

All the troops had gone on to Chattanooga except a small guard and the 107th New York Regiment, which was to guard a wagon train through to the front. We were to go with them with our horses. The third night we camped on the top of the Cumberland Mountains.

The road over the mountains was very rough, hardly passable for teams. A band of guerrillas were reported to be down in one of the valleys below, near Cowan Station, and about to attack that place which was guarded by only a small force. Guerrillas being our favorite game when there was any hunting to do, we all volunteered to go. We rode along the edge of the precipice, looking for a road down, but for a long time were unable to find any road leading from the mountain. We arrived at a point on the mountain about an hour before sunset, which afforded one of the most beautiful views I ever had the pleasure to look upon. We came out of the timber and found ourselves upon the very edge of an immense ledge of rocks at least three hundred feet in perpendicular height, then came the steep but sloping sides of the mountain covered in cedar, low and dwarfish shrubs, elder, and hemlock. The mountain ridge we were on curved gracefully around a beautiful valley, green and fair as Eden, dotted with plantation houses, with here and there a small cluster of white buildings surrounded with groves, green fields, and gardens. A small village with its dwellings, like a cluster of white water lilies in the midst of a sea of green, stood in the centre of the valley, with its little snow white church and steeple glittering in the sun light.

But the sun was low in the west, and we had been ordered to warn the garrison at the station of the danger that threatened them, and were resolved to go. We failed to find any road down but at last discovered a ravine which in wet times was doubtless a water course. This we followed down, leading our horses. It was a very difficult task, both for men and animals. We reached the bottom, however, just after dark without any serious accident.

We called at the first house and had our horses fed and a good supper for ourselves. Here we learned that there was truly a band of guerrillas numbering over a hundred in the valley. The scouts were sent out in different directions to ascertain, if possible, their locality and numbers. Having a good horse and a Rebel uniform,[2] I was one of the number. It was supposed that they were encamped in a ravine at the foot of the mountain about three miles from where we were, for so we had been informed by a Negro man who reported to have seen them go in that direction. I volunteered to act as guide. We left the house unbeknown to any of the people and rode rapidly along the narrow road by the base of the mountain until we reached to within a half mile of the place of encampment. Then we rode cautiously along, halting every few moments to listen and look around from every little hill. The night was quite dark and cloudy, and it was difficult to follow the road or, rather, path, for road it could be hardly called.

To one who has never been out on such an errand, it is difficult to understand the disagreeable sensations that creep over one as he rides along, knowing not at what moment he may meet an unexpected enemy or what dangers he may encounter, seeing the loneliness of the situation, the strangeness of the country, the dark mountains seeming to cast a deeper shade than night, and the fact of being guided by a stranger who might be seeking to lead you into danger. But my sable companion seemed to be honest and cautious, riding by my side like a shadow. "Dah, sah, just around de hill dar is de place whar day be." The hill which he pointed out was about a quarter of a mile ahead and was a low spur of the main ridge jutting out into the valley.

I thought it best to leave our horses and reconnoiter the place on foot. We led our animals back behind a hill in the woods, and leaving the darkie to wait until I came back, I went on down the road to within a short distance of the hill he had showed me. Then I left the road and proceeded cautiously along through the woods until I reached the top of the hill. The Negro had not misinformed us, for there was the guerrilla encampment just below me, entirely hid from view except from some hill in the vicinity.

They had only one small fire burning, and it was impossible to judge their numbers from my position. Wishing to have a closer inspection, I crept down the hill, crouching along behind the rocks and trees until within a few rods of the encampment. I could now see by the light of the fire several horses and some of the men sitting around the fire, while here and there dark objects could be seen up along the ravine which I judged to be horses. The low hum of voices could be heard farther up. The Negro's story was doubtless true, that there were a hundred of them. They were not intending to remain all night, as the men had their arms in their hands and the saddles had not been removed from their horses. After making a careful observation of what was before me, I returned to my colored friend, whom I found quietly waiting.

We mounted and rode rapidly back and joined our friends at the farm house. On hearing my report the captain gave the order to "mount," and we pushed on rapidly to the station, where we found only two companies of infantry guarding the place. On hearing the report of the captain, the commander of the post ordered the men to fall in under arms. Some of the mounted men were stationed out as videttes, but no enemy appeared during the night. They did not intend to attack the place, or had learned of what had happened and deemed it best to keep at a respectful distance. We ascended the mountain the next morning, following a narrow path which had been pointed out by a citizen, and joined the command.

We reached Chattanooga on the 6th of May. About five or six miles from there, we first came in sight of Lookout Mountain. This bold, high mass of rock and earth terminates abruptly on the bank of the Tennessee, rising several hundred feet in perpendicular height. The rail road runs along the river bank at the foot of the mountain. The highway winds up along a natural shelf or step, above which looms the old mountain in all the solitary grandeur of earth, rock, and forests. Below is the Tennessee, broad and deep, and to the right in the little valley, walled in by the mountain and Mission Ridge, is Chattanooga, with its vast depot buildings, the tin roofs of which gleam and glitter in the sun light. The old, spacious brick buildings, the many forts and entrenchments, the white tents of the encampments, the haze and smoke settling down over the city, the river and mountains, all gave to the scene as we looked down from the heights a very picturesque appearance, reminding one of scenes of romance.

There were but few people in the little city except soldiers and Negroes, as most of the inhabitants had gone south. The rats and mice, more bold than the people, had evidently remained, even to live among the hated Yankees. We remained until the next morning, when we resumed our journey to the front.

Willard and his comrades ride to catch up with the army, which was already in motion and, indeed, in action. He passes over the battlefields and sees many signs of recent strife.

Meanwhile, the armies were in motion. We encamped at night on the green banks of the Chickamauga, the scene of the fierce and bloody battle of the 19th and 20th of September. The trodden ground, the torn and shattered trees, scarred by bullets and mangled by shell, gave proof of the terrible contest. The Chickamauga is not, as many suppose, a dark and sluggish stream, but a clear, sparkling creek over hung with willows, with green mossy banks where the pale lilies and watercress dip their beautiful heads in the passing wave. We bathed in its crystal waters and kindled our camp fires along its margin. The gentle wind seemed to murmur and moan among the trees as though freighted with the sigh of mourners, and the stars came out in the blue sky, glimmering with mellow lustre as though they had been the spirit eyes of those who had fallen, and were looking in sorrow on their own lonely graves.

We passed through Ringold the next day, where also were to be seen traces of deadly strife. Ringold was once a fine, little town situated on a plateau, sloping gently to the west. A high ridge rises up darkly just beyond the town, casting its sombre shadows over it. A narrow pass through the mountain affords the only passage in that vicinity. It was here that the Rebels attempted to make a stand after being driven from Lookout Mountain, and it was at this place that one of the most daring charges of the war was made by a portion of the 2nd Division of Hooker's corps.

The Rebels had fortified the entrance to the pass, and Hooker rashly attempted to dislodge them. The nature of the ground and the narrowness of the pass gave but little room for the movements of troops. The Ohio brigade was formed eight lines deep and charged into the pass, meeting a storm of lead and fire that glared and flamed across the narrow defile as though a volcano had burst out in its midst. But the brave boys pushed on, though the first line was broken and went down like a forest torn by a tornado.

The first line of the enemy was driven back, and the brave Buckeyes rushed on over the heaps of dead and wounded until they had nearly cleared the gorge, when they were met by a most terrific fire of musketry and artillery, which swept them down so fearfully that they were thrown into confusion. The Rebels, seeing this, charged furiously, breaking the line and driving our men back. The trees all through the pass are scarred and torn. Hundreds of brave men are sleeping their last long sleep beneath the shades of the mountain in that dark, gloomy pass.

As the Union forces moved south, they were confronted by Confederates strongly dug in at Rocky Faced Ridge, which runs northeast to southwest and is located just west of Dalton, Georgia. Sherman had to get east of the ridge to move against Atlanta. Sensing that a direct attack on the Confederate position would fail, he attempted to bypass it, sending Gen. James McPherson's Army of the Tennessee around the Rebels' left flank with the intention of coming in from below and cutting their rail communications with Atlanta to the south. Sherman's other units then demonstrated against the Confederates to keep them pinned in their positions.

McPherson took Snake Creek Gap to the south of the Rebel entrenchments, which was just the passage that Sherman so badly needed. He marched the balance of his troops down and through the Gap and headed for Resaca to the southeast. McPherson was unable to cut the railroad, but if Sherman could take Resaca while Confederate general Joseph Johnston's army remained in Dalton, he would come between it and Atlanta, making any effective defense of that city impossible.

Johnston sized up the situation and withdrew from his virtually impenetrable works to head for Resaca, hoping to cut off Sherman. There his men built new defensive works just west of town and hoped to draw the Federals into a costly assault. Sherman, for his part, would have liked to hold Johnston there until his whole force was available, then badly defeat the Rebels and destroy them as an effective fighting force.

On May 14 Sherman attacked the right center of Johnston's line, which was stronger than he had expected, and he had to give up the assault without achieving any results. The Confederates then hit the Union far left, turning it, taking some of their works, and threatening a battery. Late in the afternoon, the 3rd Wisconsin and others in the XX Corps were rushed in; they threw back the Rebels and saved the day.

We passed on and joined our regiment near but to the south of Tunnel Hill and Rocky Faced Ridge. The dark, rough heights of old Rocky Face loomed up frowningly before us. There are several passes through this ridge, which runs north east by south west. One is known as Dog Run Gap, another as Buzzard's Roost, and another as Snake Creek Gap. On the afternoon of the 11th a part of the 20th Corps charged the enemy at Dog Run and Buzzard's Roost, and had been repulsed. Those narrow passes were so strongly fortified that it was found impossible to carry the place—indeed, the men were unable to climb the works, so high and steep were they. The boom of cannon signaled the beginning of the fierce struggle. Our brave boys swept into the narrow defiles in the most gallant manner. The works stretched across the narrow passage through the mountain. They reached the works and natural barrier that towered up before them massive and strong, meeting a most withering fire of musketry. They attempted to climb the works, but many of them were crushed by rocks and timbers rolled down on them from above. Shells were thrown by hand over the works by the enemy. It was found to be a useless task, and the men fell back—the few that escaped.

The same afternoon a portion of the 15th Corps entered Snake Creek Gap, which was found to be held by cavalry and mounted infantry. The entrance to the Gap was carried by the first charge, and then began a lively skirmish between our sharp shooters in the advance and the Rebels. Whenever a stand was made by the Rebels, a charge would be ordered, which never failed to break their lines. The pass at this place is seven miles long, dark, and narrow, one of the most gloomy places I ever saw. Before night, our men had cleared the path of enemies, save those who had fought their last fight and lay cold and dead. Many of our men fell as they pushed along the narrow defile. We passed through the Gap the next day and found many graves along the bloody pathway of battle.

We mounted men had now turned our horses over to the quarter-master and joined our companies. We camped at the eastern entrance of the defile on the night of the 12th. During the night a fierce storm came up, and such a storm! The thunder seemed to shake the mountains, and the lightning's glare lit up, at times, the dark and gloomy pass, revealing the dead timber and dark walls for an instant, then leaving all darker by contrast; and the wind blew a furious tornado that swept along between the lofty walls, hurling huge trees to the ground and scattering dead limbs at their feet. Several trees fell in our neighborhood, one in the midst of our camp, but no one was hurt.

The eastern entrance to the gorge was strongly fortified in anticipation of an attempt by the Rebels to recover what they had lost. The 14th Corps came through the Gap on the 13th and occupied the works thrown up by the 15th and 17th Corps while they and the 20th Corps pushed on to the right in the direction of Resaca.

The Rebels, finding themselves out generaled, were compelled to abandon their position at Tunnel Hill and along old Rocky Face. While their attention was called in the direction of Buzzard's Roost, Dog Run Gap, and Tunnel Hill, the greater part of the army were passing through the mountain at Snake Creek Gap. General Sherman's head quarters were moved up from Ringgold to Tunnel Hill. The Rebels hastily abandoned their strong position and fell back to Resaca. The country around Resaca is rough, hilly, and covered with a forest, mostly of dead timber, and is but sparsely settled. Resaca is a little town on the Costonoula, a narrow but deep river with high, bold banks.

On this stream rested either wing of the Rebel army, giving them a position from which they could not be flanked. Here on the banks of the Costonoula, an impassable river save by bridge or boats, Johnston drew up the Army of the Confederacy. His position was stronger than the one on Rocky Face. A perfect maze of hills and woods surrounds the town, on which the enemy were posted, strongly entrenched. After some skirmishing the enemy's position was ascertained.

Constant skirmishing was kept up along the line, with the occasional boom of cannon. The 20th Corps was held in reserve in rear of the main line, which came upon the enemy on May 13th. Some fighting occurred, but nothing serious until the 14th. An advance was made early in the morning and met with some resistance, and the enemy were pressed back. All the forenoon the rattle of musketry rang along the line, growing more rapid at times and deepening into the roar of battle, then would die away, only to break out again at some other point.

Our line extended far around to the south, gradually closing in around the town. During the day several charges were made by our men and the Rebels driven from their positions. Late in the afternoon, the firing on the left became more rapid and heavy. We were still in reserve, and as we lay "closed en masse" in rear of the line, we could hear the firing and see what was going on. All attention was turned to the left, where now the hoarse voice of battle drew more angry, rolling up with a louder tone and deepening to the deadly roar of battle. Just before sunset the bugle call sounded from head quarters and was caught up by the division, and then the brigade buglers, and then the "fall in" from regimental commanders, and in less than five minutes from the first call we were in line and moving rapidly to the left. Our rapid walk was soon changed to a double quick.

Stanley's brigade of the 4th Corps held the extreme left, and this the Rebels had resolved to crush. Their charge was so sudden and impetuous that they succeeded in driving back our line a short distance, but the men rallied and they were in turn driven back. Three other attempts were made to drive the brigade from the hill which they held.

Just before sunset a heavy column of Rebels appeared in front, while another pushed around farther to the left, striking Stanley in [the] flank and rear. The left was turned and that division of the 4th Corps thrown into confusion. The Rebel lines rushed on, cheering as they came, making the old woods ring with their yells.

It was at this critical moment, when the whole left wing seemed about to give way, that the first division of Hooker's corps swept into line, charged the advancing columns, and hurled them back, regaining nearly all the ground that had been lost. When we came on the ground, the troops were falling back through the timber in confusion. A battery which had been in reserve was captured and in a few moments more would have been lost, but was retaken. The scene would have been a fine one for an artist. The sun red and almost obscured by smoke, the blue hill and the little valley in which we fought, the red flashes of the guns, and the dark blue canopy of smoke that hung over all, would have made a grand picture of war. The Rebels were pressed back and the hill regained. The object that the Rebels had in view seemed to be to turn the left wing, throw a heavy column in the rear, and regain Snake Creek Gap, where our trains were parked. But whatever their object was, it was a failure.

The night passed away quietly. The soldiers lay on their arms that night, ready to fall in at a moment's notice. The fighting had now fairly begun and we were sure that the next day would bring victory or defeat.

On May 15, both sides went on the attack at various points and battered each other, with little gain but many men lost. At the end, Sherman did what he should have done in the first place: He bypassed Resaca and sent his forces around Johnston's left one more time, trying to get between him and Atlanta. As Sherman moved south, Johnston again had to leave his works and head in that direction.

During the forenoon of the 15th, it became evident that movement of some kind was about to be made. The skirmish line was advanced, troops were massed in rear of our line, orderlies and ADCs[3] rode here and there, officers rode along the skirmish line carefully inspecting the ground in advance, and preparations were made for a move. There was but little firing along the line, and the men were grave and quiet. About noon a brisk skirmish fire broke out in front, caused by the advance of our skirmishers.

Late in the afternoon the bugle suddenly rang out its shrill notes, and the mass of men sprang into line and soon were moving rapidly, deploying into line of battle; and sweeping forward, passed the skirmish line, which had also advanced, driving in the Rebel advance to their main line. On swept the charging column with lowered bayonets and firm steps through the woods and up the hill, never halting though their ranks were swept by a perfect tempest of death. They gained the works, springing over the entrenchments and scattering the Rebels in wild confusion. Other portions of the line advanced, meeting generally with success.

At three o'clock the Rebels attempted to retake the works. They appeared in front in line, and a sharp musketry fire began; but it was only a feint—their intention was to throw a heavy force around to the left and, by crushing that wing, compel the retreat of the other portion of the line. This move was discovered, and troops were rapidly marched to the left. The 1st Division of the 20th Corps held the left, and was in reserve to the left and a little in the rear of the 3rd Division.

We were hurried to the left still farther. There was no time to be lost—the enemy's masses with skirmishers out could be seen from head quarters moving rapidly around on the flank. They first struck our line on the left of the 4th Corps, then swept up against the 2nd Division of the 20th, meeting our line just as one blade of a pair of scissors meets the other. But their line extended far beyond our left and had already begun to swing into the rear.

The 1st Division formed on the left of the 3rd at a double quick, keeping up the alignment by forming by "the right flank into line," facing in such a way as to meet the enemy and prevent his striking our line on the flank. One brigade dashed off across the fields, forming a line at right angles with ours. The Rebels, finding that their attack had been anticipated, charged the line in fine style, and the fight raged furiously for half an hour, when they were repulsed at every point and hastily withdrew, leaving their dead and wounded in our hands.

Night came on and the sun went down, its last red gleams reflected back by the victorious arms of the Union army. Nearly half of that night was passed by us taking the Rebel wounded from the field, and when we lay down in line to sleep, it was with the grateful sensation of being victorious. Many wounded Rebels lay beyond our picket line. We could hear their groans and cries for help; the woods were filled with their moaning, dying soldiers.

Permission was granted to go beyond our lines and bring them in. It was not known how near the enemy were to us, as we had heard nothing from them since their repulse. But the men were not afraid to go out and ascertain, at least to go as far as to where they were laying. There were those who had bravely met the enemy, fighting them to the death, who could not rest now until every fallen foeman was cared for. It was a dangerous affair to go out beyond our skirmish line to pick up wounded men, but it was done; every one of them in our front was brought in.

"There is one poor devil out there yet," said one of the men, as a low, mournful wail came faintly up from far down in the dark, gloomy forest, borne on the still, cool air of night. Four of the men volunteered to bring him in and, leaving the line, disappeared in the woods, halting often to listen, then moving forward again, until at last they came near the place where he was. One of the men went ahead alone, creeping cautiously forward to within a few feet of the wounded man, and after listening a moment whispered, "Hush! Friend, do not speak. I have come to get you." Then, creeping to his side, he asked, "Where are your men?" "Oh, a right smart bit from here," said the wounded man, clasping the hands of the Federal and begging him to carry him to our lines. "Wait one moment and you shall be taken in." Then, calling the other men, he was placed on a stretcher and carried to our lines. His gratitude knew no bounds, he thanked and prayed and wept all at the same time.

During the night, from after twelve o'clock until nearly morning, the enemy were dashing against our lines, now at one point and then at another. None of their attacks, however, were made with any great force, and whether they were trying to break our line or doing it only to cover their retreat I cannot tell; but I think for the latter reason, as the next morning found their works abandoned. They had retreated during the night, leaving their dead on the field and many of their wounded.

One incident of Yankee coolness and ingenuity occurred which not only surprised the Rebels very much, but gave us one of their most important positions. When the 2nd Division charged the Rebel line, one fort was found to be so constructed and so high that the men could not climb up it, but having reached the moat, they kept up such a continuous fire that by the aid of our artillery, they were able to silence the guns and prevent the infantry from firing. The pioneers were sent for and, when they came up, commenced digging under the fort, and in less than two hours the fort was seen to tumble, the boys having dug under it. Ropes were thrown over the guns and they were dragged down.

We entered Resaca on the morning of the 16th, and a sad looking place it was, too. The buildings were torn and riddled with shell and cannon shot, the ground plowed by plunging balls, the fences thrown down, and the town deserted, save by a few who came up timidly from their cellars and basements. Some greeted us with smiles, a few perhaps with unfeigned pleasure, but most of them looked on us with sad faces and a kind of melancholy, hopeless stare, saying nothing and seeming to care for nothing, making no complaint as the soldiers (stragglers rather) helped themselves and pillaged their homes. Their spirits seemed quite broken down as they looked on us as coming between them and their last hope; for they knew that the resistless columns would sweep on, and their hope of independence would be crushed beneath the firm, brave tread of the armies of the Republic.

Long before noon our army was in motion, and the boom of a gun far ahead gave proof that we were in close pursuit. But the Rebel army, forced from the strong position and labored fortifications around Resaca, was rapidly retreating southward toward the Allatoona Mountains. A portion of our army followed the rail road, while others swept down on the right and left.

The country from Rocky Faced Ridge southward does not appear to be of the first quality. A stunted, dwarfish kind of timber abounds, and there is but a small portion of the land cultivated comparatively. Much of it is still as wild as when in possession of the natives.

Cartersville, Calhoun, and Adamsville fell into our hands without resistance. The country seemed nearly deserted save a few *old* men; there were none other of that sex to be met with. The people neither expressed loyal or disloyal sentiments, but looked on us apparently with silent indifference. At some of the houses none but Negroes could be seen, at others a woman or perhaps several, with their little ones clinging to them. Poverty seemed to have marked that country as its own, and there were none who dared to dispute his sovereignty. Want and misery seemed to have taken up their abodes in the mansion of the lordly planter, as well as in the hovels of the poor, and despair marked them all as its victims.

The Negroes alone rejoiced at the coming of the hated Yankees; many of them were wild with their exuberance of joy. Their shouts rang out everywhere—"Bress de Lord, de Yankees *hab* come!" was heard wherever our columns appeared, and "Sambo" would dance and sing, flourishing his arms in the air, while his lower extremities jerked and twisted into most dangerous crooks and angles, with head thrown back and eyes rolling, while he gave vent to his overwhelming joy by song and laughter.

We overtook the Rebels at Kingston and Cassville, two small towns, one (Kingston) on the rail road and the other on a branch road which runs from the former to the latter place, a distance of ten miles. There Johnston resolved to resist our advance and had constructed some formidable works.

No considerable battle was fought, however, at this place. We came upon their line late in the afternoon and found them strongly posted on the hills and ridges north of the town. Our line advanced, and a brisk fire was commenced by the skirmishers. Late in the afternoon and just before sunset, the 1st Brigade of the 1st Division, 20th Corps, swept around to the left and fell upon the flank of the enemy while the 3rd and 2nd Brigades charged the enemy's line in front. But the Rebels abandoned their position without hardly firing a shot and retreated to a high ridge beyond the town. It was now sunset, and as the dusk of evening stole over the scene, the firing died away, and only the occasional flash of a skirmisher's rifle, as it gleamed through the deepening twilight, gave proof of a hostile foe. The next morning found their works beyond the town deserted. They had retreated during the night and were hurrying on toward the Allatoonas.

During the march southward the "corps d'armée" did not march in one column, but moved forward on roads parallel with the rail way or pushed across the country, keeping up communications from right to left. The country was generally desolated and almost depopulated that we passed through, for what the Rebels left, our men appropriated, and often we could look back from the crest of some hill and see the blue smoke columns curling upward as the out buildings and sometimes the dwelling house of some wealthy Rebel was given to the flames. Such things were not sanctioned by the commanding general, but were always the work of stragglers and sneaks who were never seen in the ranks but were first to plunder the dead or fire a building.

Johnston halted his retreat and set his defenses in Allatoona Pass. Sherman determined to bypass this strong position, again heading south by circling to the left of Johnston. The Confederates then countered by moving west to meet the threat and dug in near New Hope Church to the west of Dallas, Georgia.

Thinking that he was faced by a small Confederate force rather than a large and well-fortified one, Sherman ordered his men to push on through the enemy

defenses. The Union regiments making the attack included the 3rd Wisconsin.
They were met by a blizzard of shot and shell from cannon and a battle-hardened
enemy set behind log and dirt entrenchments. The Union advance was stopped in
its tracks. The 3rd Wisconsin suffered nineteen killed and ninety-one wounded. To
put this in perspective, this was as many as it had lost at Chancellorsville. Among
the wounded was one Van R. Willard. This was his second wound, and it effec-
tively put him out of the war.

The Allatoona Mountains, as they are called, are irregular ranges of
high hills and isolated peaks lying north of the Chattahoochie. Allatoona
Pass is a narrow cut through this range of hills. Here the Rebel army again
faced about and, getting their back up against the mountains, prepared to
dispute our passage. But Sherman never wastes time in useless disputes,
and leaving them to hold the pass as long as they liked, quickly swung his
army around to the left and, by one of the most brilliant flank movements,
again compelled them to evacuate their position. In this flank movement
the 20th Corps took the most conspicuous part.

We were on the extreme right of the line and for three days pushed on
through a rough country, crossing over the mountains and sweeping down
towards Marietta from the west. Johnston saw that unless this movement
was met and checked, his retreat would be cut off and his communications
destroyed, as in another day we would reach the railroad in his rear. To
check this movement, the Rebel chief hastily retreated from his impreg-
nable position at the Allatoona Pass and threw his army across the path
along which Hooker was sweeping down on his flank.

It was the 25th of May. The weather was warm and pleasant, and the
sun light gleamed and glittered from the polished arms of the troops, while
the banners waved and flaunted in and out of the woodlands, rising
proudly on the spring breezes or drooping gracefully over the heads of
their bearers. The troops were in the best of spirits, and the column moved
onward, animated by the enchanting music of the bands. Early in the
afternoon the advance guard of the 2nd Division came upon the enemy's
skirmish line posted on a high ridge just beyond what is known as Pump-
kin Vine Creek. So sudden and unexpected was this that their presence
was not known until they fired into the advance where Hooker himself
was riding. One of his aides was killed by his side, but he happily escaped
unharmed. A regiment was immediately deployed as skirmishers and

dashed across the ravine, others swept into line on the right and left of the road and soon drove the enemy from their line.

To deploy a regiment as skirmishers quickly and handsomely requires drill and discipline and, when properly done, presents a fine sight to the eye of every soldier. When a whole regiment is to act as skirmishers, the right and left wings move forward a few yards, leaving the four centre companies in the rear as a reserve. The companies forming the right and left wings, being counted off from right to left by twos to form groups of fours, are ready to be deployed, which, if properly done, is one of the finest of military movements. The companies move obliquely forward, inclining to the right and left until a proper distance is attained, then the groups deploy, spreading out like the rays of a fan. The distance between each skirmisher is generally about five yards. The reserve follows, moving generally by the flank in rear of the skirmish line eight or ten rods. The four companies are arranged along the line from right to left, one on either flank and two in the centre. If strong resistance is met, the line is reinforced from the reserve.

The line was quickly formed and moved forward, driving the Rebel skirmishers before them. It was soon ascertained that the enemy was in the vicinity in force. Only the 20th Corps was in the neighborhood. Most of the afternoon was spent in skirmishing and getting the troops into position. We were formed in order of battle south of the ravine, and just before sunset the bugles "sounded the advance" and the line moved forward through the woods. The Rebel line fell back slowly, fighting as they went. Several times we found them drawn up in line. Our bugles would sound the "charge," and our lines would rush forward with cheers, breaking their line and scattering them back through the woods. This was repeated several times, and I suppose that General Hooker thought that there were no fortifications in our front, but it proved otherwise.

We had advanced over two miles from the creek when, on arriving on the crest of a densely wooded ridge, we found ourselves confronted by a large force of the enemy posted behind strong works of logs and earth, and they poured into us the most withering fire of musketry and artillery that we had ever experienced. Hundreds of our men along the line went down like grass before the mower. Their works fairly blazed with fire as it ran along their line. The woods were filled with white clouds of smoke that drifted among the trees, hiding every thing from view save the glare of the

guns. The roar of musketry was most deafening. The air seemed to vibrate
as if agitated by a hundred whirlwinds, and the earth seemed to tremble
beneath our feet. We were within a few yards of their works, and notwithstanding the terrible fire to which we were subjected, our line never
wavered, and I believe we could have carried the works if a charge had
been ordered.

We had crept up under cover of the smoke and woods to within a
short distance of their line. Their artillery could take no effect on us, their
grape and canister went whistling harmlessly over our heads; their fire had
slackened very much also, for we kept up a furious fire, and they did not
seem to wish to expose themselves. A few moments more and we should
have been masters of the works in our front. At this moment a large body
of the enemy appeared on our right and came charging down, making the
woods ring with their yells—and such a yell, I shall never forget it—how
wild, how demonic, how it rose and swelled and rang through those old
woods! A legion of devils from the infernal regions could not have surpassed it.

But Hooker had guarded against such a flank movement. The 3rd
Division, which was in the rear as support, had just been sent to the
right, and firm as a rock they met the Rebel wave, which broke like the
crested breaker against the headland. The contest was, however, for a few
moments most desperate and bloody, foot to foot and hand to hand. The
musketry firing was tremendous, the sounds that came up from the scene
of contest were appalling, and the white banks of smoke seemed to rest
over hill and wood like a shroud.

The terrible scene was soon over; a strong, manly cheer announced
that the cool, determined valor of the old 3rd Division was more than a
match for the fierce, fiery courage of the Southern legions. The enemy
had been fearfully repulsed and had gone back, and much more silently
than they came. When the Rebel column appeared on our right, we
were forced to fall back to prevent being outflanked, and had not the 3rd
Division repulsed the attack, the whole corps would have been routed. It
was now sunset and dusk stole over the scene, putting an end for the time
being to the fearful contest.

The day had been one of the most lovely of beautiful May's train of
golden days, but the sun went down in the midst of clouds and battle
smoke, and shortly after dusk it began to rain, and the night was dark and
gloomy. I received a slight wound in my hand and, after our repulse, went

to the rear. The woods were filled with the dead, the wounded, and the dying, and all along the road the groans of the stricken ones were heard. The wounded were sent back to the hospitals. This was my last battle, making in all *seventeen* engagements in which I had participated.

Willard returned to his regiment about a month later, at Kennesaw Mountain. Johnston's Confederates had a strong position on the mountain, and Sherman made the mistake of assaulting it rather than turning and going around its left. Willard witnessed but did not participate in some of the action.

My time was now nearly up, and after remaining at the Soldiers' Home at Chattanooga a few days, I returned to the regiment on June 25th. I found them at the foot of old Kennesaw Mountain, on the top of which was perched the Rebel army, its centre on the crest and the wings extending to the right and left along a high, rocky ridge, curving backward, forming nearly a half circle. It was a well chosen position on the north bank of the Chattahoochie and north of Marietta. Kennesaw is a high, bold peak hardly rising to the height of a mountain. Little Kennesaw is a smaller elevation near the main elevation

Constant skirmishing was kept up along the line, and at all hours of the day and night the sharp, ringing report of the skirmisher's rifle could be heard, with an occasional dull, heavy boom of a cannon, the sound of which reverberated and echoed among the hills, dying away in the distance. Of course, the army was not idle; hardly a day passed without a skirmish or a battle. The Rebels had been hurled from Pine Mountain and Lost Mountain, had been routed at New Hope, and now had gathered their legions on old Kennesaw's crest.

On the 27th of June, the charge was made on Little Kennesaw, which resulted in a disaster to our army, as it proved a failure owing to the height and steepness of the ascent. Rocks and logs were rolled down on our men, and it was found impossible to reach their works. The 1st Division of the 20th Corps acted as supports to the assaulting column, which was a part of the 14th Corps.

During the afternoon, a position was gained by the 2nd Division (20th Corps) on our left and in advance, from which the Rebels attempted in vain to dislodge them. At dark they still held the hill, and the old flag waved proudly out over its brave defenders, dimly seen through the blue smoke that settled down at evening over the field of battle.

At eleven o'clock A.M. the Rebels made a furious assault on this position. The onset was so sudden and impetuous that they were within a few yards of our line before we were aware of their presence, making the night air ring with their cheers. But suddenly a long, white sheet of flame rolled up along the line, and the ground fairly shook with the roar of musketry. The Rebel line was staggered, but for a few moments a furious fire ran along either line, glaring up against the sky. The Rebel onset was repulsed, and the next morning found the brave old 2nd Division still on the hill and the old flag waving more proudly than before.

Willard's regiment went to Atlanta with Sherman, then on to the sea, and served with distinction until the war's end. Van R. Willard, veteran of seventeen battles and innumerable skirmishes, was not with it, however. After three years of arduous service, he had reached the end of his enlistment term. He bade a tearful farewell to the men with whom he had experienced so much, and full of memories and the satisfaction of knowing he had fought to save his country, he headed home to Wisconsin. His future lay before him, full of promise.

It was now the 29th of June, and my term of service had expired. We were not mustered out, however, until the 1st of July, when we were relieved from duty. Late in the afternoon, we took leave of the old regiment at the foot of Kennesaw. Hands were shaken and good bys were said, and there were few eyes that were not moistened that day.

We had all been brothers together. Side by side had we marched many a weary mile, had endured hardships and faced dangers most appalling. For three long and weary years we had served under the same banner, which we had borne through many a fiery contest.

We reached Big Shanty about midnight, where we took the cars, homeward bound!

APPENDIX

Selected Poems
of Van R. Willard

A Song for the Times

Our war drum has sounded,
Our flag is unfurled,
And our vengeance of wrath
On the foe shall be hurled.

Then awaken every brave heart,
Each strong heart and true,
And strike for our country
And the red, white, and blue.

Traitors are rising our homes to deform
But dark is the tempest and dark is the storm
That shall gather about them
To blight and to harm.

Their homes and their cities to ruins shall turn
Ere Freedom shall cower or our banner be torn.
And the "Rattle snake flag"
In triumph be borne.

Hail to Columbia,
The gem of the sea,
The pride of the world,
The home of the free.

The pride of the world,
The gem of the ocean,
And the shrine of each true heart's
Earnest devotion.

We'll not forsake thee
When dangers are nigh,
We'll fight for thy honor,
We'll preserve thee or—die.

What news from the South;
Ah! The tidings forebear,
For the flag of our Union
Waveth not there.

For the Rattle Snake Flag
With its Palmetto tree,
Hath taken the place
Of the flag of the free.

Bold Ellsworth has fallen,
Brave Lyon is dead,
And the blood of a Baker
By traitors was shed.

Then awaken each brave heart,
Each strong heart and true,
And strike for our country,
And the red, white, and blue.

Oh Columbia, Columbia!
The home of the free,
The star that arose
Above the dark sea.

When the eagle came down
From his mansion on high,
From his palace in clouds,
From his home in the sky.

And perched on our banner—
The flag of the true—
Oh, the eagle, the eagle!
And the red, white, and blue.

>─┼◆>─O─<◆┼─<

Far from Home!

I'm far away from home tonight,
No cherished friend I see,
Though all the stars of heaven are bright
They're not so bright to me.

As once they seemed in days gone by
Before I learned to roam,
Bespangling all the deep blue sky
Above my native home.

Yet fate and fortune bade me go
And I will not repine,
In all my wanderings to and fro
Whatever fate be mine.

For soon, perchance, the day will come
When I no more shall roam,
And friends that sigh that I am gone,
Will bid me welcome home.

>─┼◆>─O─<◆┼─<

Lines on Receiving a Present

Thanks, dear one, for this thy token
Of remembrance here conferred,
Let the silence long unbroken
Cease, and thankfulness be heard.

Yes, I thank thee, for the treasure
For a treasure 'tis to me,
Calling mindward hours of pleasure
Which I never more may see.

Hours was youthful fancy teeming,
Hours of bliss without alloy,
Hours when hope was fondly dreaming,
Of the future shared with joy.

Oh! I wish air castle building
Had not pleased my fancy so,
Then perhaps life's real gilding
Had not worn so faint a glow.

Once a beaming sun of gladness
Brightly o'er my oath did blaze,
Now alas a cloud of sadness
Shrouds in gloom its genial rays.

Yet I will not prematurely
Deem my life a barren waste,
Nor for vain regret demurely
Shun the joys I yet may taste.

No, the waves upon life's ocean
Drifting downward with the tide,
Both the billows of commotion
And the waves of quiet tide.

Hearts may sink today in sorrow
'Neath the pressure of a grief,
Yet upon the coming morrow
Rise in fortunate relief.

What thoughts, hopes we fondly cherish
Prove elusive, false, and vain,
Soil that one neglects to nourish
Afterwards may teem again.

What though flowers of choicest flavor
Wither on the drooping sprig,
After, ones of equal savor
Bloom on the self same twig.

Then why mourn for days of pleasure past?
And will they come no more?
Aye, I'll fondly hope each treasure
Time will yet to me restore.

Restore the hours with pleasure teeming,
Hours of bliss without alloy,
Hours when hope was fondly dreaming
Of a future starred with joy.

I will keep the welcome present
Oh, the memory of the hours,
When life's pathway, smooth and pleasant,
Hid its thorns beneath its flowers.

>━┤━◆>━O━<◆━┤━<

Of the following poem, Willard wrote, "The following lines, which I have read somewhere, are so applicable that they seem to have been written while viewing the valley of the Shenandoah." It is unclear where Willard read this poem, as he sometimes recorded the musings of his fellow soldiers in addition to writing his own. It is also possible, given its style, that the poem was written by Willard but attributed to someone else.

The Valley

Behold a lovely valley
With its cottages so white,
The fields and blooming orchards,
And homes so fair and bright.

And the cutter early rising
Sang his ditty to the sound
Of the brooklet's gentle murmur
And the leaves that rustled round.

And the maiden held the distaff
And the matron twirled the wheel,
One might know that on that valley
Peace had set its golden seal.

But, lo! As upward swept the coursers,
The coursers of the sun,
A cloud above the mountain
With its visage bleak and dun.

And the thunders hoarsely rattle
And the lightning, like a chain,
Burned around that valley
And flashed long the plain.

The cutter ceased his singing
And the matron fled her wheel
One might know that on that valley
War had set his crimson heel.

>━┼━◆〉━○━〈◆┼━◁

The following poem, from Book Three, was written in the winter of 1863, while Willard was in Philadelphia recovering from his wound at Antietam.

The Nameless

Nameless this little book shall be
For it deserves no name,
You may call it what you will,
It will be to me the same.

It was not written for public eyes,
Not for fame or gold,
Not to be read by every one,
Not to be bought or sold.

Whether it is good or bad
It matters not to you,
For 'twas written in those lonely hours
When I had nothing else to do.

>-I-◄>-O-◄>-I-◄

Farewell to Summit House

Fare thee well, old Summit House,
Thy walks, thy shades, thy walls farewell,
I'm going to leave thee now, old Summit House,
Mid other scenes to dwell;

But where ere I go, old Summit House,
You I'll not forget,
Tho' I leave thee now, old Summit House,
With no feelings of regret.

For know you not, old Summit House,
That duty says "away,"
And I leave thee now, old Summit House,
And cheerfully obey.

Yes away, away, old Summit House,
I'll linger here no more,
For I long to hear the bugle's call,
And freedom's cannon roar.

Adieu, Adieu, old Summit House,
With my rifle in my hand,
I'll strike a blow for liberty
And my dear native land.

I remember well, old Summit House,
The day I first came here,
And looked upon thy sombre walls,
So cheerless and so drear.

I shuddered, old Summit House,
As I viewed the scene around,
The leafless trees, the barren fields,
And the cold and frozen ground.

The day was dark, old Summit House,
And the stormy winds were high,
And darkly lowered the tempest clouds,
And scowling was the sky.

You seemed to me, old Summit House,
Like a Lazar house of death,
Where grim disease forever breathed
His withering, blighting death.

But time since then, old Summit House,
Rolled smoothly on apace,
And though you looked so lone and drear,
I learned to love the place.

But I would not stay, old Summit House,
I could not there remain,
I long to join my dear old friends
Away on the tented plain.

Good by, good by, old Summit House,
I'll linger here no more,
I go again to the crimson plain
Where the storms of battle lower.

Then fare thee well, old Summit House,
I leave without a sigh,
For other skies and other scenes,
Old Summit House, good by.

⊰•⊱•○•⊰•⊱

The following poem Willard wrote in remembrance of his friend Ansel Edwards, who was killed at Buckton Station.

Edwards

Down in yonder valley,
By the Shenandoah's wave,
We laid young Edwards to rest
In his lonely, lonely grave.

'Twas morning and the golden sun
Above the mountains high
Shone mildly down as though 'twas sad
That one so brave should die.

Fiercely had the battle storm
Swept o'er us from afar,
And many men had fallen there
'Neath the leaden hail of war.

The shots were falling thick and fast
And hissing bullets flew,
But midst the storm without alarm,
Stood Edwards, brave and true.

On every side the rifles blazed
And the woods were fringed with flame,
While with shriek and yell, like fiends of hell,
The Rebel squadrons came.

Their bright sabres in the sun
Flashed like gleams of light,
While with clash and clang, their scabbards rang
As they came like the wind to the fight.

And not swifter could the swallow fly
Or more madly rush the wave,
Yet 'mid the storm stood Edwards' form
The bravest of the brave.

With whoop and yell and wild hallo,
To every danger blind,
With sword in hand came the Rebel band,
On sweeping like the wind.

Then rang a hundred rifles out
And a hundred bullets sped,
And not a few of that Rebel crew
Were numbered with the dead.

The sun went down, the fight was past,
And we had won the day,
But sad to tell, brave Edwards fell
In that short, bloody fray.

'Twas evening and the silvery moon
Smiled sweetly over head,
And the Evening Star looked from afar
On the face of the noble dead.

We dug him a grave in yonder glen,
Where the pine trees sadly wave,
And the birds of Spring may come and sing
Their requiem over his grave.

Silently and sadly we turned away
And left him to sleep alone,
In that valley low, where the flowers grow
And the sad winds sigh their moan.

>–•◆›–○–‹◆•–‹

Columbia

Columbia, my country,
    All bleeding and torn,
Sad is the fate
    That seems waiting thee now.

Sad are our hearts
    And sadly we mourn,
For dark are the shadows
    On America's brow.

America, Columbia!
    The land of the free,
Dark is the tempest
    That around thee does play.

Still ever shall flourish
    Fair "Liberty's Tree,"
Though the Goddess of Liberty
    Is Weeping today.

And though Freedom's proud banner
    Droops sadly and low,
Thy fame and thy glory,
    We *cannot* forget.

And though the screams of the eagle
    Are the wailings of woe,
Still the star of thy glory
    Never shall set.

And though a tempest of ruin
    Seems gathering afar,
And traitors assail ye
    On land and on sea.

Though thy bosom is bleeding
    'Neath the ravage of war,
Still will we fight on—
    For God and for *Thee*.

NOTES

BOOK ONE

1. Unpublished, from the private collection of the editor.
2. On May 7, Secretary of War Stanton informed the governor that, to be accepted in the Federal service, the men had to enlist for three years.
3. The new recruits were not yet formally accepted into the U.S. service and bided their time in drill. On May 28 the Wisconsin adjutant general informed them that they were to be called into service and ordered them to report into camp in June.
4. The camp was named after Charles Hamilton, the first colonel to command the 3rd Wisconsin. He was appointed brigadier general in August 1861 and left the regiment. He was succeeded by Thomas Ruger.
5. Illinoisans were known as "Suckers" in the same way that Wisconsin natives were called "Badgers." The term did not have the same connotation that it does today.
6. Bryant confirms that the men were not issued their first guns until reaching Hagerstown.
7. This tent city was called Camp Pinckney. According to Bryant, from there the men could "faintly but distinctly" hear the cannonade during the battle of Bull Run on July 21.
8. George W. Dodge of Neenah. He was wounded at Winchester in 1862, then discharged.
9. This is where the regiment received the blue uniform of the Union army to replace their state militia uniforms.
10. John Scott of Oshkosh, who was killed in action at Chancellorsville.
11. Ira Prouty, later wounded at Antietam.
12. Ervin Robbins and Robert Longstaff, both of Co. G. Robbins was wounded at Antietam and discharged.
13. Unpublished, from the private collection of the editor.
14. Six men of the 3rd Wisconsin had died of illness, though possibly only five of fever. They were Sgt. Amos Eid, Corp. John Steigman, and Pvts. John Gaston, Ole Osmundson, John Morgan, and John Remele.
15. Three companies of the regiment—A, C, and H—crossed the Potomac to Bolivar Heights, Virginia. They were engaged by cavalry and infantry under Confederate colonel Turner Ashby, and in the skirmish, Henry Clemens, Edgar Rose, Stewart Mosher, Henry Raymond, and Franklin Tuttle were killed. They were the regiment's first battle casualties.
16. Orlando D. Rodgers, a principal musician, who was discharged in May 1862.
17. Clark Austin of Co. C.
18. John Myers of Co. D.

19. One of these men was L. Perry Yarger of Co. C.
20. A local defense group made up principally of men too old for active service.
21. Horace Northrup of Co. C.
22. This was one of the Brainard boys of Co. A—either George or John.
23. J. W. Narracong of Willard's own Co. G.
24. Ninety-four men of the 3rd Wisconsin died of disease during the war, eighteen of them before or during Willard's stay in his hospital in Frederick. Six others were killed in action or died of wounds before hospital duty.
25. Joseph Bemis of Co. C.
26. Maj. Arnold C. Lewis was murdered on September 22, 1861, by John Lanahan of Co. I, whom the records at Camp Curtin in Harrisburg, Pennsylvania, stated was "an insubordinate soldier."
27. Levi Close, Co. D., of Lamartine, Wisconsin.
28. One of these was Richard Close, in the same company as Levi. Richard was later wounded at Chancellorsville. He survived the war but surely never forgot the moment Willard describes.
29. Willard acted as good Samaritan for either Nels or Peter Peterson, each of Co. K of the 3rd Wisconsin. Both survived the war, so Willard's efforts bore wonderful fruit.
30. Ephraim Giddings of Neenah served through the entire war.
31. Richard Foltz of Co. I.
32. Capt. Edward L. Hubbard of Neenah, who resigned in December 1863.

BOOK TWO

1. Unpublished, from the collection of the editor.
2. Ibid.
3. Col. John R. Kenly's command of a thousand men was overwhelmed at Front Royal by 8,000 Confederates.
4. This is also the version of the battle given by Bryant, though he notes that the Confederates also claimed Buckton Station as a victory.
5. The actual number of casualties was 23,000.

BOOK THREE

1. Probably the Cooper Shop Volunteer Refreshment Saloon, which both provided soldiers with free food and drink and operated a hospital for their relief.
2. During the Civil War, the Summit House was in a rural location with a vista of the Delaware River and small villages around. Today the site is located on the Darby Road in densely urbanized west Philadelphia. In 1864 all of the white soldiers were moved out to another facility, and the Summit House became a hospital for black troops.
3. Willard learned details from the front by reading reports in the *Philadelphia Inquirer*, a newspaper that is still in business and is the city's largest daily.
4. Until just prior to the Civil War, the spark used to fire a musket was produced by a piece of flint striking the pan. The phrase "pick their flints" survived well into the Civil War, however, meaning to get their guns ready for firing.

BOOK FOUR

1. Henry Wilson, later vice president of the United States.
2. Ed Moran, who shared this adventure with Willard, was also of Company G. He rose from the rank of corporal to second lieutenant during the war and was mustered out in June 1865.

3. The number, including the missing, is now thought to have been more than nine hundred.
4. Gen. Charles P. Stone, who had ordered the "demonstration" that turned into the battle of Ball's Bluff, was reviled as a traitor and court-martialed.
5. John Fesler.

BOOK FIVE

1. Clement Vallandingham was the North's most prominent opponent of the war. He was deported to Canada but in 1863 still received the Democratic party's nomination for governor of Ohio. John Brough, a "war Democrat," ran against him on a fusion ticket of prowar Democrats and Republicans. The election was expected to be close, but Brough soundly defeated Vallandingham, saving the Lincoln administration and the war effort from a stinging rebuke.
2. The fact that Willard had a Rebel uniform raises the question of whether he was a spy. Certainly he would have been treated as one and executed if he had been captured by the Confederates while wearing it.
3. An aide-de-camp, assistant to the senior officer.

INDEX